A Vision for Science Education

One of the most important and consistent voices in the reform of science education over the last thirty years has been that of Peter Fensham. His vision of a democratic and socially responsible science education for all has inspired change in schools and colleges throughout the world. Often moving against the tide, Fensham has travelled the world to promote a more democratic science education. He was appointed Australia's first Professor of Science Education, and was later made a Member of the Order of Australia in recognition of his work in this emerging field of study.

In this unique book, leading science educators from around the world examine and discuss Fensham's key ideas. Each describes how his arguments, proposals and recommendations have affected their own practice, and extend and modify his message in light of current issues and trends in science education. The result is a vision for the future of science teaching internationally.

Teachers, researchers and academics in science education around the world will find this book a fascinating insight into the life and work of one of the foremost pioneers in science education. The book will also make inspiring reading for students intending to make a career of teaching science and technology.

Roger Cross is a Senior Lecturer in the Department of Science and Mathematics Education at the University of Melbourne, Australia. He, along with so many others, has been inspired by Peter Fensham's vision.

A Vision for Science Education

Responding to the work of
Peter Fensham

Edited by Roger Cross

RoutledgeFalmer
Taylor & Francis Group

LONDON AND NEW YORK

First published 2003 by RoutledgeFalmer
11 New Fetter Lane, London EC4P 4EE

Simultaneously published in the USA and Canada
by RoutledgeFalmer
29 West 35th Street, New York, NY 10001

RoutledgeFalmer is an imprint of the Taylor & Francis Group

© 2003 Editorial and selection material: Roger Cross;
Individual chapters: the contributors

Typeset in Bembo by BC Typesetting, Bristol
Printed and bound in Great Britain by
The Cromwell Press, Trowbridge, Wiltshire

British Library Cataloguing in Publication Data
A catalogue record for this book is available from the British Library

Library of Congress Cataloging in Publication Data
A vision for science education: responding to the work of Peter Fensham/
edited by Roger Cross
      p.   cm.
Includes bibliographical references and index.
    1. Science–Study and teaching (Higher) 2. Fensham, Peter, J.
    I. Cross, Roger, 1941–

Q181.V57 2002   2002073382
507′.1–dc21

ISBN 0–415–28871–1 (hbk)
ISBN 0–415–28872–X (pbk)

To school students, for whom we hold the future in trust

Contents

Tables

Contributors

Glen Aikenhead (Canada) has always embraced a humanistic perspective on science. This perspective was honed during his graduate studies at Harvard University and has guided his research and scholarly writing ever since. His current interests relate to cross-cultural science education for indigenous students. In 1990 Glen was awarded the Canadian Education Association Whitworth Award 'Canadian Educational Researcher of the Year'. In 1992 he received the Canada 125th Commemorative Medal for his research and development in science education nationally and internationally.

Nancy Brickhouse (USA) is an associate professor at the University of Delaware and editor of *Science Education*. She was educated at Baylor University and Purdue University in the USA in chemistry and education. Her research programme has been focused on issues of epistemology, gender, and culture in learning and the science curriculum.

Roger Cross (Australia) is a senior lecturer at the Department of Science and Mathematics Education, University of Melbourne. He was educated at London University and the University of Adelaide. His interests in Australian history and the social responsibility of science have been combined in his recently published book entitled *Fallout: Hedley Marston and the British bomb tests in Australia*. He has written five other books on education and science, including a recently co-edited book with Peter Fensham entitled *Science and the Citizen: For educators and the public*.

Reinders Duit (Germany) is Professor of Physics Education at the Institute for Science Education in Kiel (the central institute for science education research in Germany). His major research interests include teaching and learning key science concepts, conceptual change, constructivist approaches, quality development, and scientific literacy. He is a member of several editorial boards of science education research journals, and reviews for ARC, NSF, and the German Science Foundation. He is a member of several professional associations, and received the Outstanding Paper Award of NARST in 1998.

Harrie Eijkelhof (The Netherlands) After a Master's degree in physics (Leiden, 1971), Harrie taught in secondary schools in Zambia and The Netherlands. Since 1975 he has been involved in curriculum development in physics and science education with an emphasis on STS. In 1990 he completed a PhD thesis on teaching and learning about the risks of ionising radiation. Since 1997 he has been Professor of Physics Education and the Director of the Utrecht Centre for Science and Mathematics Education.

Jim Gaskell (Canada) is a professor of science education in the Department of Curriculum Studies, University of British Columbia. His research interests include the social contexts of science curriculum, scientific and technological literacy, gender issues in science education, and the vocational/academic interface in school science. He is currently principal investigator of a federally funded project on 'applied academics'. He is also the North American representative to the International Organization for Science and Technology Education.

Richard Gunstone (Australia) joined Monash University in 1974 after twelve years of high school science/physics teaching. His research interests include student learning of, and engagement with science, metacognition, assessment, and teacher development. He has been most fortunate to have spent many years collaborating with Peter Fensham in research and teaching. He now holds the chair that was formerly Peter's.

Cliff Malcolm (South Africa) has been a professor in South Africa since 1997. This follows a distinguished career in Australia, where he led a major redevelopment of the science curriculum (k–12) in Victoria (1980s), and the design of the Australian outcomes-based framework (1990s). His contributions to government policies and frameworks, teacher support, and learning materials express his deep commitment to 'Science for All'.

Jonathan Osborne (UK) is a professor of science education at the Department of Education and Professional Studies, King's College London, where he has been since 1985. His major research interest lies in improving the quality of science education for the majority of students and teaching more about science. He was the co-editor, with Robin Millar, of the influential report *Beyond 2000: Science Education for the Future* and has since been involved in a number of projects on teaching the nature of science. A particular research focus is on enhancing the exploration of argument and its use in constructing and evaluating explanations and evidence.

Cristina Padolina (Philippines) Frustration at not seeing better achievement among many of her students, even after teaching as best as she knows how, led Cristina Damasco Padolina to the field of science education. She was drawn to this field soon after joining the University of the Philippines Los Baños in 1973 upon obtaining her PhD in organic chemistry from the University of Texas in Austin. This interest led to her involvement in teacher education, to a post-baccalaureate Diploma in Science Teaching, to the first formal distance education programme in the University, and later in the establishment of the UP Open University with her as its first chancellor. After serving two terms, she went back to being a professor of chemistry, a stint she thoroughly enjoyed, but which was cut short when she was appointed Commissioner of the Commission on Higher Education. (She is now back to being simply a professor of chemistry, still maintaining an active interest in science education.)

Léonie Rennie (Australia) is Professor at the Science and Mathematics Education Centre at Curtin University of Technology, and Dean of Graduate Studies at the University. She has a background in science teaching and teacher education. Her research interests relate to how students learn science and technology, in both formal and informal settings, their attitudes about science and technology, and gender-inclusive assessment of cognitive and affective learning.

Tarsisius Sarkim (Indonesia) is a physics education lecturer at Sanata Dharma University, Yogyakarta, Indonesia. He is currently researching ways of reforming science teacher training in Indonesia. He has a particular interest in developing pedagogical content knowledge and constructivist methods in teacher training courses.

Joan Solomon (UK) taught science for more than twenty-five years in different high schools, mostly in the London area, and inaugurated the first STS course for state schools. She has been at the forefront of the STS movement and has developed a theoretical framework for STS curricula. She was awarded the first post as Lecturer in Educational Research at Oxford University where she ran some ten large research projects, and taught postgraduate students. She is now Senior Research Fellow at the Open University, and Visiting Professor at King's College London as well as at the Open University.

David Treagust (Australia) is Professor of Science Education in the Science and Mathematics Education Centre at Curtin University in Perth, Western Australia. He holds postgraduate degrees in science education from the University of Iowa and undergraduate qualifications in science from England and Australia. Prior to working in universities, he taught secondary school chemistry for ten years in England and Australia. He has published articles on student learning difficulties and approaches to alternative assessment on a number of topics in the secondary chemistry curricula. His research interests are related to understanding students' ideas about science concepts, and how these ideas contribute to conceptual change and can be used to enhance the design of curricula and teachers' classroom practice. He was President of the National Association for Research in Science teaching (1999–2001) and is the regional editor of the *International Journal of Science Education*.

James Wandersee (USA) taught high school biology for ten years, and then college biology for ten years, before becoming William LeBlanc Alumni Professor of Biology Education at Louisiana State University, where he directs the largest focused biology education research group in the USA. It has produced eighteen PhDs to date, and currently has twelve doctoral students in residence. His 15° Laboratory Group investigates the effects of visual approaches on biology learning – especially plant biology. He has also visited and presented his research at botanic gardens around the world – including the Royal Botanic Garden, Kew. Jim served as North American Editor of the *International Journal of Science Education*, and as the Associate Editor of the *Journal of Research in Science Teaching*. He was recently elected a Fellow of the AAAS in the Biological Sciences section.

Richard White (Australia) taught in high schools for ten years before studying for his PhD under Peter Fensham's supervision. As lecturer and later as Professor of Educational Psychology he was a close colleague of Peter's at Monash University from 1971 until Peter's retirement. Subsequently he served as Dean of the Faculty and then as Pro Vice-Chancellor for Monash in London. He helped Peter found the Australasian Science Education Research Association. He is the author of several books, including *Learning Science*, and many articles on science education, psychology, and research methods.

Acknowledgements

This book would not have been possible without the wonderful support of the individual authors. They have given their time unstintingly to the task of projecting into the future Peter Fensham's contributions to science education. They are both representative of the vast number of professional contacts Peter has made over the years and among the leading science education researchers and teachers in their fields. It has been a pleasure to work with them on this project. They have given of their time freely and commend Peter on his choice of Amnesty International as the recipient charity of the royalties from this book. Amnesty International is especially appropriate given that the authors worked on their chapters during 2001. It is their expertise and vision that make this book a resource for those interested in furthering the cause of science education in the years to come.

I thank Professor Richard Gunstone, Faculty of Education, Monash University, Australia, long-time junior colleague of Peter Fensham and now occupying Fensham's chair at Monash, for enlightening me about Peter's work within the Faculty. My friend and mentor Ronald Price, emeritus scholar, La Trobe University, gave me support and encouragement along the way and read an early draft of my chapter.

I thank the Department of Science and Mathematics Education, University of Melbourne, for providing me with sufficient time and facilities to enable this work to be brought to completion.

Perhaps the most important person of all to thank is Peter Fensham himself. I first met Peter as a raw recruit to a sister institution (La Trobe University) and he encouraged my first tentative efforts to marry the social theory of the social responsibility of science to the science education curriculum. Increasingly, I have come, like so many others, to feel privileged to have met the man and shared ideas for the improvement of a democratic science education for all. I also thank Christine Fensham, Peter's wife, for her patience and her encouragement.

Peter knew nothing of the genesis of this project – but when informed, he willingly gave me his time. At the personal level it was a delight to learn something of Peter's life and interests. His scholarship is formidable and his memory equally impressive. To him I say thank you on behalf of all the authors, who (except Mr Tarsisius Sarkim) have been enriched both professionally and personally by Peter. For my own part, let an Australian expression convey my gratitude: 'thanks, mate'.

Finally, I wish to acknowledge the love and support of my wife, Jenny Carter, whose own writings have inspired me and from whom I have learned so much.

Roger Cross
University of Melbourne
March 2002

Preface

In 1957 some of the world's greatest scientists heeded the call of Albert Einstein and Bertand Russell and met in the little town of Pugwash in Nova Scotia in Canada to discuss the fate of the world. So began the Pugwash Conferences of concerned scientists from around the world. At this and subsequent meetings scientists, almost unwittingly, acknowledged the enormous changes that had occurred in science as a result of two world wars (sometimes referred to as the 'Chemists' War' and the 'Physicists' War', respectively). Scientists were now thrust upon the world stage as actors in the decisions that would affect the fate of the world as we know it. The threat of rising levels of global radio-activity, especially strontium-90, galvanised Linus Pauling and others – thereby destroying the myth of a value-free science.

A 30-year-old Peter Fensham had, by this time, completed PhD degrees in both the physical and social sciences, and he had returned to his home town of Melbourne to become a physical scientist. As an academic scientist he did not fit the usual mould. Almost immediately (see Chapter 1) Peter Fensham showed his true colours by becoming a leading figure in Australia's own Pugwash movement. He was warned that involvement in such a movement might well be dangerous for a young scientist hoping to make his way through the ranks. What his friendly advisor did not realise was that Peter's career would take a curious turn away from research and teaching in the physical sciences into the muddy waters of research in, and reform of, science education. What was to become typical of Peter's work in the new and emerging field of science education research was the marrying of a strong sense of a democratic and collaborative approach to the solution of the difficulties science teachers found in their own classrooms and a grand vision for how people around the world might benefit from learning science at school. This perhaps unique attribute has helped Peter to connect with so many different cultural groups. They, like the authors of these chapters, recognised that this man saw through the petty barriers that divide different people, that the common good was also their good. That, I contend, is why we have collectively recognised the importance of his work and feel that it has much to say for the development of science education in the coming decades. While we recognise that Peter Fensham's work is not yet over, the major part of his corpus of work is now available to us – and we hope that even he, with his marvellous physical energy and intellectual capacity, will agree with our assessment.

All of the contributors know and respect Peter professionally and socially (except our Indonesian contributor). Some know him very well, having been close colleagues at Monash University, others have come to know him through his internationally focused research, yet others are personal friends. We have been enriched in a variety of ways by our various contacts with him. I suspect that, like me, the authors have not always agreed with his vision for reform and have engaged in healthy debate based on different interpretations of the issues that confront us. This Peter has welcomed, and expected, for he has helped to create an open atmosphere where scholars can present ideas without the burden of a particular orthodoxy, for Peter's personal values and his training have ensured that he welcomes diversity. Indeed, rational debate is seen as a necessary feature of finding a way forward.

The authors invited to contribute to this book are among the world's foremost science educators. They have made very significant contributions to the field in their own cultural settings and beyond. The contributors represent Australia, Canada, Germany, Indonesia, The Netherlands, Philippines, South Africa, the UK and the USA. While this is not intended to be a *Who's Who* of science education research, it does represent a cross-section of people who are working in fields to which Peter has made significant contributions. They are, therefore, well placed to be able to assess critically the current issues and trends in science education.

Chapter 1, 'Living the dream: Peter James Fensham, social justice, and science education' by Roger Cross, enables the reader to gain an understanding of the man behind the ideas. This is an attempt to bridge the mind/body divide by providing the readers with sufficient knowledge to be able to determine why Fensham has acted in the way he has.

Chapter 2, 'Science for all: learner-centred science' by Cliff Malcolm, deals with the application of what is arguably Fensham's greatest achievement, championing the concept of 'Science for All' to the new South Africa. Malcolm takes the reader on a journey to the educational challenges confronting science teachers in South Africa as they reach out to their students – whose cultural expectations of the meaning of science and interpretations of phenomena are so different from the standard representations found in science textbooks around the world. Here, 'Science for All' needs to be reinterpreted in the light of enormous disparities in opportunity and cultural differences. Malcolm's answer is to learn from the public, science teachers, and their students.

In Chapter 3, 'Making science matter', Jonathan Osborne deals with what is arguably one of the most pressing issues in education for the twenty-first century. He deals with what kind of schooling of science should provide a basis for a democratic society in an era of increasing technological specialisation. He examines the key dilemmas facing us as we grapple with the issue of curriculum reform, and convincingly argues for a science education that is suitable both for those who may go on to specialise in a science-related career and for the majority who will not. This is essential reading for all who are concerned about the role of science education in social construction and the value of teaching science.

Chapter 4, '"Science for All": reflections from Indonesia', by Tarsisius Sarkim, is a valuable addition to this book. Indonesia is part of an increasingly important area of the world, as are the Philippines, represented here by Cristina Padolina. Sarkim points to the contradictions and the dilemmas of 'Science for All' when applied to an archipelago of more than a thousand islands and the diverse cultures that make up modern Indonesia.

Chapter 5, 'STS education: a rose by any other name' by Glen Aikenhead, is a well-rounded review of the history of the science, technology, and society movement. It enables the reader to understand not only how this reform movement gathered momentum but also Fensham's contribution. Aikenhead comes to the conclusion 'that changing the status quo science curriculum cannot simply be achieved by STS-like curriculum innovations based on rational philosophical grounds alone'. He notes the importance of the socio-political in future efforts to reform, which is exactly Fensham's conclusion as his involvement in the OECD PISA (Programme for International Student Assessment) demonstrates by strongly advocating a different kind of testing – one that moves towards some of the principles of STS and the public understanding of science.

Chapter 6, 'The UK and the movement for science, technology, and society (STS) education', is written by Joan Solomon, the UK's most consistent advocate of STS. She examines Peter Fensham's contribution to STS and how his science education philosophy enabled him to link this reform with the broader ideas embedded in 'Science for All'. Solomon perceptively relates these dual threads in Fensham's work to the pioneering British scientist and educator Lancelot Hogben (see his famous book published in 1938, *Science for the Citizen*). She gives a complementary history of the STS movement, from a British perspective. Importantly, Solomon looks to the future through the lens of citizenship and ethics education as a process for a more democratic form of science education.

Chapter 7, 'Science for all? Science for girls? Which girls?' by Nancy Brickhouse, is a timely up-to-the-minute appraisal of some of the issues embedded in gender and science teaching. She begins by noting Fensham's contribution in this field and then deals with the problem from a US perspective. She draws into the net of gender both colour and socio-economic disadvantage and in this way an important step forward in the debate. Of equal importance is her perceptive analysis of identity formation, especially as applied to the different cultural and economic groups within the USA. The interpretation of achievement as a form of identity is a significant step that will enable other researchers to apply revised social theory to the question of gender and science education.

Chapter 8, Léonie Rennie's chapter entitled 'Understanding gender difference in science education: Peter Fensham's contribution', deals, in part, with the enigma of the research Peter carried out into gender differences in Thailand with Sunee Klainin. This study was considered controversial at the time (1987) as it went against the accepted expectations. She points out that this study dispelled once and for all the proposition that biological differences accounted for differences in girls' performance in the physical sciences. Rennie then deals with a number of contemporary issues in this research paradigm and outlines a way forward that is complementary to Nancy's.

Chapter 9, 'Fenham's lodestar criterion' by James Wandersee, is a highly original and thought provoking development of some of Fensham's work in the theory and practice of science education. The 'lodestar' according to Wandersee is 'a star to steer by', and he states that 'Peter Fensham's sustained interest in using student-appropriate personal, societal, and technological applications of science to teach science in understandable ways indicates that he has long weighed science teaching outcomes on a "usefulness to students" balance.' Also, '[m]any of his research studies can be viewed as investigations intent on informing the construction of better science curricula and/or improving science instruction that maintain scientific integrity while insuring utilitarian value for students'. Wandersee deals with these issues from a US perspective.

Chapter 10, 'Partners or opponents: the role of academic scientists in secondary science education' by Harrie Eijkelhof, discusses the role of politics in the construction of the science curriculum. Eijkelhof's intimate knowledge of the role of politics in education in The Netherlands, especially the competing forces acting upon physics education, makes for illuminating reading. He shows us ways in which these forces might be accommodated via collaborative partnerships that allow different stakeholders to participate in future changes in what counts for the schooling of science.

Chapter 11, 'Perspectives and possibilities in the politics of science curriculum' by Jim Gaskell, provides an important analysis of the influence of academic scientists as guardians of the 'purity of school science'. Jim's account is all the more appropriate for this book because Peter Fensham himself was once an academic scientist, albeit a highly unusual one. Gaskell's analysis goes much further than this – he uses the Canadian situation to illustrate the exercise of power over what counts for the science curriculum in schools, and provides readers with thought provoking ways of engaging with powerful players in the field.

Chapter 12, 'Visions, research, and school practice', places Peter's work in the context of German students' achievements in international science testing. Reinders Duit deals with the problem of the meaning of scientific literacy in terms of a constructivist perspective and whether or not science education research has had any impact on teachers' work. He deals with Fensham's vision of 'Science for All' and illustrates how this has been interpreted in the professional work being done in Germany to bridge the gap between expectations about the results of international testing and the recent findings. This is another profoundly important statement about the possible future course of science education research.

In Chapter 13, Richard White's 'Changing the script for science teaching', he begins by explaining the meaning of 'script' – that it is knowledge of how to behave and, therefore, what our expectations are about social structures. The script of schools and schooling 'reflects the belief that schooling is for the acquisition of knowledge, which is needed for two purposes: to equip students for employment, and to prepare them for further study of the same sort of knowledge. The script guides the behaviour of teachers, students, parents, curriculum designers, examiners, administrators, and governments.' He goes on to analyse the teaching script in a way that challenges Peter Fensham's long-held articles of 'faith' regarding the possibilities for reform.

Chapter 14, 'Impact of science education now and in the future', deals with ways in which science education is seen to have contributed to life in the Philippines. Cristina Padolina is uniquely placed in the Philippines to explain the importance of Fensham's 'Science for All' as an inspiration, and as a way of developing appropriate experiences to diverse communities within one country. She provides the reader with a refreshingly different perspective on the issues with which Peter has grappled.

David Treagust writes Chapter 15 from both personal and professional perspectives. His chapter is entitled 'The importance of being able to see "the big picture": a personal appraisal of Fensham's influence on science education research and development'. In it he discusses Fensham's uncanny ability to bring 'diverse ideas together' when considering the complex problems of teaching and learning. Treagust amply illustrates the importance of the 'big picture' with respect to conceptions of scientific literacy and how we might advance scientific literacy. He offers valuable suggestions for a way forward by drawing on some of his own research.

Richard Gunstone has written the Afterword; he describes a joint project between Monash University and King's College London. It was one of Peter Fensham's visions to establish an international centre for research into the science curriculum. This has now become a reality under the guiding hand of the professors of science education at Monash and King's. Gunstone describes how the joint centre was established and the kinds of research questions it will address.

Appendix 1 is a list of selected publications from Peter Fensham's enormous output in the field. At the time of writing it is worth noting that he has just completed the manuscript of another book that describes the emergence of the field of science education research. Its title is *Evolution of Science Education as a Field of Research*. How appropriate it is that this should be written by him.

Part I

Peter James Fensham
(1927–)

1   Living the dream

Peter James Fensham, social justice, and science education

Roger Cross

In beginning to contemplate my account of Peter Fensham's life I am acutely aware that this cannot be a biography, even though his full and interesting life would make a fascinating story. It will, however, be biographical – for how else can we begin to appreciate what has driven Peter to the four corners of the world in the cause of enhancing our understanding and knowledge of science and its teaching for nearly forty years? I will try and give you an insight into this remarkable man's life without taking away from the essential purpose of this volume. Also, I must not 'steal the thunder' of the distinguished scholars who will be discussing his work and how it might be carried forward. As to literary style I am in 'no man's land' somewhere between a *Who's Who* entry and a retirement speech given by a colleague. What genre of writing can help in this dilemma? For better or worse I have laid out what seems to have been Peter's journey through life to the point of finding his métier and then dealt briefly with how one of the major intellectual themes in his quest for the reform of science education arose. It will be up to you to judge whether this gives you sufficient insight to form a judgement about the intellectual and emotional attachment that Peter has for his quest to promote a fairer world.

Finding a way: Peter James Fensham, AM, BSc Hons, MSc (Melbourne), PhD (Bristol), PhD(Cantab.), Dip Ed (Monash)

Here is a man who has lead a remarkably active life, a life that from the outside looks obsessive in its drive, and compulsive in its search for a better and fairer way ahead for all societies – a search for social justice. A man, his Monash colleagues say, who you are as likely to meet in some out of the way corner of the world promoting his vision as you are to come across in his hometown of Melbourne. In trying to understand what Peter has been endeavouring to do all these years, it is necessary to revisit how he came to be Australia's first professor of science education. I realise that in doing this there is a danger of a Festschrift – simply a celebration of his work. However laudable that might be, it is not the point of this book. Nevertheless, it is important to understand something of what drove Peter to pursue certain avenues of work, and how he came to think the way he does. This will help you in forming your own judgement about the breadth and depth of Peter Fensham's work, his obsessions, his strengths and weaknesses that have been a part of his long campaign for a more just society – through the medium of teaching science. Like us all, Peter carries the baggage of his past and projects it still into his work. Like the scientist he once was, he cannot divorce his values, his personal agenda, from the claims he makes for the improvement of science teaching.

I will try and reveal something of Peter's life's adventure, and his strong sense of calling and mission – a mission that is evident in every conversation he has about his beloved personal themes: how to make our world a more comprehensible place, and a more interesting place in which to live. Let one of his favourite books help us approach an understanding of this man: *A Fortunate Man* by John Berger and Jean Mohr (1967). This slim volume tells the struggles of a country doctor, Dr John Sassall, who worked in England among largely unschooled foresters who seemed left behind by the pace of change, and were largely despised by the changed population in the cities. Sassall gradually comes to admire their hidden strengths, their folk knowledge, and their essential goodness. In this journey Sassall finds himself in the course of a life where a feeling of adventure has nothing to do with exciting events. This is so apt for Peter – who has spent half a lifetime in the air and in airports – for each moment appears to be an adventure of the mind. It was said by his colleagues at Monash: beware Fensham fresh from a long journey from half way round the world! The ideas pour forth, gestated within the bowels of an aluminium bird (Gunstone, 2001). For Peter, as we shall see, has found (like all mortals) that time is irreversible but the mistakes in teaching science are not. They have occurred over and over, leading him on to new battlegrounds, and it seems that the defensive and offensive strategies are best formulated over a plate of plastic food and a turbulent ride.

Peter Fensham was born in Melbourne in October 1927, the year that saw Lindbergh as the first man to fly solo across the Atlantic, that the Australian Parliament first sat in Canberra, that Al Johnson starred in the first talkie film immortalising the line: 'You ain't heard nothin' yet' (prophetically capped by science's Werner Heisenberg's 'Uncertainty Principle'); no wonder, some might say, that he turned out the way he has!

He grew up at a time where universal secondary education had not yet been completely established in Victoria, and his earliest years were lived through the Great Depression. As luck would have it, he went to strongly academic schools for his primary and first years of secondary education. Gifted students could find their way to higher education, and so it was with Peter. He was awarded a scholarship to the prestigious private school, Melbourne Grammar School. This was to be an important moment in his life: MGS, along with one or two other schools, was the closest thing to an elite English public school in Australia. It immediately opened its doors to those boys with wealthy parents, or scholarship boys like Peter who provided the intellectual backbone of the school. He qualified a year early for university at the age of 17, and decided not to stay on for another year but to try his luck at university. He was fortunate that the year was 1945 and the war ended just before his 18th birthday. He was thus able to continue his studies rather than be called up for active war service. It is hard for us who were not adolescents at that time to understand how that terrible war may have affected young people's lives and their vision of what life should be. For the youth of a country that was drawn into effective nationhood through the experience of our armed forces at Gallipoli in the First World War, to have missed active service was certainly a blessing – but could it also be a burden for Australian men? I have often wondered how it affected those men, Peter included, who could never be a part of the Australian mateship of the Returned Services League (RSL) and could never share in the dubious glory of being a veteran. I speculate that this was an important factor in the life of this restless and energetic man. Many other factors have, of course, contributed to his sense of social justice, including, I believe, his personal beliefs, and his Protestant church upbringing.

Studying science rather than medicine at university – the normal choice of profession for high-flying MGS boys – must have come as something of a surprise to the School. But Peter had what he thought was a wise plan: science studies took three years at university, not six as with medicine. Never did he think that he would be studying for the next twelve years! After his Bachelor's degree he went on to do a Master's degree – Australia's top scientific qualification, at that time. As chance would have it, his supervisor was a man who was to have tremendous influence on him, so much so that, along with Peter's non-conformist Christian faith, it was crucial for his working life. Dr Walter Boas, a leading CSIRO (Commonwealth Scientific and Industrial Research Organisation) physical metallurgist, came to Australia from Switzerland in 1938. He had a strong belief in the responsibilities of science and became prominent in Australia's Pugwash movement – the peace movement initiated by Einstein and Russell in the search for peace (Russell, 1961, pp. 55–61). The Pugwash group was largely responsible for the campaign to end atmospheric testing of nuclear weapons in the 1950s. Peter says of Walter: 'He was a very great influence both scientifically and what science means in society' (Fensham, 2001). After completing his Master's degree he was successful in obtaining the prestigious Exhibition 1851 Research Scholarship. So off he went to the University of Bristol, England, to research for a PhD in the field of solid state chemistry.

While in Bristol Peter met Christine, an Edinburgh University biochemist, and they were to marry some years later. In 1952 Peter went to Princeton University as a postdoctoral fellow to work with Hugh Stott Taylor, a famous physical chemist, and his career in chemistry was launched. Perhaps it was the allure of Christine, perhaps too he was still searching for his true vocation, but chemistry was about to take a back seat for a while! While in Princeton he met Professor Hadlee Cantrill, the social psychologist, and discussed with him the idea of studying social psychology. Perhaps this idea would have come to nothing if it hadn't been for a stroke of luck – one of the strange quirks of fate that are a part of every life – when the British Nuffield Foundation advertised scholarships for people who wished to make the switch from natural science to the social sciences. At this opportune time Sir Frederick Bartlett, the famous Cambridge psychologist, visited Princeton, and on meeting him Peter was persuaded to apply for one of the Nuffield scholarships at Cambridge – a place, Bartlett told Peter, that would 'give you some freedom to find your way' (Fensham, 2001). This was a 'long shot' for Peter: the scholarships were intended for British subjects, not Australians, and he was a late applicant. He was told at the interview that he broke all the rules. With this daunting interview over he spent the rest of the day watching test cricket across the road at Lords!

The Australian must have been on a good batting wicket, however, because despite all the rules he was offered a scholarship at London University. I'm afraid Peter further confounded the Nuffield Foundation by telling them that he would have to take it up at Cambridge and not at their nominated university. One happy result of returning to England for the interview, and the new intellectual mountain he hoped to climb, was his subsequent marriage to Christine in Bristol in April 1954. He successfully completed his second PhD in 1956 after having met some of the most significant Anglo-American scholars in the field. He had by now developed a holistic approach to dealing with complex problems of human society, one that would stand him in good stead in the years to come.

But the Antipodes were calling and the search began for a post back home. Naively he thought that the premier social psychology department in Australia, at his old university, Melbourne, might provide an opening. But it was full of positivists, and they, he discovered later, found little of value in his thesis. (It is worth noting here that his thesis was published as a book, and the publishers, Taylor & Francis, through their Tavistock Press imprint, are about to reprint classic works in psychology. Not surprisingly Peter's is among the list. How many of the Melbourne positivists can claim that?!)

With bread and butter for a young family the priority, it was imperative to find a job and so social science lost him to chemistry. Determined to continue his life in Australia, he turned again to his first love and was appointed to the Chemistry Department at the University of Melbourne as a solid state chemist. His calm recording of these facts today belies what, I believe, must have been a deep sense of disappointment and frustration. Knowing Peter as we do, there was no question of letting disappointment stand in his way. He threw himself back into the world of chemistry and soon began to climb the academic ladder. At some risk to his career he became an active member of the Australian Pugwash movement in Melbourne during a time when the organisation was decidedly too radical for the Australian government. In 1963 he became aware of Bloom's taxonomy and seized on the idea of conducting an educational study on his own chemistry students – this would bring him a little closer to his work in psychology. The study was published by The Royal Australian Chemical Institute, and to his amazement the editor of *Nature* contacted him at a time when the first glimmering of interest in improving the quality of university teaching was appearing. It was quite a thrill to see the article appearing in *Nature* in 1964.

Peter became chairman of the Melbourne Pugwash Group while still a chemist, and in the 1960s he was approached by Joseph Rotblat, president of the international organisation, with the idea of holding a South East Asia Pugwash Conference. This was the time of the Vietnam War and it was thought that such a conference – without the USA or the Soviet Union – might encourage China to participate. In the end the group didn't manage to persuade the Chinese to participate, but thirteen other South East Asian countries attended.

By now he was a reader in chemistry and the possibility of a chair in chemistry was looming fast. He reluctantly declined the chair in chemistry at the new University of New Guinea, and found the new University of Lough-borough painfully slow in making the offer. Peter came to the notice of Louis Matherson, Vice-Chancellor of Monash University (having interviewed him for both of these posts), and he told Selby Smith, the Dean of the Faculty of Education. Smith was trying to establish his Vice-Chancellor's vision for the University to be at the forefront of research – and he duly appointed Peter. This was to change Peter's life again, this time in a way that would marry physical and social science in the one man. He was invited to apply for the first chair in science education in Australia, and so again he jumped ship – for the last time. He moved to Monash in September 1967 and didn't look back. Now working for young people's futures instead of with chemicals, he had come full circle, and while never a medical practitioner like so many other successful boys at MGS, he would be totally immersed in people's lives.

Before long he had five PhD students, among them Richard White, one of the contributors to this book. His job was to build up as quickly as possible his university's international reputation for research in this new and emerging field of study. The decade 1967–77 was one of frenetic activity. His initial sortie overseas in 1968, when crucial links were forged, paved the way for Monash's name to be synonymous with science education around the world. Luck again intervened on the home front. After years of neglect by the federal conservative government, Gough Whitlam's reformist Labor government opened the purse strings to school education.

As far as his work in science education is concerned he is wholly responsible for establishing science education as a legitimate field of research in Australia. His ex-students now hold chairs and senior positions around the country, and he has encouraged and helped many other academics (like myself). Perhaps the single most important event in the early years was the conference he organised in 1970, the first meeting of the Australasian Science Education Research Association (ASERA), the second such organisation in the world (the first being NARST in the USA). The first ASERA proceedings appeared in 1971. That year, too, he also became the first elected president of the Australian Science Teachers' Association.

By 1977 the Faculty of Education at Monash was producing between a third and a half of all the PhDs in education in Australia and it was the only faculty in the country that had more postgraduate enrolments than initial teacher training. This was an unbelievably vibrant academic community and at the summit was Peter, always approachable and full of ideas. As Richard Gunstone, the present incumbent of his chair at Monash, says:

> He had a huge impact on me – he improved and validated the whole research area. The great luck of my professional life has been working with Peter Fensham . . . I can't conceive of a greater professional opportunity. Peter has the capacity to consider multiple issues at once that is most impressive. The description I could never apply to Peter is Prima Donna [*sic*].
>
> (Gunstone, 2001)

In 1975 he was invited to succeed Kevin Keohane as the Director of the Centre for Science and Mathematics Education, Chelsea College, London (now part of King's College), but family ties kept him at Monash. Other job offers have come his way from time to time, but the world was coming to Monash, so why move? During the twenty years spanning 1970–90 there was a constant stream of science educators from all over the world on pilgrimage to Monash, many of them hosted personally by Peter in his own home.

He has been responsible for very many initiatives, both internationally and in his home state of Victoria. One close to my heart is his work in environmental science education. In 1973–4 he was the Australian representative for the famous UNESCO Conference in Belgrade (see 'The Belgrade Charter: A global framework for environmental education', *Connect*, 1(1), 1976), at which the founding international principles for environmental education were laid down in a historic document called 'The Belgrade Charter for Environmental Education'. Peter fondly remembers this conference for the way the ideas evolved:

> the first day the [organised] programme was totally overturned by some of the delegates from developing countries . . . we spent four of the seven days hammering out the Charter until we knew what we were talking about, and the real depth of the problem. That was a very famous moment . . . I remember the Peruvian [representative] saying [to me] could you ask that European speaker to stop speaking about 'aid' because you [the First World] have ripped us off so much that there is no way you can pay this back, so let's just forget about aid and think about some other way of expressing the relationship we are trying to have? Aid, after all, was half the problem.

Peter was in the forefront of awaking interest in Australia in environmental education. He chaired the regional meeting on environmental education for

UNESCO in Bangkok, and was the Australian government's representative at the inter-governmental conference on environmental education at Tbilisi (resulting in the Tbilisi Declaration, see *Connect*, 3(1), 1978). He became the founding president of the Australian Association for Environmental Education in 1981.

In the 1970s at the local level, in his own state of Victoria, he introduced and supported a new senior secondary science subject called physical science, and strongly supported a second, environmental science. These subjects were the beginning of the Science, Technology, and Society (STS) movement in Australia, another one of Peter's major interests – as you would expect from his personal history.

Perhaps rather reluctantly, Peter's globetrotting, promoting the causes dear to him like 'Science For All', was moderated by a seven-year stint as Dean of the Faculty, at Monash, 1982–9. During this time he received one of the highest Australian honours, an AM (Member of the Order of Australia). Four years remained before he retired from his chair in 1993. Throughout this time he continued to develop links with people in other countries. Anyone would think that after a lifetime of such intense activity Peter might put his feet up and reflect on his achievements. Not a bit of it. Since retirement he has constantly worked at promoting the cause of a more democratic and socially responsible science education for all. The undiminished stream of scholarly publications and his many travels to all parts of the world to collaborate with old friends and encourage new researchers in the field are a testament to his energy and to his personal ethics – of giving of himself unhesitatingly. It has been remarked by many that Peter will always respond to the call for help. In 1999 Peter was awarded the NARST's Distinguished Contribution Award; there can be no greater recognition than this. Here, indeed, is proof that Peter Fensham, the passionate Australian who championed the teaching of a particular kind of science in the best interests of all, has been recognised for what he is: a man of integrity and principle, and one of the few truly important figures in the field. A man for his time, bringing people together in a common cause from whatever corner of the world they live, to counteract inequality. The citation for the NARST award includes the following:

> [He] has provided outstanding leadership and direction in science education research. The remarkable and distinctive feature of his research contributions has been his capacity to discern and synthesize key issues in science education. . . . Professor Fensham's significant and outstanding accomplishments make him a worthy recipient of this prestigious award for life-time achievement in science education research.

Peter remains committed to his ideals, and, as a member of the Science Group of the OECD Programme for International Student Assessment (PISA) project has had considerable influence in ensuring that future international testing of students for science now involves the application and understanding of science in society, which he sees as necessary for a more holistic and democratic schooling of science.

Peter has enormous energy and is extremely fit – from being able to hike in the Tasmanian wilderness and 'Walking for Want' (an annual event that he always completes, ensuring that his friends dig deep). Richard Gunstone tells me that on one occasion he met Peter in Vancouver, and on arrival, instead of succumbing to jet lag, he immediately went to work contacting people and holding discussions. Richard remarked that Peter has the uncanny knack of coming off a transpacific flight as if he had walked down the corridor of the Faculty at Monash for morning tea! How does he do it?

Research: a way is found, 'Science for All'

I am very much aware that I must not pre-empt the following discussions of Peter's many contributions to science education research and theory. Distinguished writers will be placing his work in a number of different areas in the context of the possible future developments of his science education philosophy. Here I will only consider his underlying philosophical position embodied in 'Science for All'. This has meant so much to him. The fact that he has been steadfast in promoting a particular approach to the schooling of science over so many years illustrates how close to his heart it is. In other words, his commitment reveals a great deal about the nature of the man. One speaks of social justice in the same sentence as one speaks of Fensham's collective effort in science education. This is, of course, not surprising. A person's value system and vision of an ethical life, and even morality, are all to be found in a life's work. In Peter's case it is particularly clear – for more than thirty years he has been displaying what he is for anyone who cared to look. His values shine like a beacon through his writing, in his research programmes, and the causes that he holds dear show. In discussing these matters with Peter I was struck by his generosity towards all those colleagues who have, as he says, enriched his life and helped to formulate the way forward. It is fitting that his promotion of the ideas underpinning his enduring slogan 'Science For All' can represent the man as much as it can represent a new way of thinking about the teaching of science. This is the core of the rest of his work, the unifying factor that has informed all that he stands for. It is to this value statement, which now seems so self-evident, that we must turn if we are to understand how Peter's views beyond teaching have determined his way forward.

In 1968 during Peter's first full year at Monash his sense of social justice and, I suspect, his personal religious beliefs came to the fore with the twentieth anniversary of the United Nations Declaration of Human Rights. Since he was intimately involved in the United Nations Association it was natural for the Association to ask him to convene some meetings to mark the occasion. These were a great success and, importantly, a book was produced that was to become highly significant to Peter and, as it happened, to national events in Australia. *Rights and Inequalities in Australian Education* finally appeared in

1970 and quickly became a seminal text in Fensham's philosophy, guiding his work in the years to come. Nationally, Australian education was moribund; its elitist structure was a product of the colonial past. The flood of children from post-war migration from all over Europe was now entering secondary school and Australia was about to change for ever. Peter became aware that one of the greatest causes of inequality in education was science itself – it was male dominated and elitist, favouring the very few and barring many from those professions that relied on the study of science as a prerequisite for entry. For the first time, publicly at least, it was possible to explain why Fensham had 'deserted' scientific research in favour of social science and climbed the mountain required to become qualified in that field. Here, I suggest, is that moment in his life that defined the way forward. Added to his left-leaning politics and his faith, this project gave him a cause – notwithstanding that he was a product of one of the most elite schools in the country. *Rights and Inequalities* was an influence far beyond academic circles. Gough Whitlam swept into the Prime Minister's Office on the 5 December 1972; his reforming Labor government established a number of socially relevant institutions, including the Schools Commission. The book became something of a bible for that organisation which was hellbent on addressing educational disadvantage. Peter (2001) says: '[these events] alerted me very strongly to [the] conditions of social disadvantage that led to educational disadvantage'. Here, for the first time, the federal government began to take a real interest in encouraging educational programmes in schools, normally the preserve of the individual states. Peter advised the commissioners on how an innovation programme would fit into the overall philosophy of initiatives based on educational needs and disadvantage. It led to a decade of fascinating innovation and a great boost to the morale of teachers. This was a time when Australia underwent many reforms, and the climate of debate and desire for change in the country from 1972 to 1975 was conducive to Peter further developing his ideas surrounding 'Science for All'. He became increasingly aware that

> we had to create a form of science [education] that was attractive in ways, which were different to the way it had been attractive to me and to most people in the science education field, because we were the exceptions. For some reason we had stuck with science where most of our peers had rejected science at school as being boring, too difficult, or totally irrelevant.

Here we see his final transformation from the successful scientist to a science educator who recognised that what made him pursue science as a career was unsustainable in the sense of the changed world in which he lived. He acknowledges the committee who worked on the new Victorian senior science, STS-like course called 'Physical Science' (mentioned above). It was, he recalls, one of his most satisfying experiences. Traditional views of what constituted a science course were challenged: they (the teachers) 'were fantastic, because when I suggested things that could go in they said what about your criteria of relevance? Things dear to my [scientist] heart were rejected [by the teachers I worked with]' (Fensham, 2001). He had to fight tooth and nail to have the course accredited by the universities and the scars of that process illustrate how entrenched the old ways were (and are today), and how difficult the road ahead was, and still is, for that matter.

We come now to the formulation of 'Science for All' as a holistic viewpoint of the purpose of teaching science in schools. The leap across the divide of science for its own sake to science as an educational tool had been made and Peter had, by now, incorporated fully his personal values and his ideology into this conceptual framework. It can be seen as a socio-political statement, just as much as it can be seen as logical for the times in which he formulated the concept. He was greatly affected by his involvement with UNESCO, and the revelation that science could be transformed into useful knowledge came, in part, through his contacts in Bangkok. 'Science for All' has become far more than a convenient slogan with which to capture the attention of the bureaucrats – it is a way of teaching science for a broad social purpose. It involves useful scientific knowledge, and ways of thinking and doing that could help all future citizens to lead fulfilling lives. With the arrival of the 1980s, 'Science for All' was to become the dominant theme of concern among science educators around the world. 'Science for All Americans' and 'Science for All Canadians', and even the staid Royal Society of London took up the theme in 1985 in its document *Public Understanding of Science*. Its message was incorporated into the STS and the 'Girls in Science' projects of the time. It was an underlying theme of the important movements for reform throughout the period. Science was to be open to all under its banner and the elitist structure of science teaching and the curriculum began to break down.

Let us consider briefly the STS movement and the 'Science for All' theme. Peter notes that the rapid growth in the number of people wishing to be seen as part of the reform led to much confusion about the underlying principles and purpose of STS. This lack of coherence in the understanding of STS was nowhere more evident than at the famous Bangalore Conference in India in 1985. The papers presented illustrated an enormous disparity of views, from the most traditional and elitist to some highly radical and innovative programmes. The muddle and lack of coherence inhibited the implementation and the promising support of 'Science For All' – something that Professors Joan Solomon and Glen Aikenhead discuss in their chapters. Another important issue that caused him concern was the impact of the Alternative Frameworks research programme – in which he had been prominent in its early years. He states:

> In 1989 I tried to find out what had been done in terms of STS type concepts within Children's Science – there was almost nothing done . . . all the evidence was based on traditional concepts. Implying too readily that all that had to be done was to teach the old subject matter better

and all would be well! Sadly we now have a burst of new curricula, with a constructivist sort of mantra to them, but the content is still the same.

(Fensham, 2001)

The relationship between Peter's ideas and STS can perhaps be best seen by examining some of the Dutch PLON physics units. They closely relate to his own work of a decade earlier on the physical science course in Victoria. PLON gave a glimmer of how science might be taught – the similarity of purpose with Peter's early efforts is striking.

In his paper in the *International Journal of Science Education* (Fensham, 1988) dealing with approaches to STS, he proposed that if you wanted to emphasise the nature of science in relation to certain content you would focus on 'Science' in STS; if you were interested in people and social interactions you would focus on 'Society' in STS; and if you were interested in the technological innovation you would focus on the 'Technology' of STS. You allow, he says 'each to be the drivers, of the content or the focal point of the teaching of content. Whereas, so many of the so-called STS curricula were saying well just add on a bit of application in society in traditional [content].'

Conclusion

I have highlighted 'Science for All' here to illustrate what I believe is Peter's underlying educational philosophy. It is, of course, but one of the research themes to which Peter has been deeply committed. His work is ongoing, and his influence in the OECD Programme for International Student Assessment project is testament to the way his advice and his wise counsel are still at the forefront of international developments in science education. The fact that his life's work is not completed has made this slight contribution to understanding the man a more difficult task.

References

Berger, J. and Mohr, J. (1967) *A Fortunate Man*, New York: Pantheon Books.

Fensham, P. (1988) 'Approaches to the teaching of STS in science education', *International Journal of Science Education* 10: 346–56.

Fensham, P.J. (2001) Personal communication.

Gunstone, R. (2001) Personal communication.

Russell, B. (1961) *Has Man a Future?*, Harmondsworth: Penguin.

Part II
Science for all

2 Science for all

Learner-centred science

Cliff Malcolm

> Science educators face two dilemmas. The first is how to sort out from the available literature the ideas and outcomes that may apply to their own schooling contexts. . . . The second is the sheer unavailability of most of the world's experience of science education since 1960.
>
> (Fensham, 1988, p. 17)

I came to South Africa from Australia in 1997, to a land of immense cultural and physical diversity, where dreams and disappointments, generosity and crime, swirl together as blacks and whites, rural and urban, rich and poor, emerge into a democratic nation. Johannesburg, Durban, and Cape Town, in their different ways, stand as symbols of Western life, with their steel and glass, freeways and traffic lights, theatres and gardens, prosperity and slums. On the other hand, most of South Africa's blacks (and black Africans comprise 80 per cent of the population) live in rural areas, often in thatched round huts with no electricity. Young girls carry water home on their heads, young boys tend cattle and goats, and women are the mainstay of community life because so many of the men work in the cities and mines. There are many 'South Africas', in this the most inequitable country in the world, after Brazil (Department of Education, 2001a).

From the cities it is never far to the open spaces of Africa: rolling grasslands beneath vast blue skies, desert plants crackling underfoot, rock art and legends deep in the mountains, rainforests tumbling down to long beaches. Here in the land where humans, as we know them, began, it was only a moment ago that people shared these spaces with leopards, elephants, rhinos, and elands. Yet 'a colonial culture is one which has no memory. The discontinuities and impositions made it so' (Jacobson, 1971). European sciences, European technologies (of production, law, public administration, and war), and European philosophies changed Africa quite suddenly.

Myths are stronger than memories. Since the first democratic elections in 1994, the recent past and the ancient past are being reframed, as the nation looks forward. The excitement and confusion are captured in conference reports, newspapers, short stories, and novels. I enjoy especially the novels, and the ways they bring together the 'grand narratives' of struggle, liberation, and change with individual stories of hope, intimacy, and abuse. For example, *Imaginings in Sand* (Brink, 1997) centres on the 1994 elections, the rewriting of history, and the sense of 'coming home' that the elections symbolised. *Disgrace* (Coetzee, 1999) delves into the unsettling of identity – sexual, familial, cultural, political, economic – that was part of the liberation. It is no easy matter to integrate into a national programme the different traditions of Africa, the character of the land, promises of new prosperity, and political participation.

'Science for All' is important in the national vision (Department of Education, 1997; 2001b) but it is not so clear what that means in practice, or how it can be achieved.

'Science for All': a plea for access

'Science for All' is primarily a plea for access. (The theme is central in Peter Fensham's writings and educational leadership. For example, in Victoria, Australia, in 1984, a reformist government in which Peter was active made 'access and success for all' its slogan for change, at about the same time as he wrote 'Science for All, a reflective essay' (Fensham, 1985).) He writes about many dimensions of access (Fensham, 1985; 1988; 2000):

- Physical access is a basic requirement – access to teachers, facilities, courses. Exclusion arises directly and indirectly from devices such as university prerequisites and combinations, student counselling at school, streaming and stereotyping, curriculum and assessment.
- 'Science for All' is contrary to 'Science for Some' (especially potential scientists). Offering all students narrowly defined programmes focused on preparation and selection for tertiary science study is not 'Science for All': sitting at a table with food you don't want, and a language you don't speak, is not 'dining'.
- Access is partly about pedagogy – enabling different students to learn effectively, taking into account their backgrounds, contexts, learning styles, and aspirations. To follow the 'dining' metaphor, it is about having a cook and guests who understand where you're coming from, and make space for your input.
- Access is also about outcomes: to what should students have access? Access stretches beyond effective learning to meaningful learning, and issues of purpose and content: Which Science? Whose Science? Why?

Questions of purposes and content – and access itself – are deeply contestable. The politics are difficult, especially at the senior secondary level where preparation for higher education looms large, with reverberations throughout the curriculum. Change also is difficult. Existing school practice – largely defined by teachers, texts, history, and 'the system' (locally and internationally) – has enormous inertia. Reform requires strong teacher support and teacher education, all linked to system reform.

Physical access

In South Africa, access to educational resources remains far from equitable. Programmes to build classrooms and libraries, and provide electricity, telephones, clean water, and sewage in all schools, proceed, but the backlog is large (Department of Education, 2001a). Average class size nationally is coming down (forty-seven in 1994, thirty-five in 2000), as is the proportion of under-qualified teachers (36 per cent in 1994, 25 per cent in 1998). Participation rates in schooling are generally high, but achievements are often dismal, with pass rates in Grade 12 of only a few per cent (Malcolm *et al.*, 2000). But these averages mask variations. Across learning areas, science does badly. Before the mid-1980s, the apartheid government argued that black Africans did not need science and mathematics, and equipped and staffed schools accordingly (Rogan and Gray, 1999). These subjects are now receiving special attention (Department of Education, 2001b), but it will be many years before equitable access is achieved.

Two factors greatly limit progress. First, the South African economy struggles as it shifts from primary industry to manufacturing and service industries within the global economy. The demands of global competition, as they exist currently, greatly limit the funds available for social spending (Carnoy, 2001; Castells, 2001). Second, HIV/AIDS is pandemic. Current HIV incidence is about 25 per cent nationally, around 50 per cent in some rural districts (Badcock-Walters, 2001). Massive destruction is inevitable, at enormous costs financially as well as socially. Funds for schooling will be harder to find. Science teachers will be sought by other industries, similarly hit. Even to sustain a functioning education system will be a major challenge.

Given this scenario, it might be argued that 'Science for All' is not affordable in South Africa; the nation would do better to focus provision on selected students. Politically this option has already been rejected (Department of Education, 2001b) – not only on the bases of labour force and equity, but also as a response to wounds of colonialism and apartheid:

> The effect [of imperialism] is to annihilate a people's belief in their names, their languages, their environment, in their heritage of struggle, in their unity, in their capacities, and ultimately in themselves. It makes them see their past as one wasteland of non-achievement, and it makes them want to distance themselves from that wasteland. It makes them want to identify with that which is furthest removed from themselves; for instance, with other people's languages rather than their own.
>
> (Ngugi, 1986, quoted by Mbeki, 2000)

Western science and mathematics are two of those 'languages'. On the one hand they are gateways to national and international discourse, economic development, and educational status, but on the other hand they represent a foreign culture and threaten local knowledge, purporting to be 'better'. Science and mathematics as elite and exclusive subjects sounds like an echo of a 'language' that is in one breath coveted and spurned.

Who is 'All' and what do they want?

In the leafy northern suburbs of Johannesburg, some colleagues and I in 2000 trialled a Grade 8 science unit we were writing, on what it means to 'work scientifically' (Malcolm and Keane, 2001). From a variety of cultural backgrounds, the twenty-seven students were all proficient in English (the language of the playground as well as the classroom). In class, they were imaginative and enthusiastic, analysing, drawing pictures, writing stories, enacting role-plays, completing and even creating homework for themselves. Part of our unit was about science-based jobs. The students worked on it deeply, optimistic about doing well at school and becoming part of the global economy – yes, perhaps in science careers. The conversations at home that many recounted indicated that their families and friends supported these options, as did their teachers. Through hefty school fees and fundraising, the school was well equipped with spaces and playing fields, laboratories, and libraries. In the foyer, paintings, photographs, and trophies in glass cupboards celebrated people, and security gates kept everyone safe.

A hundred kilometres east of Cape Town, Mrs Dee (not her real name) teaches forty-five students in a Grade 4/5 composite class, in a 'farm school' (Malcolm, 2001c). Farm schools such as this are common in South Africa, built on private land, often by the (white) farmer, originally for the children of (black) workers and their families. Government involvement in farm schools varies, usually providing staff and administration costs, but not necessarily building maintenance and utilities. From the road, the line of rooms looked tired in the rocky grounds, but inside, the Grade 4/5 classroom was alive with children, posters, and winter sun. In this school community, none of the parents has employment, and there is no dole. Some 85 per cent still pay the school fees – a meagre R25 (US$2.50) per year.

The lesson was about dissolving, using powders Mrs Dee had brought from her kitchen, seven jars of water, forty-five sheets of paper and thirty pencils, shared. The children worked comfortably, chattering in isiXhosa and English. 'Dissolve' was a new word for everyone (as was its isiXhosa equivalent), and Thabo was proud to report: 'So the water dissolves!' When all presentations were done, Mrs Dee took up the claim: 'In English', she explained, 'We can say: "The salt dissolves", or better: "The salt dissolves in the water". Or we can say: "The water dissolves the salt", but we don't say: "The water dissolves".' My head was spinning! A second language is not only new words, but new grammar, and in isiXhosa, subject–verb–object relationships are expressed differently.

Did the students talk about 'science' at home, and what did they talk about? Mostly, they told me, they talked to older 'brothers', about things they were doing in school, such as water and energy, and things their brothers told them about plants and animals, such as names, characteristics, relationships, and stories.

In October 2001, I visited a rural secondary school a hundred kilometres north of Durban, to talk to a class of Grade 8 students about their interests. In this region, HIV infection is above 40 per cent (Badcock-Walters, 2001), and I wondered how this might influence our conversation. The school stands alone, its large, rectangular buildings out of place among scattered huts that are round with thatched roofs. Many students walk many kilometres to school, and it was raining so heavily that some routes were impassable. No sooner had school started than it was cancelled. Forty of the students in the class were happy to stay for our appointment. Their teachers estimate that over half of the children in the area claim African religion as their belief system and the others Christianity (though usually strongly mixed with African religion). African traditions are strong in people's daily lives.

The students worked for two hours, talking and writing mostly in isiZulu. What were their science interests? Many of their questions were hard, with a sense of the awesome:

- What enables a single moon to light up the whole world?
- What makes the rain fall in one place and not in other places?
- What causes thunder and lightning?
- What causes the waves and the noise they make in the sea?
- Why does a stone fall quicker than paper?
- If it is raining, small frogs appear. Where do they come from?
- What makes radio and television able to collect all announcements?

Multiculturalism is different in South Africa from countries such as Australia and The Netherlands. First, it stretches across a wide range of beliefs, traditions, socio-economic conditions, physical environments, and lifestyles. Second, the major cultural groups still tend to live in their own areas, often with a strong sense of 'place'. While the nation has many cultures, most individual schools do not. Third, many ethnic groups (and there are eleven official South African languages) properly claim South Africa as their land – they are not recent immigrants expecting to 'integrate' into a dominant culture. They bring their traditions and hopes to the science curriculum.

One science or many?

'Science for All', scientific literacy, and STS in the international literature tend to view science as an object and singular. Even as language shorthand, the singular carries a subtext: a single, objective definition of science exists. Inspection of outcomes statements and standards in the UK, New Zealand, Canada, Australia, the US *Project 2061* and the US National Standards reveals a definition that is heavily positivist and mechanistic, centred on the 'basics' from physics, chemistry, biology, and geology. Overlays of STS are added, but with science still a definable entity, interacting with technology and society like point charges in a physics problem. This assumption, of a single (Western) science, often arises in cultural approaches, such as those of Jegede, Aikenhead, Ogunniyi, and Coburn: Western science is a particular culture with a particular worldview (Coburn, 1996) that demands border crossings (Costa, 1995; Aikenhead, 1996), collateral learning (Jegede, 1995, 1998), and contiguity strategies (Ogunniyi, 2002). This is a fair position in so far as these authors are talking about 'school science' as it is usually defined, as a result of negotiations and history. But school science can be changed!

The consensus in Western countries on the nature of science in the curriculum can be challenged from many perspectives. These range from the political (whose interests are served?) to the practical (are distinctions between sciences, applied sciences, engineering, medicine, and environmental management worth the effort?), to the educational (are such oversimplifications justifiable?) and the philosophical (does Western science offer 'truth'?). All of these debates are real in South Africa, as the nation seeks not only economic transformation, but to articulate its cultural heritages and ways of knowing. For example, reductionism and Cartesian dualisms of seventeenth-century Western philosophy – with their separations of subject/object, mind/matter, physical/spiritual – are deeply embedded in Western science curricula. This is in spite of assaults on them from within physics – begun more than 100 years ago through quantum theory and relativity, and continued through fundamental particle research and the thermodynamics of far-from-equilibrium systems (Bawa, 1997). It is in spite of critiques by social scientists (whose work becomes increasingly relevant as science becomes more applied and socially accountable), feminists, and post-structuralists (Harding, 1998; Gough, 2001). It is in spite of constructivism, which science education embraced in the 1980s as learning theory (Fensham *et al.*, 1994; Fensham, 2000), but not as epistemology and ontology.

African worldviews are incompatible with the axioms of positivist science. Though details vary from one tradition to another, all African worldviews emphasise the continuity of subject and object, matter, mind and spirit, human and non-human, living, once-living and non-living, natural and supernatural, individual and community (Jegede, 1995; Ogunniyi *et al.*, 1995). These ideas are central to *ubuntu*: 'I am through others; because we are, therefore I am'. In *ubuntu*, the definition of 'other' stretches beyond people to encompass ancestors, animals, plants, and the physical environment. *Ubuntu* is about harmony (Boon, 1996; Schneider, 1997). Further, contrary to the usual scientific axiom of reproducibility, African experience is that some people have 'special hands', so that one cook will always produce better food than another, one gardener better vegetables than another, one experimenter different results from another (Khumalo, 2001). These variations are not reducible to chance or failure to follow instructions, but depend on powerful influences (for which supporting evidence is available). Chance and coincidence are dismissed as causal explanations: the interesting question is not simply whether the anopheles mosquito spreads malaria, but why that mosquito bit that woman. Thus, for many Africans, Western sciences are limited at heart by their axioms, their compartmentalisation, and the relatively narrow scope of their explanations.

Reductionism and learning

In science education, reductionist simplifications arise also in the triads knowledge–skills–values, and content–process–context: the elements are not discrete, but part of a dynamic whole (Fensham, 1985; 1991). They surface similarly in the polarisations of cognition/behaviour, and constructivism/behaviourism. 'Learning' is neither cognition (inner mental action) nor behaviour (outward action), nor merely an interplay between the two: it involves affective, subconscious, unconscious, and irrational processes and influences, often captured in notions of 'practice' (Morrow, 2001).

Approaches to learning as practice are well developed in sports, crafts, apprenticeships, and religious observance. In all these cases, novices work with teachers who are skilled practitioners in a community of learners. Learning occurs through immersion – practising, analysing, theorising, training, explaining, and copying. Soccer players, for example, study the rules and purposes of the game; learn directly and indirectly from coaches, models, and peers; develop physical skills, strategic thinking, and teamwork; analyse, reflect, and theorise about their own performances and those of others; work together in set plays, mini-games, and full matches. The subtleties of performance, and learning, are often beyond analysis: what confluence of perception, imagination, excitement, skill, and magic led that striker to score that goal at that moment? In science education, ideas of tacit knowledge and teaching as practice are acknowledged in teacher education (Roth, 1998; Tobin, 1998), but not often for students in schools. They could be.

We need to be clear about what 'practice' refers to: is it the practice of science, or the practice of education? It is both: becoming a better practitioner in science, learning to work scientifically, and to understand and use the strengths and limitations of working scientifically, are part of becoming more educated. It remains to contend with many different practices in the sciences, and many different practices of education. In South Africa, these choices need to be made in a multicultural context, acknowledging that for much of their time *sangomas* and *inyangas*, herbalists, engineers, industrial chemists, psychologists, marine biologists, and chefs all work scientifically in their domains.

It is always difficult to throw out bath-water without there being a baby in it somewhere. In accepting the complexity of 'practice', the problematic nature of 'science', and the subtleties of becoming a skilled practitioner, we need to accept the value of analysing a practice and theorising about it. This takes us back to 'Which practices?' and the philosophies, procedures, knowledge, and techniques that underlie them, but need not reduce practice to a single 'object'. Turnbull (1997) helps, in his distinction between representational knowledge and performative knowledge. Representational knowledge consists of concepts, metaphors, and conceptual schemes (and their underlying world-views, assumptions, and processes of legitimation) used to explain the world. Performative knowledge is experience, and what people do to get results. Both performative knowledge and representational knowledge are culturally determined and deeply entwined. Different cultures can have similar performative knowledge (throwing a stone, growing corn, preserving food, developing a scientific theory, or behaving compassionately to others) but underpin it with different representational knowledge. In science education, Western science representations, interpretations, and processes of legitimation are usually the focus of the classroom: they are treated as 'truths' more than representations or models. As noted earlier, this position is problematic for many African students. On the other hand, African students have no problems with similarities in performative knowledge and its centrality in all sciences.

Ideas of knowledge as culturally defined representations, like approaches to learning, cannot be separated from language. At the level of words, in isiZulu for example, one word suffices for force, energy, momentum, and pressure. In English there are many words. Meanings are carried also by grammar and syntax, the metaphors that underpin adjectives and nouns, and the nuances that express humour and irony. Meanings are multiple and often subtle. (Consider, for example, the prejudices, from an African viewpoint, in such English terms as 'supernatural', 'traditional beliefs', and 'tribe'.) English is the language of instruction in most African schools, African language is their language of thinking and identity, so students work back and forth (Rollnick, 2001; Malcolm *et al.*, 2000). Code switching is increasingly advocated, but a more complete cultural perspective to language is required (Rollnick, 2001). This echoes the Ngugi (1986) passage quoted earlier, and slogans that are part of the revival of African languages in South Africa, such as: 'Me and my language are one.'

South African students and their teachers negotiate these conflicts and prejudices in various ways. In the primary school, much of the science in the curriculum is descriptive, technical, and non-controversial – its focus is performative knowledge. Students (like those in my accounts earlier) find science interesting and link it to their lives. Further, teachers such as Mrs Dee are prepared not to be dogmatic about, for example, whether water is 'alive'. Through secondary school, the conflicts become more demanding as the focus shifts to representational knowledge. Here many students – and their teachers – resolve the issues by treating the syllabus, textbook, and examination as a closed system, working to pass, without much concern for believing the science they learn (Costa, 1995; Jegede, 1995; 1998; Aikenhead, 1996). Even so, individual students make different choices. For example, Sibusiso Manzini (1999) worked with a group of Grade 11 students, incorporating Zulu experience into the classroom. In one activity, the class burned incense (as is done in religious rites), and talked about why the smoke rose. At the end of the sequence, in the context of the science classroom, some students insisted that the smoke rose to find ancestors; some said it rose because of convection and air currents that ancestors controlled; and some discounted any roles of ancestors. As Sibusiso noted, all these students belonged to the same school class, the same community, and so had similar backgrounds in and beyond school. Nevertheless, they made personal choices, with more of less conviction, according to their own criteria and purposes at that time of their lives.

Globalisation, localisation, and isolation

Issues of multiculturalism in the science curriculum might be more easily negotiated but for three pressures:

- The predictive powers of Western scientific theories – and their openness to change – are indisputable. Whatever their limitations, whether or not they 'represent reality', they surely say something about reality and warrant serious study as a system of thought. Western science as a system of thought fits with the long-standing ideals of liberal education and its more recent expressions in critical pedagogy.
- Western scientific theories and practices have demonstrated the contributions they can make to technological developments in manufacturing, communication, medicine, agriculture, etc. – blunders notwithstanding. Western science has instrumental value personally and nationally.
- Western sciences and technologies are pivotal in the globalisation of economies and industries, and to international discourse in these domains – entangled though they are with economic, military, and political manouvres. Western science has pragmatic value.

Globalisation, in its current form, is deeply problematic for South Africa and groups within it, such as rural Africans. Economic competitiveness depends on 'value-added labour', especially in-service-based and knowledge-based industries, management, science, and technology. Education is more critical than ever, with science education centre stage. Current levels of science education in South Africa, coupled with weaknesses in communications infrastructure and electrical supply, make it hard for the nation to compete. Further, international competitiveness and discourse tend to produce (and require) common frameworks and standards in the science curriculum. (For example, the Third International Maths and Science Study (TIMSS) applied the same tests all around the world, tests in which South Africa performed badly. On 27 November 2001, the national Minister for Education announced with pride that a Scottish authority had evaluated South African Grade 12 examinations and pronounced them of 'world standard'.) On the other hand, localisation of identity and control suggests science education attuned to local cultures and economies. For most South Africans this involves small–scale industries and entrepreneurial activity, often linked to traditional practices in remote settings. This implies science education quite different from that homo–genised in TIMSS and 'world standards'.

In South Africa, this tension between global and local, more than between 'Science for All' and 'Science for Some', dominates educational planning. Resolution is immensely difficult. To play the globalisation game (as currently defined) is to risk exploitation, growing poverty, and decreasing government control over national affairs; not to play is to risk isolation and, once again, poverty. So the nation walks a tightrope, hoping to 'leapfrog' into the devel–oped world, trying to balance social development and economic development, wondering about 'trickle-down effects' as the gap grows between rich and poor, optimistic that the rules of the global economy will change. The rules are bound to change (Carnoy, 2001; Castells, 2001; Illbury and Sunter, 2001). But it is not clear how and when, nor whether developing countries will have any say.

'Science for All' or 'learner–centred science'?

'Learner–centred science', with its emphasis on inclusion, is implicit in concep–tions of 'Science for All' such as Peter's (Fensham, 1985), but 'learner–centred science' is more overtly multicultural, and avoids the notion of 'one science'. Learner–centred education is central to South African policy:

> Educational and management processes must therefore put the learners first, recognising and building on their knowledge and experience, and responding to their needs.
>
> (Department of Education, 1995, p. 21)

For teachers and curriculum designers in South Africa, it is helpful to think of levels of learner–centredness: (1) caring for students, (2) learner–centred pedagogy, and (3) learner–centred outcomes (Malcolm and Keane, 2001). For teachers, the levels are developmental, encouraging teachers to extend their skills from level 1 to level 3, but acknowledge level 1 is a start. For curri–culum designers and policy makers, the levels guide development of activities and structures that provide spaces for level 3 as well as levels 1 and 2.

The first level, caring for students, is basic. It commends belief in students' curiosity to know, their abilities, the knowledge and learning strategies they have already acquired, their participation in their communities, their rights to think, be, and become. Even in classrooms dominated by chalk-and-talk (as is typical in South African classrooms where forty to sixty students are crowded together), students can be highly successful (in examinations and in broader outcomes) when they feel that 'the teacher loves us and believes in us' (Malcolm *et al.*, 2000; Malcolm and Keane, 2001).

The second level focuses on pedagogy – choosing examples and contexts that relate to students' interests, helping them to extend and reconstruct their knowledge in ways that engage diversity. It draws especially from constructivist approaches and conceptual change theories as they dominated science education through the 1980s and 1990s (Driver, 1988; Hewson *et al.*, 1998; Fensham, 2000). As with Sibusiso's class, students might learn about the separation of mixtures by filtering beer in traditional and modern ways, or study phase changes through the ritual of body steaming (Manzini, 1999). Whether these approaches favour personal or social constructivism (Solomon, 1987) or mastery learning, their concern is to lead students to particular explanations. Differences in backgrounds and purpose are largely limited to pedagogical considerations, but nevertheless bring students' lives into the classroom. Many of the textbooks written recently in South Africa fit into this level (GICD, 2001a).

The third level extends beyond pedagogy to the knowledge itself, permitting students to form different constructions (personally and within groups) and give different emphases to the outcomes available. Constructivism in the classroom is now more than a learning theory; it reaches into epistemology and ontology. It steps outside the closure of usual 'objectives' approaches ('By the end of this lesson all students will be able to . . .'), and questions the 'truths' of school science. In doing so it raises for discussion issues of viability and comparability of alternative explanations (including Western sciences). As a first step, the class can test ideas through criteria of 'being' (Taylor, 1998) – measuring theories against experience (including personal experience of physical phenomena, other people's experiences and ideas, and trusted authorities). This brings into the open underlying assumptions, the nature of evidence, the design of experiments, and ways in which scientific ideas are tested and accepted. Students see that their own and others' knowledge claims are problematic, pro-scribed not only by experience, but by histories, social structures, and cultures. In Turnbull's (1997) terms, they can relate agreed performative knowledge to alternative representational knowledges. To choose between representations, a further test may be required: valuing (Taylor, 1998). Valuing points to the cultural and moral dimensions of testing ideas – whether via systems of thought (Western science, African religion, Buddhism), emancipatory ethics (advocated in critical pedagogy), or ethics of care (advocated by feminists such as Harding, 1998). Science is thus placed into larger frameworks of human thought and action.

The classroom now is a complex space. It has moved from goals of closure on particular representational or symbolic knowledge to science education as 'practice'. Sibusiso's example of burning incense (Manzini, 1999) offers an example. His students pondered two explanations of why the smoke rose: by convection or to find ancestors. The classroom experiment did not help –

for a start, the smoke did not rise continually in a vertical stream, as predicted by the school rule 'Hot air rises'. Second, attempts at more carefully controlled experiments were unlikely to be convincing – for example, to do the experiment in a box would have contrived a situation that no longer represented the room and did not have the same interest for ancestors. Resolution, for the class, had to depend on authorities – whether distant scientists and their frameworks, or cultural elders and theirs – and valuing.

Learner-centred education at level 3 makes new demands not only on teaching but also assessment. At levels 1 and 2, classroom processes are directed to closure on particular understandings and skills, so that students' achievements can be assessed against expectations. However, at level 3, assessment is complicated by the richness of opportunities, the variety of outcomes available, the diversity of students, and the extent to which outcomes are personalised. In the case of the burning incense, what 'mark' does Sibusiso give a student who favours the 'seeking ancestors' explanation? Does he ask students to provide the convection argument, regardless of their own beliefs? Or does he ask for critique of the various explanations (Malcolm, 2001b)? There are three issues here: the nature of the outcome desired (or achieved), the personalisation of outcomes, and the richness of outcomes. Who decides which outcomes are important for whom, what should be reported, and what should be the basis of 'accountability'?

Choosing the content of science

It is remarkable that such universal agreement exists on the 'essential' content of school science, that the choices are seldom justified against alternatives, and that they are so hard to change (Fensham 1985; 1988; 2000). Curriculum designers debate whether electrostatics should precede current electricity, whether there should be more thermodynamics, and whether there is 'time' for history and sociology of science. But the 'science basics' remain, even in STS and cultural approaches. History, politics, and the sociology of science education are powerful forces in the curriculum, internationally as well as nationally.

The choice of content is critical in designing 'Science for All', and many approaches have been developed and debated. I will focus on two aspects: the inclusion of 'culturally relevant sciences', and the freedom that students and their teachers might have in choosing content.

Inclusion of African experience and traditional knowledge can occur in a number of ways. At level 2 of learner-centredness, examples of African technology and African wisdom can be used as contexts for the development of Western science concepts and theories. The examples can be drawn from daily life, the local environment, cooking, health, agriculture, manufacturing, mining, transport, etc. (Moodie, 2001). This is straightforward, but has not been common: science texts and curricula, until recently, have been heavily slanted to urban life and Eurocentric experience, to abstractions (such as point charges and smooth surfaces) and laboratory equipment. In connecting to daily life, examples are chosen largely because of their consonance with Western sciences. Many examples are suitable and appropriate, able to bring together African knowledge and Western science knowledge. However, the approach soon becomes complicated. First, in its selection of instances, it takes particular performative knowledge and interprets it through Western science representations ('Is that how you brew beer? I can explain why that works.') thus privileging Western science. Second, there are numerous instances where African beliefs and Western science, even at the performative level, are contradictory, with moral implications. For example, many Africans believe that covering water containers, or sprinkling *muthi* (special potions) around a house, helps prevent lightning strikes. More serious is the oft-quoted (but poorly sourced) African belief that having sex with a virgin cures HIV/AIDS. Such instances bring the science curriculum face to face with moral responsibilities; level 2 learner-centredness moves to level 3.

Level 3 is clearly more than an intellectual critique of worldviews and philosophies. Its explorations of the validation of theories and choices between theories have consequences. Its regard for 'ethics of emancipation' and 'ethics of care' concern health, safety, human rights, and environmental conservation – as well as broad notions of social class, gender, and culture. Science education is singularly placed to address issues of health, survival, and human rights. How far should it go? As a moral activity, what is its proper scope in the total education of the child? To what extent should students believe (as against merely understand) the science we teach (Gould, 2001)? How should issues of content be resolved (politically and conceptually) in policy and curriculum design? These are important questions in the current redevelopment of the national curriculum (Moodie, 2001) – questions for which Western nations offer limited guidance.

In a learner-centred framework, especially in schools as diverse in their physical environments, resources, and communities as in South Africa, teachers and students must have considerable freedom to decide curriculum content. Choice can range upwards from selecting examples and contexts to develop set outcomes, through the interpretation of outcomes, to the design of outcomes. Each of these options is problematic in South Africa. At a practical level, most teachers lack the content knowledge and design skills to develop high-quality curricula, and need guidance, structures, and models (as well as in-service education). Textbooks have been, and remain, important resources for teachers and for students. However, textbooks designed for a national market cannot accommodate the diversity of environments and students. At a policy level, a balance has to be struck between equity in the sense of common outcomes (equitable access to higher education and employment), and equity in responding to students' individual backgrounds and aspirations. In South Africa, both options have histories. Under apartheid, different ethnic groups and regions had different education, determined to limit the access of blacks to higher education and employment. At the same time, curricula (for all ethnic groups) gave scant regard to African experience and culture, again privileging whites. Policy has to provide for common national outcomes, and at the same time accommodate diversity.

A policy framework for learner–centred science

Curriculum 2005 (Department of Education, 1997) was heralded as a symbol of the new South Africa (Jansen, 2000). Following countries such as the USA, Canada, Australia, and the UK, it opted for an outcomes-based approach, in which outcomes and standards are set centrally, and curriculum design and assessment are largely devolved to schools. The outcomes enabled redefinition of 'content'. They also provided a technology to support learner-centred education, in so far as they could be defined narrowly enough to claim common achievements, but broadly enough to allow local variation.

Design of the outcomes framework is no easy task! Too few outcomes limit the scope of the curriculum; too many make it unmanageable. If outcomes are too tightly defined, they limit local interpretation; if they are too loose, the goal of common achievements is sacrificed. If they are too close to current practice, there is no change; if they are too far away implementation is at risk. The design is further complicated by requirements of accountability. If accountability is to be achieved, in part through national testing programmes, variations in content (even at the detail of instances) from class to class are problematic. Teacher-based moderation processes can be established, but require long time frames.

Curriculum 2005 proceeded boldly, with a set of overarching critical outcomes (including problem solving, critical thinking, communicating, personal management, and teamwork), and specific outcomes in each of eight learning areas. The science outcomes are broadly defined. Adding to the conceptual knowledge and process skills of Western science the relationships of science are: culture, environment, and economic development; ethics, and bias and inequities (that arise from the sciences; responsible decision making in science); and the contested (problematic) nature of knowledge in science (Department of Education, 1997). It was accompanied by policies on teacher education that emphasised the roles of teachers as subject experts and curriculum designers (Department of Education, 1999a; 1999b), and major programmes of in-service education.

Curriculum design: curriculum as story

Complex outcomes and learner-centred education (especially at level 3, but even at level 2) cannot be satisfied by linear 'instructional' curriculum designs. The metaphor of curriculum as 'story' offers a way forward. Narrative (as opposed to exposition) is able to communicate complex ideas, fold in various themes and outcomes, carry many levels of meaning, provide a secure and directed structure (organic, not linear), and maintain interest. It is open ended, enabling students to respond in different ways, shaping meaning through their experiences, actions, interactions, and imagination (Egan, 1976; 1988; Gough, 1993; Gudmunsdottir, 1991; Malcolm, 1998). Curriculum as story can be approached in a number of ways. One strategy makes direct use of narratives (whether as fiction, historical accounts, or case studies) as inputs to classroom activity. Another considers students' lives (and the curriculum itself) as an unfolding story, in which the students are writers/actors. A third uses the structure of stories as a model for the structure of curriculum. The story below offers an example (Malcolm, 2001a). Phoka was teaching energy to a Grade 3 class:

> Phoka introduced ideas of energy through a game. 'What happens if the cow runs out of grass?' The students responded easily: 'It dies'. 'Yes, it stops', said Phoka. 'What if the car runs out of petrol?' It stops too, the students replied. This started the game. The students had to think of other situations where something runs out, and causes the animal, object or machine to stop. Phoka asked them to draw pictures, and write below: 'If ___ runs out of ___ it stops'. Their pictures showed animals and people running out of food, machines running out of fuel, appliances running out of electricity, plants running out of sunlight and water, soccer players running out of energy. (Indeed some of the students used the word energy.) As they worked, Phoka moved among them, talking with them, helping with words, checking that they had pencils.
>
> Some students explained their pictures to the class. The class talked about different ideas, and Phoka introduced some words: fuel, food, electricity, sunlight. He explained that these were different sources of energy, and that scientists would summarise the results by saying that 'If ___ runs out of energy, it stops'. Energy can make things grow, make things move, and produce heat or light.
>
> He asked the students to go to three corners of the room with their drawings, depending on whether, in their pictures, the energy was for growing, moving, or making heat/light. In their groups, the students checked each other's pictures. Phoka asked them, within their groups, to say what was 'running out'. Was it fuel, food, electricity, sunlight? The students saw that different sources of energy could sometimes have the same effect. They regrouped according to sources, rather than effects. Finally, Phoka asked the students to write answers to two questions: What were some of the sources of energy? What were some of the things energy did? Phoka moved around, looking at what students were writing, helping students who didn't understand.
>
> The next day Phoka took the students on a walk through the nearby shops. They had to identify instances of 'If ___ runs out of energy, it stops'. They saw buses, bicycles, walkers, grass, shops, cash registers, lights, radios. They talked about possible sources of energy in each case, and were amazed at the idea that almost everything that happens around us depends on energy. They also realised that buying energy was one of

the important things people did with money. During the walk, Phoka talked to students about what they were finding, and helped them understand about energy and energy sources.

Back in class, Phoka showed some pictures from magazines and newspapers. In some places, cows are running out of grass, cars out of petrol, people out of food, trees out of sunlight. He asked the students to choose a picture they felt strongly about, and write a sentence about that picture. The students talked about the importance of sharing and saving energy.

To end the unit, Phoka raised with the students that they could take steps to share energy, and save energy in their own houses. He set them into groups of four, and asked each group to design a poster that could be put up in the school, to help everyone think about saving energy. They made a variety of posters – put on a jersey instead of lighting a fire; eat fresh fruit rather than cooking; don't waste; walk to the shop instead of going in the bus. Some of the posters were put up in the school foyer, some in the corridor, and some in the classroom. Phoka looked through the posters carefully, to see which students seemed to understand about energy and energy sources, and made notes on a checklist.

Linked to the idea of curriculum as story is the view of the curriculum designer as story-writer/teller (Egan, 1988). Many teachers and curriculum writers find this a liberating idea: it encourages imaginative thinking (there is no 'correct' place to start), a sense of audience, attention to subtext as well as text, and the incorporation of waves of divergence and convergence developing plot, interest, and progression (Malcolm, 1998). It is also a conceptualisation of teaching that resonates with the traditions and roles of story-telling in African societies. Further, there are many stories that can be written, with different degrees of complexity and open-endedness, some more linear in their structure than others (Fleer *et al.*, 1995; GICD, 2001b; Malcolm, 1996). More experimentation and research are required to develop these approaches.

Concluding remarks

Peter Fensham has been a champion of 'Science for All' and learner-centred education, arguing for it on an international scale, drawing from research, policy documents, and published curriculum materials in many cultures. He hasn't simply written about it and talked about it. He has involved himself directly in policy formation, curriculum development, and the politics of change. From this deep experience, he has promoted the dream, but also understood the difficulties.

I have tried to show how the ideas and problems he articulated, combined with other writings, have been taken up in South Africa, added to, and interpreted in the local context. The problems are far from solved! While there is wide professional and public support for the underlying principles of *Curriculum 2005*, weaknesses in the technical aspects of the initial documents (especially their open approach to content) and lack of capacity for implementation are deep concerns (Chisholm, 2000). A review of the policy and rewriting of the documents is in progress. The revision is likely to draw back somewhat from the original policy, as it struggles with content, globalisation/localisation, and devolution of curriculum and assessment. But perhaps not too far.

A story is never finished. Teachers and thinkers such as Sibusiso and thousands like him have responded to the notions of learner-centred, culturally inclusive science and teachers as curriculum designers, and will continue to explore, experiment, and imagine. They enjoy sharing authority and power with their students, are stimulated by their students, and learn from them.

The children I talked with recently in rural KwaZulu Natal, in many ways, capture the lives and hopes of South Africans when they ask: 'What makes the rain fall in one place and not in other places?' and, in almost the same breath, 'What enables a single moon to light up the whole world?'

References

Aikenhead, G. (1996) 'Science education: border crossing into the subculture of science', *Studies in Science Education* 27: 1–52.

Badcock-Walters, P. (2001) 'HIV and its impact on the education sector: the management challenge', Health Economics & HIV/AIDS Research Division, University of Natal, Durban, seminar presented at University of Natal, 14 September 2001.

Bawa, A.C. (1997) 'Knowledge production and curriculum research strategies in South Africa', in N. Cloete, J. Muller, M.W. Makgoba, and D. Ekong (eds) *Knowledge, Identity and Curriculum Transformation in Africa*, Cape Town: Maskew Miller Longman, pp. 43–51.

Boon, M. (1996) *The African Way: the power of interactive leadership*, Sandton: Zebra.

Brink, A. (1997) *Imaginings in Sand*, London: Vintage.

Carnoy, M. (2001) 'The role of the state in the new global economy', in J. Muller, N. Cloete, and S. Badat (eds) *Challenges of Globalisation*, Cape Town: Maskew Miller Longman, pp. 22–34.

Castells, M. (2001) 'The new global economy', in J. Muller, N. Cloete, and S. Badat (eds) *Challenges of Globalisation*, Cape Town: Maskew Miller Longman, pp. 2–21.

Chisholm, L. (chair) (2000) *The Ministerial Review of Curriculum 2005*, Department of Education, Pretoria.

Coburn, W.W. (1996) 'Constructivism and non-western science education research', *International Journal of Science Education* 18: 295–310.

Coetzee, J.M. (1999) *Disgrace*, London: Vintage.

Costa, V.B., (1995) 'When Science is "another world": relationships between worlds of family, friends, school and science', *Science Education* 79: 313–33.

Department of Education (1995) *White Paper in Education*, Pretoria, South Africa.

Department of Education (1997) *Curriculum 2005*, Pretoria, South Africa.

Department of Education (1999a) *Assessment policy in the General Education and Training Band*, Pretoria, South Africa.

Department of Education (1999b) *Norms and Standards of Teacher Education*, Pretoria, South Africa.

Department of Education (2001a) *Education in South Africa: achievements since 1994*, Pretoria: South Africa.

Department of Education (2001b) *National Strategy for Mathematics, Science and Technical Education in General and Further Education and Training*, Pretoria, South Africa.

Driver, R. (1988) 'Theory into practice II: a constructivist approach to curriculum development', in P. Fensham (ed.) *Development and Dilemmas in Science Education*, London: Falmer Press, pp. 133–49.

Egan, K. (1976) *Educational Development*, New York: Oxford University Press.

Egan, K. (1988) *Teaching as Story Telling: an alternative approach to teaching and curriculum*, Chicago: University of Chicago Press.

Fensham, P.J. (1985) 'Science for All', *Journal of Curriculum Studies* 17: 415–35.

Fensham, P.J. (1988) 'Familiar but different. Some dilemmas and new directions in science education', in P.J. Fensham (ed.) *Developments and Dilemmas in Science Education*, London: Falmer Press, pp. 1–26.

Fensham, P.J. (1991) 'Science and technology', in P. Jackson (ed.) *Handbook of Research on Curriculum*, Chicago: AERA, pp. 789–828.

Fensham, P.J. (2000) 'Providing suitable content in the Science for All curriculum', in R. Millar, J. Leach, and J. Osborne (eds) *Improving Science Education: the contribution of research*, Buckingham: Open University Press, pp. 147–64.

Fensham, P.J., Gunstone, R.F., and White, R.T. (eds) (1994) *The Content of Science: a constructivist approach to its teaching and learning*, London: Falmer Press.

Fleer, M., Hardy, T., Bacon, K., and Malcolm, C. (1995) *They Don't Tell the Truth About the Wind: a K-3 science program*, Carlton, Australia: Curriculum Corporation.

GICD (2001a) Unpublished report on the evaluation of recent school texts, Johannesburg: Gauteng Institute of Curriculum Development.

GICD (2001b) *Working together – Scientifically*, Johannesburg: Gauteng Institute of Curriculum Development.

Gough, N. (1993) *Laboratories in Fiction*, Geelong: Deakin University Press.

Gough, N. (2001) 'Thinking globally in environmental education: some implications for internationalizing curriculum inquiry', in W.F. Pinar (ed.) *Handbook of International Curriculum Research*, New York: Lawrence Erlbaum Associates.

Gould, C. (2001) 'Knowledge, belief and understanding in science education', Paper presented at the Sixth International History and Philosophy of Science and Teaching Conference, Denver, USA, 7–10 November 2001.

Gudmunsdottir, S. (1991) 'Story-maker, story-teller: narrative structures in curriculum', *Journal of Curriculum Studies* 23: 207–18.

Harding, S. (1998) *Is Science Multicultural? Postcolonialisms, Feminisms and Epistemologies*, Bloomington and Indianapolis: Indiana University Press.

Hewson, P.W., Beeth, M.E., and Thorley, N. (1998) 'Teaching for conceptual change', in B.J. Fraser and K.G. Tobin (eds) *International Handbook of Science Education*, Dordrecht: Kluwer Academic Press, pp. 199–218.

Illbury, C. and Sunter, C. (2001) *The Mind of a Fox*, Cape Town: Human and Rousseau Tefelberg.

Jacobson, D. (1971) 'Introduction' to Schreiner, O. (1883, reprinted 1982) *The Story of an African Farm*, Harmondsworth: Penguin, p. 7.

Jansen, J. (2000) 'Setting the scene: historiographies of curriculum policy in South Africa', in J.D. Jansen and P. Christie (eds) *Changing Curriculum: studies on outcomes-*

based education in South Africa, Kenwyn, South Africa: Juta Academic Publishers, pp. 3–21.

Jegede, O. (1995) 'Collateral learning and the eco-cultural paradigm in science and mathematics education', *Studies in Science Education* 25: 97–137.

Jegede, O. (1998) 'The knowledge base for working in science and technology education', in P. Naidoo and M. Savage (eds) *African Science and Technology Education into the New Millennium: practice, policy and priorities*, Kenwyn, South Africa: Juta, pp. 151–76.

Khumalo, G. (2001) Master's work in process, University of Durban Westville, private communication.

Malcolm, C. (ed.) (1996) *Could We? Should We? Year 10 Science*, Carlton, Australia: Curriculum Corporation.

Malcolm, C. (1998) *Making Curriculum 2005 Work*, Johannesburg: RADMASTE Centre, University of the Witwatersrand.

Malcolm, C. (2001a) 'Learning from stories: meet Phoka and Elsie', Proceedings, SAARMSTE Conference, Ninth Annual Meeting, January 1999, Maputo, Mozambique, pp. 128–36.

Malcolm, C. (2001b) 'Shopping for culture', *Lab Talk* 45(June): 33–7.

Malcolm, C. (2001c) 'Deep thinking', *Lab Talk* 45(October): 25–38.

Malcolm, C. and Keane, M. (2001) 'Working scientifically, in learner-centred ways', Paper presented at the Sixth International History and Philosophy of Science and Teaching Conference, Denver, USA, November 2001.

Malcolm, C., Keane, M., Hooloo, L., Kgaka, M., and Ovens, J. (2000) *Why Some Disadvantaged Schools Succeed in Mathematics and Science: A study of feeder schools*, Pretoria: Department of Education.

Manzini, S. (1999) 'The influence of culturally-relevant science curriculum on African learners', unpublished MEd thesis, University of Durban Westville.

Moodie, P. (2001) Private communication.

Morrow, W. (2001) 'Scriptures and practices', *Perspectives in Education* 19: 87–107.

Ngugi Wa Thiong'o (1986) *Decolonising the mind*, quoted by South African President Thabo Mbeki, in The Second Oliver Tambo Lecture, 11 August 2000, Port Elizabeth, South Africa.

Ogunniyi, M.B. (2002) 'Science learning and the contiguity hypothesis', Paper presented at the 10th Annual Conference of the Southern African Association for Research in Mathematics, Science and Technology Education, Durban, January 2002.

Ogunniyi, M.B., Jegede, O.J., Ogawa, M., Yandila, C.D., and Oladele, F.K. (1995) 'Nature of worldview presuppositions among science teachers in Botswana, Indonesia, Japan, Nigeria and The Philippines', *Journal of Research in Science Teaching* 32: 817–31.

Rogan, J. and Gray, B. (1999) 'Science education as South Africa's Trojan Horse', *Journal of Research in Science Teaching* 36: 373–85.

Rollnick, M. (2001) 'Current issues and perspectives on second language learning of science, *Studies in Science Education* 35: 93–122.

Roth, W.-M. (1998) 'Teaching and learning as everyday activity', in B.J. Fraser and K.G. Tobin (eds) *International Handbook of Science Education*, Dordrecht: Kluwer Academic Press, pp. 169–82.

Schneider, C.G. (1997) 'From diversity to engaging difference: a framework for the higher education curriculum', in N. Cloete, J. Muller, M.W. Makgoba, and

D. Ekong (eds) *Knowledge, Identity and Curriculum Transformation in Africa*, Cape Town: Maskew Miller Longman, pp. 101–33.

Solomon, J. (1987) 'Social influences on the construction of pupils' understanding of science', *Studies in Science Education* 14: 63–82.

Taylor, P.C. (1998) 'Constructivism: value added', in B.J. Fraser and K.G. Tobin (eds) *International Handbook of Science Education*, Dordrecht: Kluwer Academic Press, pp. 1111–26.

Tobin, K. (1998) 'Issues and trends in the teaching of science', in B.J. Fraser, and K.G. Tobin (eds) *International Handbook of Science Education*, Dordrecht: Kluwer Academic Press, pp. 129–52.

Turnbull, D. (1997) 'Reframing science and other local knowledge traditions', *Futures* 29: 551–62.

3 Making science matter

Jonathan Osborne

Peter Fensham's life and work has been characterised by two features: an enduring sense of inner commitment to the notion that science education matters; and a grave dissatisfaction with existing provision. In the international arena, his is one name that has been strongly associated with the drive for systemic reform in science education and to offer a science education that would genuinely be for all. The outcome of his, and others', efforts, has been a dramatic change in the structure of school science but, sadly, not its form. Whereas, forty years ago, school science was essentially an offering for the elite – those who would become the future scientists of the next generation – now it is something which is seen as universal value and, perhaps more importantly, an essential component of the core curriculum for all. This achievement, to which he has made a significant contribution, has shifted science to the curriculum high table making it a subject of equal status to mathematics and, in many countries, an obligatory component from elementary school to the final stage of compulsory education. Moreover, this accomplishment has gone some way to removing the inequities of a science education which previously sustained unacceptable gender stereotyping.

Yet, as he would be the first to acknowledge, insisting on universal science education for all can only be justified if such a science education offers something which is of universal value to all. Thus, whilst there exists much common international consensus that science education matters, there is much less, if any, consensus, about the nature of the curriculum offering that would meet both the needs of future scientists and future citizens. Indeed, some, like Peter himself (1985) would question whether it is possible for it to do both (Collins, 2000; Millar and Osborne, 1998). Therefore, what I seek to do in this chapter is to take stock – to ask where have we come from in science education, what were the successes of such an approach, where are we now, where might we want to go and why, and finally, what are the implications? Much of this chapter will be an examination of the arguments in what I consider to be a seminal essay by Peter Fensham published in 1985 (Fensham, 1985) but still, alas, unheeded. In that work, the dilemmas confronting science education were clearly and articulately delineated. In addressing my questions then, I shall seek to explore what are the obstacles to the reforms offered by Peter

Fensham's visions. However, I also want to take the argument further to suggest that sustaining science curricula which attempt to serve two masters is, ultimately, a ruinous policy serving neither science nor society well.

Such a view is inevitably partial, limited by the fact that my views have been formed by the unique set of cultural circumstances in which I have been situated. Nevertheless, given that many of the dilemmas raised in this chapter, in particular the flight from science, are to be found in many societies across the globe, the evidence would suggest that, at least within the confines of a Western culture that permeates much of contemporary life, my argument may have much that may resonate more universally.

Science education: a retrospective look

The roots of science education lie in the noble, if somewhat wishful, aim that the study of science might develop the same attributes and intellectual abilities as the humanities. Briefly science education, in its inception, aimed to develop a knowledge and understanding of the significance and importance of the cultural achievements of the sciences. Moreover, advocates for formal education in science argued that its study would be an essential component to developing the intellectual and critical abilities of the educated and rational individual. That is somebody who is open minded, holds a commitment to evidence, and is persuaded by argument rather than dogma. However, even with its origin in the middle of the nineteenth century with influential champions such as Huxley and the then secretary for science education, Lyon Playfair, both major proponents of such a view, there remained many who, like Matthew Arnold, felt that scientific training as a form of education would pro-duce only a 'useful specialist' and not a truly educated man. Science education in Victorian England was always battling against the hegemony of the two Cs – the Classics and Christianity – and the curriculum that emerged into the twentieth century was modelled on the highly academic curriculum of the public school where these two were highly influential. In such a context, nothing so vulgar as mere technology and engineering education – applied knowledge of lower status, and which for many still is – could fight its way onto the curriculum. Rather 'the needs of the bookish few determined the education of the UNbookish many' (Barnett, 2001). Hence science education was forced into providing an academic course of science for scientists, largely divorced from its technical applications.

Indeed the efforts of Henry Armstrong and his emphasis on the value of the scientific method as a heuristic for critical thinking can be seen as an attempt to repudiate the argument of the traditionalists like Arnold. The event that changed much of this argument was the First World War. Emerging from the mire and mud of the battlefields of Europe was the recognition, within many European countries, that wars of the future would be dependent not on the insight and genius of their generals but, rather, on the technological superiority of their armaments and military equipment. Such products were, in contrast, dependent on a cadre of highly able and well-educated scientists and engineers. School science education was, therefore, to become subservient to the dominance of this singular need and the production of scientists and engineers that sustain and defend our society. The Allied success in the Second World War, dependent as it was on the superior technology of the Americans, the development of the atomic bomb, and the decoding of the German Enigma machines, served only to reinforce this view. By the middle of the twentieth century, as a consequence of these influences, the die that formed the framework of school science was well cast. Evidence that this was so comes from an examination of opportunities for scientific employment which were dominated by the needs of the defence industries. Granted, there were notable attempts by individuals such as Lancelot Hogben with his book *Science for the Million* to offer a vision of what a science education for all might be. This book, and others inspired by the general science movement of the 1930s and the 1950s, were essentially voices in the wilderness which went unheeded in the socio-political milieu of the era. Likewise attempts to give school science education a more technological and vocational dimension were still hampered by the dominance of the requirements of university entrance.

In his 1985 article Peter Fensham suggests that school science education of the 1960s and 1970s took place in a 'social and political vacuum'. This is a mistake. All of us, knowingly or unknowingly, are actors in a socio-political context. Those engaged in formulating policy and curricula for school science simply chose to meet the needs of a minority because the culture in which they were situated valued them more highly. In so doing, they chose to ignore any issues of social equity or considerations of what the entitlement of the majority of school students might be. Their needs, in the society of the time, were simply considered to be either marginal or best served by the education of an elite.

In such a context, any lingering view that such a science education might also be of value for the future citizen was further demolished by Cohen's (1952) articulate lament about the fallacies under which conventional science education laboured. Principal amongst Cohen's telling critique, which I have chosen to expand beneath in the light of contemporary scholarship, were:

1 The fallacy of transfer: this is a belief that knowledge and processes gained within science would be transferable to other domains. Cohen displays here a prescience of the seminal philosophical argument advanced by Hanson (1958) that theory and observation were interdependent. Hence skills in one domain would not transfer readily to another.
2 The fallacy of critical thinking: this is the argument that the study of science teaches students reflective thinking and logical analysis which may then be applied to other subjects of study and the conduct of ordinary living. However, as Collins (2000) has pointed out, contemporary science education is reliant on a long period of apprenticeship which requires a dogmatic and authoritarian education. Dependent as it is on transmission and rote

learning, such a science education does little to develop the critical faculties that are the hallmark of education in the humanities. Yet, given that science and mathematics might be considered to be the epitome of rational thought, surely such skills must be developed in the education of the scientist? Indeed, evidence that scientists do have such general faculties can be found in the work of Kuhn *et al.* (1988) and more recently the work of Hogan and Maglienti (2001). Hogan and Maglienti's work is valuable in providing some insight into this apparent contradiction showing that it is those who are engaged in the 'doing' of science – the professional scientists – that exhibit the characteristics of successful critical thinkers. The message of this research would suggest that developing knowledge without the opportunity to use it is akin to offering young people the opportunity to learn how to drive a car on a simulator. The inherent ersatzness of such activities fails to develop the cognitive capabilities of the professional scientist. Thus, any belief that formal school science education as currently constituted will develop the ability to think critically must remain, for all but a tiny minority, a chimera.

3   The fallacy of the scientific method: this is the belief that all the greatest discoveries in science had been the result of the consistent application (without much imagination, thought, or judgement) of a simple set of rules (often six in number) to every situation as it arose. Again, Cohen's arguments showed a remarkable foresight of the debate that was to emerge about the nature of science education stimulated by the sociological turn in the work of Kuhn, to be followed by that of Feyerabend, Latour, Collins, and others. All of these scholars have, step by step, destroyed any notion that there is any consistent method applied throughout the sciences. Even as recently as 2000, Ziman was forced to conclude:

> The function of science is to produce knowledge. What sort of knowledge does it produce? Until recently, this question was supposed to be essentially 'philosophical'. Unfortunately, the philosophers of science have not come up with a convincing answer. In spite of heroic efforts, they have simply failed to come up with a satisfactory definition of 'science'.
>
> (Ziman, 2000, p. 83)

Rather, the study of science now shows that those who have made the important discoveries of the past have never attempted anything such as those who teach the scientific method might suppose.

More fundamentally, such a formulaic conception of science is in danger of downplaying, or even denying, those very qualities of imagination, creativeness, and drama which lie at the intellectual heart of science. It is the creativity of Newton or Darwin and the ability to see the familiar in new ways that make their intellectual achievement so wondrous. And it is the potential of science to create new knowledge and to free us from the shackles of received wisdom that makes it such an intellectually liberating discipline. Yet it is hard to find such ideas conveyed within the often prosaic approach to the teaching of school science. If, as Cossons (1993) argues, the most significant determinants of our culture are science and technology, then an appreciation and understanding of the achievements of science is essential to decoding our culture and enabling public participation, whether it be protest or rejection.

4   The fallacy of miscellaneous information: once science education is conceived of in terms of a pre-professional training, rather than a general cultural education, it acquires a fundamentally different character. Rather than attempting to paint, in broad strokes, the major features of the scientific landscape and explain their significance and import, it becomes a process of training, rather than education. The hallmark of its emphasis on training is that it is foundationalist, emphasising what appears to be a set of basic concepts and unrelated, miscellaneous information. On such foundational knowledge is constructed the next layer of conceptual information and underpinnings – all of which are essential knowledge for the practising scientist. For the overwhelming majority, the problem is twofold. The first is that the lack of any interrelatedness makes this dish of dry facts unpalatable for many, killing a more general interest in science or, even worse, creating a hostility towards science and its further study. Second, and more tragically, is that:

> in focussing on the detail (for example, by setting out the content as a list of separate 'items' of knowledge as does the English and Welsh National Curriculum), we have lost sight of the major ideas that science has to tell. To borrow an architectural metaphor, it is impossible to see the whole building if we focus too closely on the individual bricks. Yet, without a change of focus, it is impossible to see whether you are looking at St Paul's Cathedral or a pile of bricks, or to appreciate what it is that makes St Paul's one the world's great churches. . . . Consequently, it is perhaps unsurprising that many pupils emerge from their formal science education with the feeling that the knowledge they acquired had as much value as a pile of bricks and that the task of constructing any edifice of note was simply too daunting – the preserve of the boffins of the scientific elite.
>
> (Millar and Osborne, 1998)

Sadly Cohen's arguments constituted yet another voice in the wilderness that was simply ignored.

Thirty-three years later, Peter Fensham was to document the attributes of such a science education in a different but sufficiently succinct and cogent form to merit reiteration here. School science, he said, has the following characteristics:

(a) it involves the rote recall of a large number of facts, concepts and algorithms that are not obviously socially useful;
(b) it involves too little familiarity with many of the concepts to enable their scientific usefulness to be experienced;
(c) it involves concepts that have been defined at high levels of generality among scientists without their levels of abstraction being adequately acknowledged in the school context, and hence their consequential limitations in real situations is not adequately indicated;
(d) it involves an essentially abstract system of scientific knowledge, using examples of objects and events to illustrate how the system is rather than those aspects of science of factual phenomena that enables some use or control of them to occur;
(e) it involves life experiences and social applications only as exemplary rather than as the essence of the science learning;
(f) the role of practical activity in its pedagogy is associated with the belief that this activity enhances the conceptual learning rather than being a source for the learning of essential skills;
(g) its content gives a high priority, even in biology, to the quantitative, and in chemistry this priority is probably greater than it is for many practising chemists;
(h) it leaves to the continued study of these disciplines at the tertiary level the balance, meaning and significance that is lacking in (a) to (g).

(Fensham, 1985, p. 418)

The essential question for the reader at this point is – in what way, since then, has the state of affairs both in science education and the society it serves changed, if at all?

Science education – the contemporary landscape

Any consideration of the role of science education must begin not with an internalist view of its content and curricula, but rather with an externalist perception of the society it serves. As stated previously, school science does not exist in a social and political vacuum. Today's society is, if anything, dominated by science and technology, and perhaps even more so. Increasingly our lives depend on a set of technological artefacts such as cars, washing machines, computers, mobile phones, and other communications technology. Most of the inner functioning of these items is no longer accessible to the laypeople – an aspect which has created for all of us a greater dependency on science, technology, and expertise. However, the vision of science and technology offered in the 1960s – 'the white heat of the technological revolution' – has turned sour. For as Beck (1992) and others such as (Giddens, 1990; 1999) have pointed out, not only have science and technology been a source of solutions to the problems confronted by humanity, but they have, ever since Rachel Carson voiced her premonitions of doom associated with the unrestricted use of DDT, also become a source of risks and threats. The litany of environmental problems from the *Exxon Valdeez*, Chernobyl, Bhopal, ozone depletion, the greenhouse effect and BSE (to name but a few) are all seen as the product of the unrestricted march of science and technology. Second, there has been a transformation from a society based on nation states, and the competing ideologies of capitalism and communism, to one in which capitalism, in one form or another, has become hegemonic across the globe. Francis Fukiyama has described this state of affairs as 'the end of history' in that society has reached a state in which there are no longer any competing ideologies of what society might be. Moreover, with the growth of multinationals, an awareness that the problems confronting contemporary civilisation are often universal, and the growth of international travel, there has been an increasing globalisation of many of the issues challenging societies today. This has led to an increase in the power of international regulatory bodies and a weakening of the nation state. In such a context, there has been a diminished perception of external threats and less need for extensive investment in defence and, concomitantly, the scientists and technology needed to support such endeavour. Rather, the current emphasis on science and technology and, in turn, on the science education that provides the skilled personnel, is a product of the recognition that the competitiveness of international economies is now dependent on the value-added component that such a well-educated and highly qualified populace brings. Thus the problem of ensuring a sufficient supply of scientists and technologies identified by the Dainton and Swan Reports in the UK in the 1960s and the post-Sputnik response embodied in the Rickover Report in the USA remains, even though the reasons may have changed somewhat.

One indication of the growing emphasis of the political significance of science and technology to society can be seen in the importance attached to the TIMSS and PISA studies. Despite the attempts of educationalists to question the credibility of these studies (Gibbs and Fox, 1999; Wang, 2001), the results have had substantive policy implications in countries such as Germany where the political response has been to invest considerable sums in research to improve the quality of their educational output. Likewise in the USA, the recent Glenn Report (National Commission on Mathematics and Science Teaching for the 21st Century, 2000), *Before It's Too Late*, raised similar concerns. And here in the UK, the decision of the Parliamentary Committee on Science and Technology to investigate science education is a reflection of similar national concerns. Nevertheless, whilst there is some recognition of the extent of the problem inherent to science education, much of the political response is still couched in the naive belief that the problem is simply one of supply or performance. And that the answer lies simply in improving the quality of science teachers or of making scientific careers more attractive to young people. Sadly, there is simply a blind refusal to recognise that the science education offered to the majority of pupils is singularly unattractive fare –

inappropriate to their needs and interests. In addition, there is no awareness that the primary limitation of tests is that, having decided to make what is important measurable, an inevitable consequence is that only the measurable becomes important – that, in short, the need for such international tests to function effectively in a wide range of contexts means that they are simply a reflection of a system of science education which suffers from all the attributes of Peter Fensham's 1985 analysis.

At the root of the problem is that such a science education is intrinsically hard and unappealing. With the growth of mixed A-levels, students have simply chosen to vote with their feet rather than endure more of the same. Consequently the numbers taking only science A-levels post-16 in the UK has declined from 30 per cent in 1980 to 16 per cent in 1993, the last time such statistics were collected (Department of Education, 1994). During this period, the range of A-levels on offer has increased to include economics, business studies, psychology, sport science, and more. Science, in contrast, lacks the appeal and relevance of such courses. Moreover, it has fallen to a scientist (Shamos, 1995) to make the important point that as much as we like to think that we live in a society dominated by science and technology, the lives of people are actually more heavily influenced by a set of humanistic concerns embodied in the genres of tragedy, comedy, romance, and irony – issues to which science and technology with their unfamiliar genres and concerns with objects not humans only play second fiddle. Interest in humanities has also grown as the nature of society has changed (Giddens, 1990) to become one where individuals are increasingly reflexive. No longer does tradition and authority play such a significant role in structuring the social order. Rather, the nature of contemporary life is that social practices 'are constantly examined and reformed in the light of incoming information about those very practices, thus constitutively altering their character'.

Such a reflexive society produces a reflexive young mind that finds itself at odds with the authoritarian nature of science. Confronted with a subject that is heavily reliant on the learning of a large number of abstract facts and concepts of secondary or dubious relevance, school students have little enthusiasm to pursue further study. Such perceptions were most clearly articulated in a focus-group study we undertook to examine pupils' and parents' views of the school curriculum (Osborne and Collins, 2001). Attempts to frogmarch students across the scientific landscape, to offer no time to stand and stare, or to explore the issues that even school science can raise, are profoundly alienating for many students:

> If you, like, give suggestions they just ignore it and go – 'No it's written in the syllabus that you've got to do this'. And it's just kind of fixed upon the syllabus and you're like, 'Well can't we just find a gap for it?' And they're, like, 'No'.

And, as well, in an era where the science in the media is that of informatics and computers, lasers, biogenetics, materials technology, and cosmology, school science offers windows on what appears to most students to be yesterday's technology, elegantly articulated in the following comment:

> The blast furnace, so when are you going to use a blast furnace? I mean, why do you need to know about it? You're not going to come across it ever. I mean look at the technology today, we've gone onto cloning, I mean it's a bit away off from the blast furnace now, so why do you need to know it?

Many additional problems exist – such as that highlighted by Munro and Elsom (2000) that science teachers persist in marketing the value of studying science in terms of its instrumental value for a restricted subset of scientific careers rather than its general cultural value. However, the message is clear: that school science has continued to act as if it exists in a social and political vacuum and chosen to ignore the changing social context in which it finds itself. Thus, Canute like, it has persisted in offering an education for the majority which is based on a model developed for a minority. Granted there has been some tinkering at the edges – some attempts in simplification, or some welcome attempts to teach more about science such as the addition of the component 'Ideas and Evidence' in the most recent version of the English National Curriculum for Science (Department for Education and Employment, 1999). However, the attempt to sustain its foundational breadth rather than selective depth may, ironically, have made the problem of engaging the intellectual able with science worse as the treatment has become more superficial, less challenging, and less engaging. The best that can be said is, at least within the higher echelons of academic science, that such a policy has finally been recognised as bankrupt by the UK deans of science who in a recent press release stated:

> Broadly we agree with the analysis presented in the report *Beyond 2000: Science Education for the Future*. . . . We are acutely aware that the style of specialist school science curriculum has not changed for many years. We thus have to recognise that an approach that worked satisfactorily in the past as a preparation for higher education no longer does so in the changed social and communications environment of today. . . . From a higher education science perspective, therefore, we would happily see the general approach advocated in the Beyond 2000 report applied to the entire secondary science curriculum.
>
> (UK Deans of Science Committee, 2001, p. 29)

What, then, might an alternative vision of science education be?

Science education for 'All'

My wish here is not to reiterate the ideas and principles that can be found in *Beyond 2000: Science Education for the Future*. Rather, it is to return to and explore the ideas that Peter Fensham raised in his 1985 article. There he argued that the rationale for the content of the curriculum should be either that:

(a) the content (science knowledge and associated skills) should have social meaning and usefulness to the majority of learners;

or

(b) the content (science knowledge and associated skills) should assist learners to share in the wonder and excitement that has made the development of science such a great human and cultural achievement.

I would suggest that such principles emerge from asking a fundamentally different question: that is, rather than asking the traditional question 'what should school students learn about science?' we must, in contrast, take the radical step of asking 'what makes students want to learn science?' It is only an effective answer to the latter question that would enable us to design a curriculum and associated assessment system that sought to leave, as its residue, not a body of unrelated facts but an enduring interest and engagement with science and the knowledge it has to offer. It would differ in that its fundamental and primary aim would be affective and not cognitive. This is not to deny the value of some of the potentially cognitive outcomes of science education but simply to point to the fact that all knowledge has little value unless embedded in a framework where its value and utility are recognised by the recipient. Then, and only then, is there any chance that the cultural and intellectual achievement of scientific knowledge might be recognised. The science education that we have now is akin to attempting to grow seeds on stony ground – little takes root and much is a futile waste of both students' and teachers' efforts.

The answer to the question of what would make students want to learn science, emerging from the 1985 Cyprus workshop, was a list of 'umbrella topics' which might constitute a minimum science education and which might satisfy one or both criteria. These were the senses and their measurement, the Universe, the human body, health, nutrition, and sanitation, food, ecology, resources (natural and manufactured), population, pollution, use of energy, technology, and quality of life. Most if not all of these topics have an easily identifiable locus of interest – their ability to relate to the world and concerns of the adolescent. So, for instance, the study of the Universe – the only topic which we found to be of universal appeal to all students (Osborne and Collins, 2001) – provides some insights into the existential questions of who we are, what we are, and where we are. Likewise, because young people are egocentric, they are interested in their bodies and their functioning, how they get ill, and why some diseases are incurable and others not. Yet some of the diseases that will afflict either them or members of their families, such as cancer, heart disease, and drug dependency, are only given marginal treatment by the existing curriculum, if at all.

Moreover, technological artefacts surround young people's lives and they do not differentiate between science and technology – yet where are the explanations of mobile phones, digital imaging, and other technologies that permeate their daily lives? Thus, to take the Ausubelian mantra that the art of teaching is first to ascertain what the learner knows a little further, the art of developing successful courses in science education is first to ascertain what interests the average 14 year old and then design the curricula appropriately. Some might object that to put young people's interests first is an abrogation of the responsibility of society to determine what is worth knowing and the need to design a curriculum that introduces young people to the major ideas and explanatory themes that science has to offer. After all, most native language curricula include some exploration of their own great writers. It would be difficult to imagine an English literature curriculum which included no mention of Shakespeare. But there is a difference – Shakespeare and other great writers deal with the great problems of life, love, and the moral dilemmas posed by human existence. Their literature has become part of the canon because their writing has a timeless, universal quality and can be read at several levels. For instance, on one level, *Romeo and Juliet* is a simple love story between two young people. On another level, it is tale of two families competing for power where marriage and family connections are important bonds that bind individuals in a complex web of relationships. Moreover, the sayings of Shakespeare are still common cultural referents of common discourse. What, then, are the products of science that likewise permeate our common culture? My answer would be some or all of the following:

- a working understanding of the body and its parts;
- a comprehension of the nature of disease and its causes and their prevention;
- the particulate nature of matter and the idea that all materials are made of only ninety-two elements;
- the mechanisms of conception and reproduction;
- a cosmology based on the notion of a singular but very large Universe that had its inception about 13 billion years ago;
- the idea that species have evolved through a process of adaptation and natural selection;
- the notion that at least our phenotypic characteristics, and potentially more, are determined by the genetic coding to be found in the DNA that exists in every cell in a living organism;
- that ideas produced by science are rooted in a commitment to evidence as the basis for belief; and that ideas gain acceptance through a process of critical examination and argument within the scientific community.

But more than this? Embodied in the following young person's comments is the essence of a telling critique of contemporary science education (Osborne and Collins, 2000).

Student A: 'A lot of the stuff isn't relevant. You're just going to go away from school and you're never going to think about it again.'
Student B: 'Yeah.'
Student A: 'Yeah, bonding, you're not going to think, "How do I bond?"'

Whilst it is, perhaps, self-evident that pupils of this age (16) are unlikely to be able to judge the future value of any knowledge, the significance of the comment lies in the fact that it is difficult for this adult, and I dare say most others, to refute. Unlike the examples that I have drawn from English literature, it is hard to imagine a context in which a knowledge of atomic or molecular bonding might be either useful or of significant value to any one other than the future scientist. Hence to continue with such a curriculum is simply a culturally bankrupt policy both for scientists and for science: for scientists because it renders their work remote, complex, and inaccessible; for science because it is alienating, making it less likely that young people will pursue further study of science past the point of compulsion. The important message here is that for many, if not the majority, science education needs to become far more vocationally orientated to endow what it has to offer with much more relevance and significance.

Hence, all we must ask of any curriculum is that it is comprehensive in ensuring that it covers those aspects that are an essential component of the cultural background that permeates the daily life of most people. In such a curriculum, it must be said that it is likely that physics or chemistry will make only incidental appearances where some knowledge is needed to explain the behaviour of simple electrical circuits or the material properties of carbon fibre in comparison to steel. Students will not emerge, therefore, with a broad grounding in all the sciences, other than that they might have attained by a more traditional science education to age 14. Rather, their knowledge will be partial and limited. But, and this is the major point of my argument, they would emerge with some sense of appreciating what science is, the nature of its intellectual achievement, and why its significance in today's society. Moreover, such an approach would be the opportunity to liberate school science from the yolk of breadth and, rather, to pursue a small number of topics in some depth.

In his 1985 paper, Peter Fensham offers three alternatives for education in sciences. Science might be offered only for a chosen elite – a choice which is simply indefensible in today's world. His second alternative is a limited and particular form of science education which is a precursor to a more specialised vocational education – essentially what we have now. His third suggestion is that 'science for all' should be one of several different forms of science education offered to school students. Here I would disagree – 'Science for All' must be mandatory for all – including those who form the elite group that will become future scientists. Only then would such an education gain political acceptance and not be condemned as something which is second rate or academically inferior. Such a course, typically offered post-14, would seek to show what are the major cultural contributions that science has to offer about the nature of the world, how science works, and why its achievements represent major intellectual achievements. In short, a kind of science for citizenship. Academic science would then be one of the additional courses available for students alongside courses for those who sought an extended but more vocational science education – a component of science education which, at least in the UK, has long been neglected and undervalued.

My argument now is that we have tried the second of these options and, as a policy, it has been found wanting. Science for the few is simply not adaptable with modification to meet the needs of 'Science for All'. That it ever could be is, with the benefit of hindsight, almost incomprehensible. In short, this is a policy which is broke and in desperate need of fixing. Even the major stake-holders in such a system – science and the scientists themselves – are now beginning to wonder about its value. The way forward is to start anew with a course that is genuinely aimed at the needs of the majority, which must also be compulsory for the minority who will become scientists as well. There is no other discipline where those engaged in its practice know so little about its history, its social practices, or hold an overview of its major explanatory themes. To permit this minority to pursue courses that provided early academic specialisation would be to sustain the separation between science and its publics and to rob future scientists of a knowledge and understanding of the cultural significance of their own discipline.

Needless to say, such a change in direction requires major changes both within the culture of science teaching, the curricula and agencies that structure their work, and the methods of teaching science. Some would say that the scale of change required is simply insurmountable, requiring resources that are simply not available. My own view is that the seeds of dissatisfaction exist already – teachers of science know that the curriculum they offer in the latter stages of compulsory science education offers little of permanent value for the majority. In short these seeds have taken root in the practice of a policy that even science teachers, who like any practitioner naturally find it difficult to stand outside their work, recognise has no credibility. Building a new structure within that context is the responsibility of all those who genuinely care about offering a relevant and important science education for all. In summary, to attaining the vision that has motivated the life and work of Peter Fensham.

References

Barnett, C. (2001) *Prelude to an industrial defeat from the 1944 Education Act to the 1956 White Paper on Technological Education*, London: Royal Society of Arts.

Beck, U. (1992) *Risk Society: towards a new modernity*, London: Sage.

Cohen I.B. (1952) 'The education of the public in science', *Impact of Science on Society* 3: 67–101.

Collins, H. (2000) 'On beyond 2000', *Studies in Science Education* 35: 169–73.

Cossons, N. (1993) 'Let us take science into our culture', *Interdisciplinary Science Reviews* 18: 337–42.

Department of Education (1994) *Science and Maths: a consultation paper on the supply and demand of newly qualified young people*, London: HMSO.

Department for Education and Employment (1999) *Science in the National Curriculum*, London: HMSO.

Fensham, P. (1985) 'Science for all: a reflective essay', *Journal of Curriculum Studies* 17: 415–35.

Gibbs, W.W. and Fox, D. (1999) 'The false crisis in science education', *Scientific American* October, 87–93.

Giddens, A. (1990) *The Consequences of Modernity*, Cambridge: Polity Press.

Giddens, A. (1999) *The Reith Lectures: Risk*, London: BBC.

Hanson, N.R. (1958) *Patterns of Discovery*, Cambridge: Cambridge University Press.

Hogan, K. and Maglienti, M. (2001) 'Comparing the epistemological underpinnings of students' and scientists' reasoning about conclusions', *Journal of Research in Science Teaching* 38: 663–87.

Kuhn, D., Amsel, E., and O'Loughlin, M. (1988) *The Development of Scientific Thinking Skills*, San Diego: Academic Press.

Millar, R. and Osborne, J.F. (eds) (1998) *Beyond 2000: Science Education for the Future*, London: King's College London.

Munro, M. and Elsom, D. (2000) *Choosing Science at 16: the Influences of Science Teachers and Careers Advisors on Students' Decisions about Science Subjects and Science and Technology Careers*, Cambridge: Careers Research and Advisory Centre (CRAC).

National Commission on Mathematics and Science Teaching for the 21st Century (2000) *Before It's Too Late*, Washington, DC: US Department of Education.

Osborne, J.F. and Collins, S. (2001) 'Pupils' views of the role and value of the science curriculum: a focus–group study', *International Journal of Science Education* 23: 441–68.

Shamos, M.H. (1995) *The Myth of Scientific Literacy*, New Brunswick, NJ: Rutgers University Press.

UK Deans of Science Committee (2001) 'Support for radical change in the secondary science curriculum across the UK', *Education in Science* 195: 29.

Wang, J. (2001) 'TIMSS primary and middle school data: some technical concerns', *Educational Researcher* 30: 17–21.

Ziman, J. (2000) *Real Science: what it is, and what it means,* Cambridge: Cambridge University Press.

4   'Science for All'

Reflections from Indonesia

Tarsisius Sarkim

I will discuss the concept of 'Science for All' from the perspective of Indonesia, a country in transition politically to a democratic society. It is also a developing country undergoing rapid changes within the global economy. I will begin with a brief snapshot of Indonesian schooling and science education in Indonesian schools, and then deal with the dilemma of 'Science for All' for Indonesia – a non-Western country.

Indonesian schooling: uniformity versus diversity

One of the major features of Indonesian schooling is uniformity, for example in the curriculum, classroom setting, learning assessment, and students' uniform. Uniformity is shaped by government policies, and is symptomatic of a deeper and more pervasive conformity of the schooling system in Indonesia. These policies, on the one hand, have established a standard system of education, but on the other hand they deny the fact of the diversity of Indonesian society.

In the whole of Indonesia there is only one curriculum for each level of education. The curriculum is the responsibility of a committee appointed by the Ministry of National Education. It consists of the goals for teaching, topics and sub-topics to be taught in every term (a four-month period), and suggestions about teaching methods. Teachers try to teach all of the suggested topics and sub-topics, but they can modify the sequence of the topics to be taught within each term.

Science, as a subject, is taught to all Indonesian students from year 3 of primary school until level 2 of senior high school. Therefore, almost all of Indonesian students, except those who take vocational education at the senior secondary level, learn science for nine years (four years at primary level, three years at junior secondary level, and two years at senior secondary school).

At the primary school level, the science taught consists of topics including the human body and environments (plants, animals, and physical environments). At this level, several basic scientific concepts such as force, electricity, and magnetism are introduced. In junior high school (three years), two subjects of science are taught: physics and biology. In senior high school, all students at levels 1 and 2 learn physics, biology, and chemistry, while at level 3 only students in the science stream learn these three subjects.

Student learning assessment is organised at the provincial or national level. The end of term tests, or end of year tests are organised at the provincial level, while the end of programme tests, that is at the end of year 6 of primary school, and year 3 of junior and senior school, are organised at the national level. The tests are multiple-choice tests with a few essay-type questions added.

The centralised curriculum and assessment have a strong impact on teaching and learning practices. Teachers strive to teach all of the content suggested in the curriculum within the available time frame. In doing this, it is often not possible to select pedagogically appropriate teaching methods, since they are seen to be time consuming. Teachers use the methods that will help students answer the test questions successfully.

In contrast to the artificially imposed uniformities is the diversity of Indonesian society. Indonesian students come from many different cultural and economic backgrounds; they have different mother languages, and they live in diverse natural and physical environments. These cultural groups hold different beliefs about particular natural phenomena. For example, there are ethnic groups that believe that the rainbow is a ladder used by fairies to bathe in the river. Several ethnic groups believe that earthquakes are caused when the giant bull that is believed to be holding the earth rocks its head. These cultural beliefs need to be taken into account in science teaching (see the South African situation, Chapter 2). However, the prescribed curriculum does not encourage teachers to think and act creatively about students' cultural understandings.

The diversity of Indonesian students can also be seen from their daily lives. There are students who live in cities, small towns, villages, or even remote areas. Students in the country are familiar with natural environments such as forests and with occupations such as farming and the use of simple technology. Yet these students may not be familiar with public transport, electronic appliances, books, and even electricity. In contrast, students who live in the cities may be familiar with IT and other modern technologies, but they do not know about agriculture and village life. The differences in students' daily lives determine what is meaningful to them. Science education should take these differences into account if it is to be meaningful to all students.

Only a small proportion of students can continue their study of science and have a career in science-related jobs. According to the data published by Statistics Indonesia (1998), although the primary school enrolment rate was high (95.7 per cent), there were only about 49 per cent of the Indonesian population aged 16–18 enrolled at senior high schools. This means that there is about 51 per cent of the population aged 16–18 terminating education at the junior high school level. These students mostly go to work in jobs that need a minimum level of scientific knowledge. In terms of science education, a crucial question can be raised: has their science instruction been meaningful to them? If only one curriculum is implemented throughout Indonesia, regardless of the future career of students, can we expect a meaningful science education for all students?

Hence, the uniformity policies are not appropriate for culturally and economically diverse societies such as Indonesia. Moreover, the centralised policies do not accord with the national legislation. The national education legislation states that the curriculum should be developed in accord with the national educational aims for students' development, environment, and science and technology development (Indonesia, 1989). This legislation implies that the content and methods of teaching should be appropriately selected to give a meaningful education to all students. However, the notion that local authorities can develop local curricula for their students, within national guidelines, has not been realised.

Therefore, the centralised uniform schooling system in Indonesia contradicts the nature of its diverse society, and seems to contradict some of the national legislation regarding the school curriculum.

There are also contradictions between the intended goals of science education and the content of the curriculum. For example, one of the goals of science education in primary schools is to help students develop simple technology to solve problems in daily life. In fact, the daily life of students in Jakarta is vastly different from that of students in Aceh or Papua. The type of simple technology for fishing is different from the simple technology for farming.

'Science for All': the Indonesian dilemma

In the past, one of the major features of Indonesian developmental policies was that they were centralist oriented (Java oriented). The policies resulted in disparities among Indonesian areas in many respects. Some of the most apparent disparities concern infrastructure facilities such as water, electricity, roads, hospitals, and schools.

In many remote areas of Indonesia the school facilities are at minimal levels. In teaching aids many village schools have only a blackboard and chalk. These schools may not have libraries or laboratories. The quality and quantity of teachers in the villages are also a problem. *KOMPAS*, the Indonesian newspaper, often reports the situations of schools in remote areas. The teachers in these areas have never been touched by professional development programmes. They have been teaching for years with a similar style, and their teaching strategies have become routine. This has resulted in low student learning achievement. In contrast to the above situation is the school situation in big cities. The students are taught by better qualified teachers in well-equipped schools and, as is predictable, these students can reach high levels on national assessment. They have access to better and higher education levels, and they become members of the technological elites. Therefore, the centralistic-oriented policies have produced inequalities in education, social, and economic development. Good education, which is supposed to be a vehicle for social mobility, is in fact only available to a fraction of Indonesian students.

This situation shows that the current educational policies in Indonesia do not match the nature of its diverse society. Within the current existing education policies, the differences in the learning environments and the students' needs for schooling are not accommodated. The needs of the students are not equally fulfilled, and the educational contexts of students are not equally recognised as important aspects of education. The current science education curriculum does not take into account the students' needs. All students obtain a similar science education, whatever their future prospects. The current science curriculum, especially in high schools, seems more appropriate for students who are going to continue their studies at university. Yet, as mentioned above, less than 50 per cent of students go to university. The current single science curriculum does not fit the needs of all students.

Hence, the issue of 'Science for All' for Indonesia, rather than say for the UK (see Chapter 3), is an issue not only of equality but also of appropriateness. For science education to be appropriate to students' needs, science education for prospective university students should be different from science education for students who will probably work in trades and low-skill jobs. This differentiation would limit access to universities for students from the second group. Hence, science education would not treat students equally. In the short term, giving more appropriate science education seems the better option. Such a 'Science for All' education would help students to obtain the best possible science education within the available learning resources and would enable them to make use of their school science experience. It can be expected that an appropriate science education would contribute to the development of a skilled workforce that is needed by Indonesian society. As indicated by Statistics Indonesia, in 2000 there were over 89 million people in the workforce, and 40 million of them work in the agriculture, forestry, and fishery areas. Thus, 'Science for All' in this situation means appropriate education but unequal opportunity for further education.

If reform is to take place several initiatives need to be undertaken. First, the central educational authorities should only develop general guidelines for the curriculum at the national level. The national guidelines would establish a national standard that should be achieved by all education units in Indonesia. These guidelines will enable students to move easily from region to region and to enter higher education wherever they wish. Provinces, or districts, should be allowed to develop curricula based on these guidelines with appropriate local contexts. For science education, this would mean that the question about what is meaningful science education for the students can be discussed. The decentralisation of curriculum development also accords with the current government policies regarding local autonomy. The national legislation concerning district autonomy was endorsed in 1999 (Indonesia, 1999). In addition, two provinces, Aceh and Papua, have received the status of special autonomy for their special situations.

Second, the curriculum for students who intend to continue their studies at university should be different from the curriculum for those who do not.

The science curriculum for students who will go straight to work on leaving high school would be more general rather than specialised, emphasising the utility of science and how it will help students in their daily lives. If science education is to be meaningful to all Indonesian students, the curriculum should be modified not only in accordance with local contexts, but also with students' psychological development in mind. The current science curriculum has been criticised for its level of difficulty for the majority of students. Drost (2000) argues that only 30 per cent of Indonesian high school students can learn the existing, traditional Western-type curriculum.

Third, learning assessment should be reformed. The centralised and multiple-choice tests have reduced the task of teachers to train the students to answer these questions correctly. The elimination of centralised learning assessment at all levels contradicts the ideas of standardisation, the concept that enables students to achieve a high standard of education and access the educational resources available. Therefore, the centralised learning assessment should be redesigned. The learning assessment should encourage teachers to improve their teaching quality creatively within the available learning resources, and at the same time enable students to achieve the national standard of learning achievement.

Although these recommendations sound reasonable, there has, however, always been a struggle to unite Indonesia as a nation. The government is reluctant to encourage the provinces or districts to develop their own curriculum. The centralised curriculum is a powerful tool for unity. Also, the more than thirty years of experience with the centralised system is the major obstacle for local authorities who wish to develop local curricula because of the dearth of experience in curriculum development in the provinces.

Past work practice may be another impediment. Schools and teachers are used to following instructions from the central authorities. Creativity has not been highly appreciated in the past. This way of working may have been seen as part of the culture. If science education is to be reformed, then teachers should be encouraged to think and act creatively.

Conclusion

A science education that is more appropriate to students' current situation and needs will be meaningful in the short term – until equality of opportunity can be established. Yet a meaningful science education for all students will, in the current Indonesian situation, lead to inequality of opportunity. The question remains: can the principles of 'Science for All' be ethically justified if it means a science education appropriate to the actual needs of students in a country of such diversity of opportunity?

References

Drost, J. (2000) *Sekolah: Mengajar atau Mendidik*, Yogyakarta: Kanisius dan Universitas Sanata Dharma.

Indonesia (1989) *Undang-undang No. 2 tentang Sistem Pendidikan nasional* (Legislation concerning National Education System, published in Jakarta by the Indonesian government).

Indonesia (1999) *Undang-undang No. 22 tahun 1999 tentang Otonomi Daerah* (Legislation concerning District Autonomy published in Jakarta by the Indonesian government).

Statistics Indonesia (1998) http://www.bps.go.id (accessed January 2002).

Part III

Science, technology, and society

Learning for the modern world

5 STS education

A rose by any other name

Glen Aikenhead

Peter Fensham's life's work in science education has embraced the complexities that define science education in schools. These complexities were addressed in Fensham's (1988a) edited volume *Developments and Dilemmas in Science Education*. In its last two chapters, Joan Solomon (1988) and Harrie Eijkelhof and Koos Kortland (1988) described a promising movement whose slogan 'science–technology–society' (STS) brought together an assortment of innovative science and technology educators. At the time, STS science education confronted competing views on issues such as: the purpose of schools, the politics of a curriculum, the nature of the science curriculum, instruction and assessment, the role of teachers, the nature of learning, the diversity of learners, and what 'science' means. STS was seen by some as a radical departure from the status quo – it promoted a holistic view of science education.

Peter Fensham has, in a variety of ways, contributed to the emergence and evolution of STS, and he continues to participate in its current transformation into science for 'public understanding' and/or 'citizen science'. Fensham (1988b) recognised that curriculum change occurs within, and responds to, changes in social realities. For STS, these realities included (Fensham, 1983; 1988c; 1992; 1996a): the Second World War, the Pugwash movement (science for social responsibility), the environmental movement, women's movement, the post-Sputnik science curriculum reforms (and the 1970s' critical reaction to that reform movement), research into science instruction and student learning, decreasing enrolment in physical science, and a nagging persistence, by a minority of science educators, to present science to students in a more humanistic way (rather than elitist pre-professional science training).

STS science required fundamental changes to the status quo of science education (Gaskell, 1982). In North America, Paul Hurd (1986) assessed, from an historical perspective, several major attempts during the past century to change the status quo by humanising the science curriculum – so that it had relevance for a majority of students. All attempts at reform failed to achieve their original goals. However, in the 1980s Fensham, among others, believed that social conditions had changed sufficiently to support a fundamental change to the science curriculum.

My chapter reviews, from a Canadian perspective, how science educators settled on the slogan 'science–technology–society' (STS), how the field has matured over the past two decades, and how the slogan might continue to change as new social and political realities challenge science educators.

The emergence of STS in school science

It was a historical coincidence in the late 1970s and early 1980s that the phrase 'science–technology–society' was current in a number of venues at the same time as a broad consensus developed among science educators about the need for innovation in science education. At this time new and diverse proposals for school science were advanced, stimulated by a number of factors including: a reassessment of Western culture and the subsequent role of school science in its transformation, an emerging need for political education for action, a call for interdisciplinary approaches to science education organised around broad problems, and a new type of demand for vocational and technocratic preparation (Fensham, 1992; 1996a; Solomon, 1988; 1994; this volume). All of these proposals seriously challenged the status quo.

As early as 1971 in the journal *Science Education*, Jim Gallagher proposed a new goal for school science:

> For future citizens in a democratic society, understanding the interrelationships of science, technology and society may be as important as understanding the concepts and processes of science.
>
> (Gallagher, 1971, p. 337)

His blueprint presciently mapped out a rationale for teaching scientific concepts and processes embedded in the sociology of science, relevant technology, and social issues. Gallagher's early publication was, perhaps, overshadowed by Paul Hurd's seminal article (1975) entitled: 'Science, technology, and society: new goals for interdisciplinary science teaching', which delineated a curriculum structure for STS science. Support for this new goal came soon after in 1977 from Harms and Yager's Project Synthesis (1981) in the USA. Project Synthesis organised science education into five domains, one was entitled: The interaction of science, technology and society (S/T/S). Derek Holford (1982) cited this project in his lecture 'Training teachers for science-technology-society roles', presented at the Second IOSTE (International Organization for Science and Technology Education) Symposium in Nottingham, UK. The abbreviation STS was used by Holford, perhaps influenced by a book by John Ziman (1980). In another IOSTE paper Bill Hall (1982) discussed the challenges of S/T/S programmes in schools, drawing heavily on the work of both Ziman (1980) and Hurd (1975). Hall's ideas were also influenced by Rip's 1979 article about higher education programmes ('The social context of science, technology and society courses'); this in turn drew upon the book by Spiegel-Rösing and Price (1977), *Science, Technology and Society: a cross-disciplinary perspective*. The book was influential in tertiary education circles at the time – indeed it is credited with popularising the STS slogan in higher education (Solomon, 1988).

University STS programmes in the USA were formally initiated in 1969 at Cornell University and Pennsylvania State University (Cutcliffe, 1989). Their central focus was the analysis and explication of science and technology as complex social constructs entailing cultural, political, economic, and general theoretical questions (Cutcliffe, 1996, p. 291). Their content is generally more theoretical than the STS content applicable to school science. Cutcliffe pointed out that the establishment of professional societies, journals, and newsletters in the 1970s gave STS a permanent home in higher education. This certainly influenced science educators who came into contact with its literature – particularly Piel's (1981) S/T/S group within Project Synthesis.

By 1982, however, international science educators had not reached a consensus on a name for their new movement. Papers presented at the 1982 IOSTE Symposium reflected a preoccupation with a diversity of viewpoints: science and/in society, science and technology, the interaction of science and technology with society and culture, along with Holford's STS and Hall's S/T/S, mentioned above. The symposium fortuitously brought together reform-minded science educators from Australia, Canada, Italy, The Netherlands, and the UK who in various ways were developing (or had developed) new science curricula influenced by various proposals to change the status quo in science education (see Fensham, 1992; 1996b; Solomon, 1988; 1994; 1996). At an informal gathering within the symposium, several attendees agreed to initiate a special interest group within IOSTE under the banner STS.

Probably the strongest influence on the group's choice of STS as the slogan for the new approach came from John Ziman's (1980) seminal work, *Teaching and Learning about Science and Society*. In spite of its title, the book consistently referred to STS in its articulation of the rationale, directions, and challenges for STS in school science. The book quickly became required reading for STS science educators everywhere. Although Bob Yager (1996a, p. 5) claimed that Ziman coined the term STS, the term was recognized in the UK by the STSA (Science Technology and Society Association) which existed under the auspices of the Council for Science and Society, of which Ziman was chairman.

In the fall of 1982, at an international science teachers' conference in Saskatoon, Canada, people from the IOSTE special interest group attempted to join forces with the USA group (Joe Piel, Bob Yager, and Rodger Bybee). An 'invisible college' was formally established in Saskatoon and named the STS Research Network. It was an international group of mainly university science educators and it published regular newsletters called *Missives* throughout the 1980s (Fensham, 1992). The US delegates at the Saskatoon meeting continued independently to develop their own versions of STS science within: the National Science Teachers' Association (Bybee, 1985), the University of Iowa (Blunck and Yager, 1996), the environmental movement (Rubba and Wiesenmayer, 1985), and the Science Through STS project (Roy, 1984). Over the years IOSTE has continued to be an effective international venue for advancing STS science education worldwide.

Other influences on STS school educators in the 1980s also came from a number of other sources, including:

1   Higher education projects and programmes, such as: Science in a Social Context, SISCON (in the UK), the Deakin University course Knowledge and Power (Australia), the Science and Society units in an Open University science course (UK), and Schroeer's (1972) *Physics and Its Fifth Dimension: Society*.

2   School projects, such as the Schools Council Integrated Science Project, *Patterns*, in the UK (Hall, 1973), *Science: a way of knowing* in Canada (Aikenhead and Fleming, 1975), *Science in Society* in the UK (Lewis, 1981), the PLON project in The Netherlands (Eijkelhof and Kortland, 1982), and *SISCON-in-Schools* in the UK (Solomon, 1983; this volume).

3   Journals, such as the *Bulletin of Science, Technology and Society* inaugurated in 1981, and *Science, Technology and Human Values* (originally a newsletter). Publications, such as Jim Gaskell's (1982) insightful analysis of science education for citizens, the NSTA's (1982) position statement, *Science-Technology-Society: Science Education for the 1980s*, Glen Aikenhead's (1980) *Science In Social Issues: implications for teaching*, Graham Orpwood and Doug Roberts's (1980) key article 'Science and society: dimensions of science education for the '80s', Fletcher Watson's (1979) keynote address at the First IOSTE Symposium, and the ASE's (Association for Science Education) (1979) position statement *Alternatives for Science Education*.

4   Centres for humanistic approaches to science education in North America, principally at Harvard University (e.g. Klopfer and Cooley, 1963); Stanford University (e.g. Hurd, 1970); the Ontario Institute for Studies in Education (e.g. Roberts and Orpwood, 1979); University of Iowa (e.g. Yager, 1996a); Berkeley University (e.g. Thier and Nagle, 1994); and a 1977 initiative by US social studies professionals to help teachers, students, and others deal effectively with science-related social issues (McConnell, 1982, p. 10), an initiative they called science/technology/society.

It seems clear that the slogan STS came from different sources from different people influenced by different circumstances and was embraced for different purposes. For almost every writer there will be a different citation for the original source of STS. More importantly, however, the slogan created networks of science educators dedicated to changing the status quo of school science (Durbin, 1991; Ziman, 1994).

The evolution of STS

Peter Fensham (1985; 1988c; 1996c) contributed directly to the evolution of STS by forging links between science education and technology education, embedded in social contexts relevant for all students. The role of technology in STS programmes has been an ongoing concern (Cheek, 2000; Fensham 1988a; Layton, 1994). It is interesting to look back to 1982 and acknowledge that most educators who had been socialised into academic science were not comfortable with the inclusion of technology in STS. This explains their initial reticence to embrace the slogan STS. Their narrow view of technology as applied science needed to be confronted and reconceptualised into a more authentic view (Fensham and Gardner, 1994). I recall Geoffrey Harrison's (1979) challenge to my own narrow thinking on technology at the First IOSTE Symposium. One theme in the evolution of STS has been the degree and sophistication to which technology is featured in the conceptions of STS programmes.

Another theme to emerge from the evolution of STS is the complexity to which STS programmes embrace the social context of science. Interestingly, Fensham's early writings on STS were characterised, I believe, by a one-way influence of science/technology on society, while in his 1990 writings a two-way mutual interaction was expressed. His apparent reconceptualisation of the interaction mirrors a similar development for many colleagues who were originally schooled in the sciences with their science-centric view of the world. From project to project and from country to country, the scope of the social context of science in STS materials has, for many reasons, been limited. For instance, some STS projects focused on science-related issues in society but left unchallenged the out-of-date positivistic notions of science found in many science curricula (Bingle and Gaskell, 1994). A more comprehensive treatment of STS includes the internal social context (the epistemology, sociology, and history of science itself) as well as the external social context of science (Ziman, 1984). Again I recall my early biases favouring the epistemology of science. I thank Jim Gaskell (1982) among others for advancing more sophisticated ideas about the external social context of science.

The maturation of STS can also be traced through the developments in the assessment of student learning STS content: from a quantitative paradigm (Aikenhead, 1973), to a qualitative paradigm (Aikenhead, 1979; 1988; Aikenhead and Ryan, 1992; Driver *et al.*, 1996), to a situated cognition paradigm (Gaskell, 1994; Solomon, 1992; Welzel and Roth, 1998).

The evolution of STS within school science is a complex story of the professional and intellectual development of individual science educators. Each country has its own story to tell. For instance, in Canada and Israel, the environment was emphasised by adding an E to STS, producing STSE and STES respectively, with numerous school implementations achieved (Aikenhead, 2000; Zoller, 1991). In The Netherlands, the PLON project grew by embracing environmental education, while at the same time, moving into the secondary schools and continuing the project's tradition of in-depth research studies with participating students (Eijkelhof *et al.*, 1996). Some of these PLON units directly influenced the development of similar STS modules in Australia and Canada. In the UK, a variety of state-of-the-art projects and syllabuses were developed (Solomon, 1996; this volume). These inspired and guided science educators worldwide. In Australia, a link to industrial technology became evident in some projects, in addition to the more conventional STS courses (Fensham and Corrigan, 1994; Giddings, 1996). In Belgium under the guidance of Gérard Fourez, ethics was added to STS, the journal *Sciences Technologies Ethique Societé*, published by the University of Namur, being influential. In Italy, STS developed towards a more scientific-discipline-oriented approach to society issues (Prat, 1990). In Spain, Maria Manassero-Mas, Ángel Vázquez-Alonso, and José Acevedo-Díaz (2001) have approached STS from an evaluative perspective, described in their book *Avaluació dels Temes de Ciència, Tecnologia i Societat*. The story from Japan involves science educators being influenced by projects in the UK and USA, but developing their own version of STS, along with considerable research (Nagasu and Kumano, 1996).

At various times, yearbooks and special issues of journals have focused on STS science education and have advanced our collective thinking. Examples are found in Table 5.1. In-depth discussions of STS science are also located in key education books, listed in Table 5.2. The full story about the emergence and evolution of STS is found by reading these publications.

STS for schools in the USA in the mid-1980s was greatly influenced by Rustum Roy's (2000) 'Science Through STS' project – centred at Pennsylvania State University. In the 1970s, he had been on the editorial board of the British Science in a Social Context (SISCON) project. In 1988 in the USA, Roy founded the National Association for Science Technology Society (NASTS), which continues to meet annually and to produce a newsletter. These national meetings are a forum for multidisciplinary discussions, bringing together school

Table 5.1 Yearbooks and special issues of journals dedicated to STS

Publications	Reference
NSTA yearbook, *Science-Technology-Society*	Bybee 1985
AETS yearbook, *Science, Technology and Society: resources for science educators*	James 1985
Special STS issue, *International Journal of Science Education*	Holman 1988
Two special STS issues, *Theory into Practice*	Gilliom *et al.* 1991, 1992
ICASE yearbook, *The Status of STS: reform efforts around the world*	Yager 1992
Special issue, *Melbourne Studies in Education*	Cross and Fensham 2000

Table 5.2 Key STS science education books

Publications	Reference
Teaching and Learning about Science and Society	Ziman 1980
Thinking Constructively About Science, Technology, and Society Education	Cheek 1992
Teaching Science, Technology and Society	Solomon 1993
STS Education: international perspectives on reform	Solomon and Aikenhead 1994
Science/technology/society as Reform in Science Education	Yager 1996b
Science, Technology, and Society: A sourcebook on research and practice	Kumar and Chubin 2000

educators, industrialists, ethicists, engineers, social activists, and professors of STS programmes in higher education. NASTS was the nexus of STS development in North America for science educators.

Unfortunately, two major US science education initiatives, *Project 2061* (AAAS, 1989) and *Standards* (NRC, 1996), have completely dominated the science curriculum agenda in the USA. There is only lip service paid to STS perspectives in these reform documents (Koch, 1996). Moreover, the agency responsible for funding most science education research and curriculum development in the USA, the National Science Foundation, has appropriated the STS acronym to mean science and technology studies (Hackett, 2000). While STS continues to have a strong minority presence in higher education, its influence on pre-college science courses in the USA is minimal. One exception to this trend is the STS project SEPUP (Science Education for Public Understanding Project; Thier and Nagle, 1994). SEPUP has recently produced two substantial STS textbooks for Grades 9–11, *Issues, Evidence and You* and *Science and Sustainability.*

One positive aspect to a slogan such as STS is its ability to garner the allegiance of a fairly diverse group of people (Roberts, 1983; Ziman, 1994). Given this diversity, however, there can be no agreement on the precise meaning of STS, as there is, for example, on the meaning of biochemistry. As a consequence, one particular STS project developed in a country can define STS science for educators of that group or country. Criticism of STS in that country can actually turn out to be a critique of a particular type of STS project, a type that other STS educators may find wanting as well. In one critique of STS, for example, Edgar Jenkins (1994) based his evidence largely on one project in the USA. In another critique, Jenkins (2000, p. 220) characterised STS courses as supporting and enriching conventional science courses. He concluded that something more radical than STS programmes is needed to humanise school science. His arguments rest on a certain type of add-on STS project (e.g. *Science and Technology in Society, SATIS*; Hunt, 1988) but ignores other projects whose radical materials have been publicly banned from some school systems (e.g. *Logical Reasoning in Science and Technology*; Aikenhead, 2000). It is refreshing, however, to hear Jenkins's voice in a forum where STS projects are usually criticised and rejected for being too radical (e.g. Harding and Hare, 2000).

One way to ameliorate the problem of stereotyping STS is to describe systematically the multiple meanings it has. Guided by Fensham's (1988c) scheme that showed degrees of integration of science and technology in the context of social issues, I attempted to design a scheme that represented a spectrum of meanings found in STS courses and programmes (Aikenhead, 1994a; 2000). The spectrum expresses the relative importance afforded to STS content, according to two factors: (1) content structure (the proportion of STS content versus canonical science content, and the way the two are integrated), and (2) student assessment (the relative emphasis on STS content versus canonical science content). I proposed eight categories along this spectrum of STS perspectives. These categories are listed in Table 5.3. Category 1 represents the lowest priority for STS content, while category 8 represents the highest priority. A dramatic change in content structure occurs between categories 3 and 4. In category 3, the content structure is defined by the discipline. In category 4, it is defined by the technological or social issue itself (learning canonical science on a need-to-know basis). Interdisciplinary science begins at category 5. Rather than discuss STS programmes based on stereotypes as critics tend to do, we should identify various programmes by the eight categories, or by some other descriptive systematic scheme. This advice extends to the most recent science for public understanding projects (mentioned below). Table 5.3 provides, I believe, a language for talking about STS curricula, classroom materials, and classroom practice. Roberts (1998), Jeans (1998), and McClelland (1998), for example, used this eight-category scheme to investigate both experienced and novice teachers' views on curriculum change and how curriculum change might affect their teaching.

All education movements seem to be overtaken by time. In 1994, David Layton surmised that this had already happened to STS. His comments are interesting because they demonstrate Peter Fensham's (1988b) observation that changes in a curriculum occur within, and respond to, changes in social realities. Layton (1994, p. 42) stated that in the UK, a change is taking place

Table 5.3 Categories of STS in school science

1	Motivation by STS content
2	Casual infusion of STS content
3	Purposeful infusion of STS content
4	Singular discipline through STS content
5	Science through STS content
6	Science along with STS content
7	Infusion of science into STS content
8	STS content

in the overall mission of schooling in the direction of privileging the practical (i.e. relating students' experience more closely to the acquisition of practical capability in the world outside school). Layton's expectation of the demise of STS, shared by others at the time, was based on (1) the low priority afforded to technology education in many STS programmes, and (2) the increasing importance of technology education for practical capability. The social realities of the twenty-first century, however, with crises related to, for example, genetically modified foods, the human genome project, human cloning, mad cow decease, and pharmaceuticals, have not clearly supported the ascendance of technology education. However, sound criticism of STS over the years, such as Layton's and Jenkins's, has nurtured the evolution of STS in the past, and it is to be hoped will continue to refocus the STS movement in the future.

In retrospect

One general theme found in the emergence and evolution of STS in school science has been the way in which cultural contexts make a difference to proposals to change the status quo. For example, Peter Fensham, David Layton, and Dennis Cheek, among others, have consistently advanced the subculture of technology education for STS, while Roger Cross and others have consistently advanced the subculture of ethics (Cross, 1997; Cross and Price, 1992; 1999). These and many other subcultures within academe and within educational institutions worldwide will continue to influence school science in the future.

Slogans come and go as social realities change. Nevertheless, in every era or in different political settings, it seems essential to use a slogan to rally support for fundamental changes to school science (Roberts, 1983). For instance, the slogan science–technology–society–environment has galvanised a diverse cluster of provincial ministries of education into collaborating on Canada's first national framework for a science curriculum (Aikenhead, 2000). This document has already motivated curriculum revisions in some provinces and guided the production of new science textbooks (e.g. Doug Roberts, Senior Programme Consultant, *Science Power* series for Grades 7–10, from McGraw-Hill Ryerson). Science–Technology–Citizenship is a slogan used in Norway where the culture tends to accentuate students' relationships with nature and with national citizenship (Royal Ministry of Church, Education and Research, 1995). Innovative Norwegian projects dedicated to teaching school science for an informed citizenry have been completed (Knain, 1999; Kolstø, 2000; Ødegaard, 2001; Sjøberg, 1997). Frequently today we read the slogans 'Science for All' (Fensham, 1985), 'Science for Public Understanding' (Eijkelhof and Kapteijn, 2000; Fensham and Harlen, 1999; Jenkins, 1999; Millar, 1996; 2000), 'Citizen Science' (Cross et al., 2000; Irwin, 1995), 'Functional Scientific Literacy' (Ryder, 2001), or variations thereof. Which slogan will the next generation of innovative science educators adopt?

The future

Based on the past history of STS in science education, we can anticipate that several slogans will continue to garner support for changing school science. We can also anticipate that these slogans will change over time as innovators develop their own understanding of their field, adjust to changes in their local culture, distance themselves from stereotype perceptions of past slogans, and need to be seen doing something different. In short: STS, 'a rose by any other name . . .'.

In this chapter, I have sought to sketch out the complexity of subcultures, allegiances, self-interests, and concepts associated with the emergence, evolution, and reformulation of STS science in schools. What underlies this complexity? STS educators seem to coalesce around diverse interests and goals. This paradox begs an explanation. They agree on the need to reform school science (though they are not reformist enough for some critics), and they value terms such as humanistic, relevant, or student-centred. What coalescent force draws these science educators into the STS movement?

Throughout the past fifty years, science educators have unsuccessfully wrestled with the same dilemma: how do we prepare students to be informed and active citizens, and at the same time, how do we prepare future scientists, engineers, and medical practitioners? Some philosophers of education, such as Kieran Egan (1996), conceptualise the dilemma as two irreconcilable voices competing for the curriculum (two profoundly different ideas about the purpose of science education). One voice, a voice of pragmatism with a lineage of thought from Jean-Jacques Rousseau, to John Dewey, to Jean Piaget, to Ros Driver, speaks of encouraging the development of each student's individual potential. For example, learning how to learn, and being able to use what one has learned (for social reconstruction, perhaps) is considered superior to amassing academic knowledge. This pragmatic voice defines the nucleus of STS educators' professional values and is, I submit, a solution to the paradox above.

However, a second voice analysed by Egan speaks to privileging Plato and the truth about reality. For example, students will amass knowledge that will ensure that their thinking conforms with what is real and true about the world (Egan, 1996, p. 8). An academic curriculum can develop a privileged, rational view of reality (Egan, 1996, p. 13). Egan points out that any proposal for changing the school curriculum must resolve the theoretical incompatibility between the two, otherwise the proposed innovation will be futile. Egan also argues that by including both ideas within a curriculum, we continue the dysfunctionality that causes fundamental tensions and failures in schools today.

Some STS educators have attempted to resolve this incompatibility. They have claimed that by not transmitting Platonic-truth knowledge to students, teachers do not necessarily undermine the pre-professional training goal of science education, given the current structure of university science and engineering programmes (Aikenhead, 1994b; Fensham, 1996a; Tobias, 1990;

Yager and Krajcik, 1989). Talented students, with an interest in the sciences, can succeed in university science-related programmes irrespective of their experiences in school science. On the other side of the coin, the consequences of transmitting a Platonic-truth science curriculum turns out to have an overall negative impact on those talented students with an interest in science and they leave science after graduating (Bond, 1985; Majumdar et al., 1991; Oxford University, 1989). Therefore, on philosophical grounds, the privileged voice of Platonic truth can either be ignored by, or be a nuance within, a science curriculum dominated by pragmatic thought (Aikenhead, 1980). Philosophical grounds, however, are not the social and political realities inhabited by most science educators. Marginalising Platonic truth is a political act.

It seems clear to me that changing the status quo science curriculum cannot simply be achieved by STS-like curriculum innovations based on rational philosophical grounds alone (i.e. successfully arguing with empirical evidence that a pragmatic curriculum is superior to a privileged curriculum). Changing the status quo also requires political interventions based on creative and power-brokering politics (Aikenhead, 2002). To ignore the politics, to shrug them off, to leave them to others, or to avoid them in whatever manner is to make a pact with futility, no matter what slogan we live by. Yet again, Peter Fensham (1988d; 1992; 1998a; 1998b) has helped lead the way.

References

AAAS (1989) *Project 2061: Science for all Americans*, Washington, DC: American Association for the Advancement of Science.

Aikenhead, G.S. (1973) 'The measurement of high school students' knowledge about science and scientists', *Science Education* 57: 539–49.

Aikenhead, G.S. (1979) 'Using qualitative data in formative evaluation', *The Alberta Journal of Educational Research* 25: 117–29.

Aikenhead, G.S. (1980) *Science in Social Issues: implications for teaching*, Ottawa: Science Council of Canada.

Aikenhead, G.S. (1988) 'An analysis of four ways of assessing student beliefs about STS topics', *Journal of Research in Science Teaching* 25: 607–29.

Aikenhead, G.S. (1994a) 'What is STS teaching?', in J. Solomon and G. Aikenhead (eds) *STS Education: International perspectives on reform*, New York: Teachers College Press, pp. 47–59.

Aikenhead, G.S. (1994b) 'Consequences to learning science through STS: a research perspective', in J. Solomon and G. Aikenhead (eds) *STS Education: international perspectives on reform*, New York, Teachers College Press, pp. 169–86.

Aikenhead, G.S. (2000) 'STS in Canada: from policy to student evaluation', in D.D. Kumar and D.E. Chubin (eds) *Science, Technology, and Society: a sourcebook on research and practice,* New York: Kluwer Academic/Plenum Publishers, pp. 49–89.

Aikenhead, G.S. (2002) 'The educo-politics of curriculum development', *Canadian Journal of Science, Mathematics and Technology Education* 2(1): in press.

Aikenhead, G.S. and Fleming, R.W. (1975) *Science: a way of knowing*, Saskatoon: Curriculum Studies, University of Saskatchewan.

Aikenhead, G.S. and Ryan, A.G. (1992) 'The development of a new instrument: views on science-technology-society (VOSTS), *Science Education* 76: 477–91.

ASE (Association for Science Education) (1979) *Alternatives for Science Education*, Hatfield: Association for Science Education.

Bingle, W.H. and Gaskell, P.J. (1994) 'Scientific literacy for decision making and the social construction of scientific knowledge', *Science Education* 72: 185–201.

Blunck, S.M. and Yager, R.E. (1996) 'The Iowa Chautauqua program: a proven in-service model for introducing STS in K-12 classrooms', in R.E. Yager (ed.) *Science/technology/society as Reform in Science Education*, Albany, NY: SUNY Press, pp. 298–305.

Bond, H. (1985) 'Society's view of science', in G.B. Harrison (ed.) *World Trends in Science and Technology Education*, Nottingham: Trent Polytechnic, pp. 10–13.

Bybee, R.W. (ed.) (1985) *Science-Technology-Society. 1985 NSTA Yearbook*, Washington, DC: National Science Teachers Association.

Cheek, D.W. (1992) *Thinking Constructively About Science, Technology, and Society Education*, Albany, NY: SUNY Press.

Cheek, D.W. (2000) 'Marginalization of technology within the STS movement in American K-12 education', in D.D. Kumar and D.E. Chubin (eds) *Science, Technology, and Society: a sourcebook on research and practice,* New York: Kluwer Academic/Plenum Publishers, pp. 167–92.

Cross, R.T. (1997) 'Ideology and science teaching: teachers' discourse', *International Journal of Science Education* 19: 607–16.

Cross, R.T. and Fensham, P.J. (eds) (2000) *Science and the Citizen: for educators and the public* (special issue of the *Melbourne Studies in Education*), Melbourne: Arena Publications.

Cross, R.T. and Price, R.F. (1992) *Teaching Science for Social Responsibility*, Sydney: St Louis Press.

Cross, R.T. and Price, R.F. (1999) 'The social responsibility of science and public understanding', *International Journal of Science Education* 21: 775–85.

Cross, R.T., Zatsepin, V., and Gavrilenko, I. (2000) 'Preparing future citizens for post Chernobyl Ukraine: a national calamity brings about reform of science education', in R.T. Cross and P.J. Fensham (eds) *Science and the citizen: for educators and the public*, Melbourne: Arena Publications, pp. 179–87.

Cutcliffe, S.H. (1989) 'The emergence of STS as an academic field', in P. Durbin (ed.) *Research in Philosophy and Technology, Vol. 9*, Greenwich, CT: JAI Press, pp. 287–301.

Cutcliffe, S.H. (1996) 'National association for science, technology, and society', in R.E. Yager (ed.) *Science/Technology/Society as Reform in Science Education*, Albany, NY: SUNY Press, pp. 291–305.

Driver, R., Leach, J., Millar, R., and Scott, P. (1996) *Young People's Images of Science*, Buckingham: Open University Press.

Durbin, P.T. (1991) 'Defining STS: can we reach consensus?', *Bulletin of Science, Technology and Society* 11: 187–90.

Egan, K. (1996) 'Competing voices for the curriculum', in M. Wideen and M.C. Courtland (eds) *The Struggle For Curriculum: education, the state, and the corporate sector*, Burnaby, British Columbia, Canada: Institute for Studies in Teacher Education, Simon Fraser University, pp. 7–26.

Eijkelhof, H.M.C. and Kapteijn, M. (2000) 'A new course on public understanding of science for senior general secondary education in The Netherlands', in R.T. Cross and P.J. Fensham (eds) *Science and the Citizen: for educators and the public*, Melbourne: Arena Publications, pp. 189–99.

Eijkelhof, H.M.C. and Kortland, K. (1982) 'The context of physics education', Paper presented to the 2nd IOSTE Symposium, Nottingham, UK, July 1982.

Eijkelhof, H.M.C. and Kortland, K. (1988) 'Broadening the aims of physics education', in P.J. Fensham (ed.) *Development and Dilemmas in Science Education*, New York: Falmer Press, pp. 282–305.

Eijkelhof, H.M.C., Kortland, K., and Lijnse, P.L. (1996) 'STS through physics and environmental education in the Netherlands', in R.E. Yager (ed.) *Science/Technology/Society as Reform in Science Education*, Albany, NY: SUNY Press, pp. 249–60.

Fensham, P.J. (1983) 'A research base for new objectives of science teaching', *Science Education* 67: 3–12.

Fensham, P.J. (1985) 'Science for all', *Journal of Curriculum Studies* 17: 415–35.

Fensham, P.J. (ed.) (1988a) *Developments and Dilemmas in Science Education*, New York: Falmer Press.

Fensham, P.J. (1988b) 'Familiar but different: some dilemmas and new directions in science education', in P.J. Fensham (ed.) *Developments and Dilemmas in Science Education*, New York: Falmer Press, pp. 1–26.

Fensham, P.J. (1988c) 'Approaches to the teaching of STS in science education', *International Journal of Science Education* 10: 346–56.

Fensham, P.J. (1988d) 'Physical science, society and technology', *Australian Journal of Education* 32: 375–86.

Fensham, P.J. (1992) 'Science and technology', in P.W. Jackson (ed.) *Handbook of Research on Curriculum*, New York: Macmillan, pp. 789–829.

Fensham, P.J. (1996a) 'Post-compulsory education and science dilemmas and opportunities', in P.J./Fensham (ed.) *Science and Technology Education in the Post-compulsory Years*, Melbourne: Australian Council for Educational Research, pp. 9–30.

Fensham, P.J. (ed.) (1996b) *Science and Technology Education in the Post-compulsory Years*, Melbourne: Australian Council for Educational Research.

Fensham, P.J. (1996c) 'Conclusion', in P.J. Fensham (ed.) *Science and Technology Education in the Post-compulsory Years*, Melbourne: Australian Council for Educational Research, pp. 317–21.

Fensham, P.J. (1998a) 'Student response to the TIMSS Test', *Research in Science Education* 28: 481–506.

Fensham, P.J. (1998b) 'The politics of legitimating and marginalizing companion meanings: three Australian case stories', in D.A. Roberts and L. Östman (eds) *Problems of Meaning in Science Curriculum*, New York: Teachers College Press, pp. 178–92.

Fensham, P.J. and Corrigan, D. (1994) 'The implementation of an STS chemistry course in Australia: a research perspective', in J. Solomon and G. Aikenhead (eds) *STS Education: international perspectives on reform*, New York: Teachers College Press, pp. 194–204.

Fensham, P.J. and Gardner, P.L. (1994) 'Technology education and science education: a new relationship?', in D. Layton (ed.) *Innovations in Science and Technology Education*, *Vol. 4*, Paris: UNESCO, pp. 159–70.

Fensham, P.J. and Harlen, W. (1999) 'School science and public understanding of science', *International Journal of Science Education* 12: 755–63.

Gallagher, J.J. (1971) 'A broader base for science education', *Science Education* 55: 329–38.

Gaskell, J.P. (1982) 'Science, technology and society: issues for science teachers', *Studies in Science Education* 9: 33–46.

Gaskell, P.J. (1994) 'Assessing STS literacy: what is rational?', in K. Boersma, K. Kortland, and J. van Trommel (eds) *7th IOSTE Symposium Proceedings*, Endrecht: IOSTE Conference Committee, pp. 309–20.

Giddings, G. (1996) 'STS initiatives in Australia', in R.E. Yager (ed.) *Science/Technology/Society as Reform in Science Education*, Albany, NY: SUNY Press, pp. 271–9.

Gilliom, M.E., Helgeson, S.L., and Zuga, K.F. (eds) (1991) *Theory into Practice* (special issue on STS) 30: No. 4.

Gilliom, M.E., Helgeson, S.L., and Zuga, K.F. (eds) (1992) *Theory into Practice* (special issue on STS) 31: No. 1.

Hackett, E.J. (2000) 'Trends and opportunities in science and technology studies: a view from the National Science Foundation', in D.D. Kumar and D.E. Chubin (eds) *Science, Technology, and Society: A sourcebook on research and practice*, New York: Kluwer Academic/Plenum Publishers, pp. 277–91.

Hall, W.C. (1973) '*Patterns: teachers' handbook*', London: Longman/Penguin Press.

Hall, W.C. (1982) 'Science/Technology/Society education: reasons for current interest and problems to overcome', Paper presented to the 2nd IOSTE Symposium, Nottingham, UK, July 1982.

Harding, P. and Hare, W. (2000) 'Portraying science accurately in classrooms: emphasizing open-mindedness rather than relativism', *Journal of Research in Science Teaching* 37: 225–36.

Harms, N.C. and Yager, R.E. (eds) (1981) *What Research Says to the Science Teacher, Vol. 3*, Washington, DC: National Science Teachers Association.

Harrison, G. (1979) 'The role of technology in science education', Paper presented to the 1st IOSTE Symposium, Halifax, Canada, August 1979.

Holford, D. (1982) 'Training science teachers for science-technology-society roles', Paper presented to the 2nd IOSTE Symposium, Nottingham, UK, July 1982.

Holman, J. (ed.) (1988) *International Journal of Science Education* (special issue on STS) 10: No. 4.

Hunt, J.A. (1988) 'SATIS approaches to STS', *International Journal of Science Education* 10: 409–20.

Hurd, P.D. (1970) 'Scientific enlightenment for an age of science', *The Science Teacher* 37: 13–15.

Hurd, P.D. (1975) 'Science, technology and society: new goals for interdisciplinary science teaching', *The Science Teacher* 42: 27–30.

Hurd, P.D. (1986) 'Perspectives for the reform of science education', *Phi Delta Kappan* 67: 353–8.

Irwin, A. (1995) *Citizen Science: a study of people, expertise and sustainable development*, New York: Routledge.

James, R.K. (ed.) (1985) *Science Technology and Society: resources for science educators* (1985 AETS Yearbook), Columbus, OH: Association for the Education of Teachers in Science.

Jeans, S.L. (1998) 'Teacher images of the intent of science curriculum policy: experienced and novice teachers at work', Paper presented at the annual meeting of the Canadian Society for the Study of Education, Ottawa, Canada, May 1998.

Jenkins, E. (1994) 'Public understanding of science and science education for action', *Journal of Curriculum Studies* 26: 601–11.

Jenkins, E. (1999) 'School science, citizenship and the public understanding of science', *International Journal of Science Education* 21: 703–10.

Jenkins, E. (2000) 'Science for all: time for a paradigm shift?', in R. Millar, J. Leach, and J. Osborne (eds) *Improving Science Education: the contribution of research*, Buckingham: Open University Press, pp. 207–26.

Klopfer, L.E. and Cooley, W.W. (1963) 'The history of science cases for high school in the development of student understanding of science and scientists', *Journal of Research in Science Teaching* 1: 33–47.

Knain, E. (1999) 'Sense and sensibility in science education: developing rational beliefs through cultural approaches', *Studies in Science Education* 33: 1–29.

Koch, J. (1996) 'National science education standards: a turkey, a valentine, or a lemon?', in R.E. Yager (ed.) *Science/Technology/Society as Reform in Science Education*, Albany, NY: SUNY Press, pp. 306–15.

Kolstø, S.D. (2000) 'Consensus projects: teaching science for citizenship', *International Journal of Science Education* 22: 645–64.

Kumar, D.D. and Chubin, D.E. (eds) (2000) *Science, Technology, and Society: A sourcebook on research and practice*, New York: Kluwer Academic/Plenum Publishers.

Layton, D. (1994) 'STS in the school curriculum: a movement overtaken by history?', in J. Solomon and G. Aikenhead (eds) *STS Education: international perspectives on reform*, New York: Teachers College Press, pp. 32–44.

Lewis, J. (Proj. Dir.) (1981) *Science in Society*, London: Heinemann Educational Books.

Majumdar, S.K., Rosenfeld, L.M., Rubba, P.A., Miller, E.W., and Schmalz, R.F. (eds) (1991) *Science Education in the United States: issues, crises and priorities*, Easton, PA: The Pennsylvania Academy of Science.

Manassero-Mas, M., Vázquez-Alonso, Á. and Acevedo-Díaz, J. (2001) *Avaluació dels Temes de Ciència, Tecnologia i Societat*. Les Illes Balears, Spain: Conselleria d'Educació i Cultura del Govern de les Illes Balears.

McClelland, L.W. (1998) 'Curriculum change: what experienced science teachers say about it', Paper presented at the annual meeting of the Canadian Society for the Study of Education, Ottawa, Canada, May 1998.

McConnell, M.C. (1982) 'Teaching about science, technology and society at the secondary school level in the United States: an education dilemma for the 1980s', *Studies in Science Education* 9: 1–32.

Millar, R. (1996) 'Towards a science curriculum for public understanding', *School Science Review* 77: 7–18.

Millar, R. (2000) 'Science for public understanding: developing a new course for 16–18 year old students', in R.T. Cross and P.J. Fensham (eds) *Science and the Citizen: For educators and the public*, Melbourne: Arena Publications, pp. 201–14.

Nagasu, N. and Kumano, Y. (1996) 'STS initiatives in Japan: poised for a forward leap', in R.E. Yager (ed.) *Science/Technology/Society as Reform in Science Education*, Albany, NY: SUNY Press, pp. 261–70.

NRC (National Research Council) (1996) *National Science Education Standards*, Washington, DC: National Academy Press.

NSTA (National Science Teachers Association) (1982) 'Science-technology-society: science education for the 1980s', Washington, DC: National Science Teachers Association.

Ødegaard, M. (2001) 'The drama of science education: how public understanding of biotechnology and drama as a learning activity may enhance a critical and inclusive science education', Unpublished dissertation, University of Oslo.

Orpwood, G.W.F. and Roberts, D.A. (1980) 'Science and society: dimensions for science education for the '80s', *Orbit* 51: 21–5.

Oxford University (1989) *Enquiry into the Attitudes of Sixth-formers Towards Choice of Science and Technology Courses in Higher Education*, Oxford: Department of Educational Studies.

Piel, E.J. (1981) 'Interaction of science, technology, and society in secondary school', in N.C. Harms and R.E. Yager (eds) *What Research Says to the Science Teacher, Vol. 3*, Washington, DC: National Science Teachers Association, pp. 94–112.

Prat, A.B. (ed.) (1990) *Scuola Scienza e Società*, special issue of *La Fisica nella Scuola* 23: No. 3.

Rip, A. (1979) 'The social context of science, technology and society courses', *Studies in Higher Education* 4: 15–26.

Roberts, D.A. (1983) *Scientific Literacy*, Ottawa: Science Council of Canada.

Roberts, D.A. (1998) 'Toward understanding how science teachers think about a new science curriculum policy', Paper presented at the annual meeting of the Canadian Society for the Study of Education, Ottawa, Canada, May 1998.

Roberts, D.A. and Orpwood, G.W.F. (1979) *Properties of Matter: a teacher's guide to alternative versions*, Toronto: OISE.

Roy, R. (1984) *S-S/T/S Project: teach science via science, technology, and society material in the pre-college years*, University Park, PA: Pennsylvania State University.

Roy, R. (2000) 'Real science education: replacing 'PCB' with S(cience) through-STS throughout all levels of K-12: 'Materials' as one approach', in D.D. Kumar and D.E. Chubin (eds) *Science, Technology, and Society: a sourcebook on research and practice*, New York: Kluwer Academic/Plenum Publishers, pp. 9–19.

Royal Ministry of Church, Education and Research (1995) *Core Curriculum: for primary, secondary and adult education in Norway*, Oslo: Akiademika a/s.

Rubba, P.A. and Wiesenmayer, R.L. (1985) 'A goal structure for precollege STS education: a proposal based upon recent literature in environmental education', *Bulletin of Science, Technology and Society* 5: 573–80.

Ryder, J. (2001) 'Identifying science understanding for functional scientific literacy', *Studies in Science Education* 36: 1–42.

Schroeer, D. (1972) *Physics and Its Fifth Dimension: Society*, Don Mills, Ontario: Addison-Wesley.

Sjøberg, S. (1997) 'Scientific literacy and school science: arguments and second thoughts', in E. Kallerud and S. Sjøberg (eds) *Science, Technology and Citizenship: The public understanding of science and technology in science education and research policy*, Oslo: Norwegian Institute for Studies in Research and Higher Education, pp. 9–28.

Solomon, J. (1983) *Science in a Social Context* (SISCON)-*in-schools*, Oxford: Basil Blackwell.

Solomon, J. (1988) 'The dilemma of science, technology and society education', in P.J. Fensham (ed.) *Development and Dilemmas in Science Education*, New York: Falmer Press, pp. 266–81.

Solomon, J. (1992) 'The classroom discussion of science-based social issues presented on television: knowledge, attitudes and values', *International Journal of Science Education* 14: 431–44.

Solomon, J. (1993) *Teaching Science, Technology and Society*, Buckingham: Open University Press.

Solomon, J. (1994) 'Conflict between mainstream science and STS in science education', in J. Solomon and G. Aikenhead (eds) *STS Education: international perspectives on reform*, New York: Teachers College Press, pp. 3–10.

Solomon, J. (1996) 'STS in Britain: Science in a social context', in R.E. Yager (ed.) *Science/Technology/Society as Reform in Science Education*, Albany, NY: SUNY Press, pp. 241–48.

Solomon, J. and Aikenhead, G.S. (eds) (1994) *STS Education: international perspectives on reform*, New York: Teachers College Press.

Spiegel-Rösing, I. and Price, D. (eds) (1977) *Science, Technology and Society: a cross-disciplinary perspective*, London: Sage.

Thier, H. and Nagle, B. (1994) 'Developing a model for issue-oriented science', in J. Solomon and G. Aikenhead (eds) *STS Education: international perspectives on reform*, New York: Teachers College Press, pp. 75–83.

Tobias, S. (1990) *They're Not Dumb, They're Different*, Tuscon, AZ: Research Corporation.

Watson, F.G. (1979) 'Science education for survival', keynote address to the 1st IOSTE Symposium, Halifax, Canada, August 1979.

Welzel, M. and Roth, W.-M. (1998) 'Do interviews really assess students' knowledge?', *International Journal of Science Education* 20: 25–44.

Yager, R.E. (ed.) (1992) *Status of STS: reform efforts around the world*, Knapp Hill, South Harting: ICASE.

Yager, R.E. (1996a) 'History of science/technology/society as reform in the United States', in R.E. Yager (ed.) *Science/technology/society as Reform in Science Education*, Albany, NY: SUNY Press, pp. 3–15.

Yager, R.E. (ed.) (1996b) *Science/technology/society as Reform in Science Education*, Albany, NY: SUNY Press.

Yager, R.E. and Krajcik, J. (1989) 'Success of students in a college physics course with and without experiencing a high school course', *Journal of Research in Science Teaching* 26: 599–608.

Ziman, J. (1980) *Teaching and Learning about Science and Society*, Cambridge: Cambridge University Press.

Ziman, J. (1984) *An Introduction to Science Studies: the philosophical and social aspects of science and technology*, Cambridge: Cambridge University Press.

Ziman, J. (1994) 'The rationale for STS is in the approach', in J. Solomon and G. Aikenhead (eds) *STS Education: international perspectives on reform*, New York: Teachers College Press, pp. 21–31.

Zoller, U. (1991) 'Teaching/learning styles, performance, and students' teaching evaluation in S/T/E/S-focused science teacher education', *Journal of Research in Science Teaching* 28: 593–607.

6 The UK and the movement for science, technology, and society (STS) education

Joan Solomon

Peter Fensham wrote about the rise of the STS movement (Fensham, 1988a) both in his own home territory and in several other countries. As if that did not display a great enough breadth of scholarship he also fitted in some of the other curriculum movements of the 1970s and 1980s (Fensham, 1992; 1988b). Together with his sound grasp of the underlying research base (Fensham, 1983), he illustrated the range of cultural forces at work behind these innovations in science education. As I reread these and others of Peter's papers I thought how very valuable it is that the history of these educationally turbulent times should be recorded. The changes began, one might say, very soon after the Second World War, although it will later be shown that this is not a sharp starting point, and mirrored a truly enormous range of anxieties, hopes, and fears of the public at large in the government in particular. It also encompassed a swing in the understanding of the nature of science. We may not at that time have realised the nature of the revolution we were living through, popularly known as the move to postmodernism, but in retrospect and armed with ever-convenient hindsight, it is not difficult to see.

About fifty years before this period John Dewey (1916) had written his great book, *Democracy and Education*. This recognised, long before the events of the second part of the century, that the educational future of a really liberal democracy had to re-examine the borderline between the school and the world, and between abstract science and practical technological activity. Jumping to the last decade of the twentieth century we can see only a little of the progress with technology that Peter has always tried so hard to incorporate into science, which still remains isolated and without the respect that Dewey would have accorded it for its 'social intelligence'.

So when Carr and Hartnett (1996) set out to examine the politics of educational ideas they concluded that the tide had turned against a truly participatory democracy of the kind that Dewey had envisioned. They wrote that it was only history that could show

> that these educational traditions could not have evolved the way they did unless and until the classical conception of democracy as an educative form

of social life, had been replaced by the contemporary conception of democracy as a mechanism for selecting the political elite.

(p. 66)

From this pessimistic passage I want to draw several rather more optimistic general lessons. First, that the social and political history of a period can cast a most interesting light on its educational innovations. Second, that the ideas about the nature of democracy which are prevalent in the society have a strong effect on the kind of science education imposed, and third, that continuous change has already, in the last five years, brought about yet another change which is of great interest. Of course all these effects are exceptionally strong when the concept of society is an explicit part of the educational course, as it always is for STS.

British innovations in science education – before STS

Writing about STS as it developed in the UK, for scholars from other countries, is always slightly embarrassing. 'No educational innovation', one might write in imitation of the poet John Donne, '*is an island*'. We need to begin by owning up to the parlous state of our science education and the reasons, as far as I can see them, for these during the period 1960–70.

The science curriculum changes of the 1960s, launched with generous help from the Nuffield Foundation, were comparatively easy to understand. Their promoters, people like Eric Rogers whom Peter mentioned in his paper (1988a) were clear that it was all to be about 'clever thinking' and 'being a scientist for a day'. So if you believed that, which in itself was by no means a mean achievement, you would already be half way to the finishing post. But the idea also had its drawbacks. Scientific thinking was very clever, probably cleverer than that of any other discipline if you read all the promotional literature of the times, and being a scientist was only open to those who were clever and had been taught the appropriate syllabus. Here we must add some peculiarly English social information. These Nuffield curricula were intended for pupils from the old public schools, or from the grammar schools which were built in their image. In such establishments students were educated for *leadership*, not for *citizenship*, and the classics were still rather more popular than the sciences at that time, as they are in Italy today. It was still important to reassure parents who had paid so much for their child's education that science was a suitable subject. Notice that, thus far in the reconstruction of science education, the word 'society' had not even been mentioned.

But this was a time of almost painful cultural change in schools as the first British comprehensive schools were opening. At first children of different ability were strictly segregated with the top stream identified as 'grammar' and following much the same curricula as the public schools. Primary schools had grappled rather better with the notion of education for all in a democratic setting (only to find that their idea of 'child-centred education' was to be used, years later when Mrs Thatcher was Prime Minister, as a term of opprobrium). However, there was a slowly growing amount of science being taught in the primary schools, although it was still not compulsory, and the real question was what should be done for the non-grammar students in the new comprehensive secondary schools.

The curriculum innovators decided to bite the bullet. These students might not be capable of very clever thinking but at least they could look forward to employment in which a limited amount of applied science might figure. So a new course, 'Science at Work', was born. It was full of simple experimental work, had less abstract content, and was nearer to more everyday questions such as 'how can we show that there is energy in food?' (The hugely enjoyable answer was to burn a peanut and use the heat to boil some water!) As Peter mentioned in his contribution to the *Handbook of Research on Curriculum* (1992), advocacy for practical work, either for apprenticeship for employment or for academic science, harked back to the earliest days of the twentieth century and to the work of the early chemistry educator Henry Armstrong (Jenkins, 1979).

Lastly, before we start on the route to STS curricula, it seems important to trace out the progress of another group of British science educators who were unconnected to schools. From the 1930s to the present day there has been an intermittent effort to teach science to lay adults. Here, as for the Nuffield scheme, the usual objective was to demonstrate the clever and logical nature of scientific knowledge. The movement that emerged in the UK during the 1930s is often referred to as 'Scientific Humanism'. It aimed at a 'scientific education' for all the people – which was certainly not available at that time. This, then, was when the movement for 'Science for All', which is so strongly connected with the name of Peter Fensham, first began in the UK. Despite the title of Lancelot Hogben's (1938) famous book *Science for the Citizen*, it now reads as no more than yet another text in general science with numerical questions, answers in the back, and some added history of a paste-on kind. The series was subtitled, with the euphoric optimism typical of the man, 'Primers for the age of plenty'. If all was going so well it may have seemed to Hogben that there would be no citizenship problems left. His next book, called *Mathematics for the Million*, was a similar text for mathematics. Hogben (1938) thought nothing of contemporary writings on 'popular science', and, as we shall see, there are plenty who feel much the same to the present day:

> The clue to the state of mind which produces these week-kneed and clownish apologetics is contempt for the common man.
>
> (Hogben, 1938, p. 11)

According to Hogben science had to be taught to 'the common man' in the same way as it might be taught to a potential scientist. Some of these scientific humanists, like the Irish socialist J.D. Bernal, did have an understanding that laypeople might want a different 'citizen's science' which addressed special questions like the role of science in society and in history. His most famous book in this vein (Bernal, 1954) was written after the war when such optimism about science could no longer count on popular support, a time in STS which will be described in a later section.

After the war Charles Snow propagated his notion of the clash between science and the humanities in his famous lecture entitled 'The Two Cultures' in much the same spirit as Hogben. He wanted to put science on the same cultural level as the classical languages, and started with the rather trivial idea that knowing the second law of thermodynamics, difficult as that might be, would somehow make a non-scientist as scientifically literate as a knowledge of the plays of Shakespeare would make a scientist literate. He completely ignored the whole question of why laypeople who were not going to be scientists might want or need to learn that, or indeed any other piece of formal science knowledge.

The scientistic comments of Hogben can be compared to similar comments made decades later by Lewis Wolpert (1993). He, and his American counterpart Morris Shamos (1995), tried to label scientific knowledge as 'unnatural' and especially difficult. This was the same feature of science that the Nuffield reformers had struggled with, but Wolpert, and to some extent Shamos, were satisfied with the exclusion that their perspective implied.

There are some very sharp and useful distinctions in Table 6.1 which has been compiled in the way advocated by the French sociologist Alain Touraine (1997). What has been omitted includes three of the features common to them all:

1 a huge pride in science as a way of thinking,
2 a contempt for most other kinds of knowledge, and
3 no special interest in science for the ordinary citizen.

We may conclude from this that for democratic thinking to penetrate into science education some very special event would be needed. We shall see in the next section that this special event had indeed occurred during the period, but that its strident message has yet to be recognised by all scientists.

Table 6.1 Forms of scientific knowledge

Type	Identity	Adversary	Goal
Scientific humanists (1930s)	Marxist educators	Social elitism in science	Relieving the oppressed (e.g. Irish)
Charles Snow (1950s)	Speaking for science as a culture	Humanism as the only culture	Recognition of two cultures
Wolpert, Shamos (1990s)	Scientific literacy is impossible	Popularisers	Preserving elite science

The first phase of STS

The launching of Sputnik, which proved to be so powerful in US science education, had little or no effect on curricular reform in the UK. It was the dropping of the atomic bomb together with the fear of a forthcoming 'nuclear holocaust' in which just one missile, dropped by the Soviet Union in retaliation for some hostility in the Cold War, might wipe out half the population of the UK that was ever present. It is hard now to look back at that time and recognise its real terror. Perhaps the bombing of London in the early years of the war, together with repeated showings of films from a devastated and radioactive Hiroshima, were visually responsible for its magnitude. Week by week journals like *New Scientist* published ever higher levels of atmospheric radiation and it was the left-wing scientists of the time who drew their own lesson from this. If neither politicians nor the general public understood the threat, was it not the scientists' responsibility to inform them?

One response was to launch the British Society for Social Responsibility in Science in 1958. This mirrored the American journal *Bulletin of the Atomic Scientists*, and the International Pugwash organisation that actually succeeded in running meetings attended by scientists from almost all countries, including the Soviet Union. It is tempting to see these as an extension of the old scientistic line of thought in which scientists as superior thinkers could solve problems that other ways of thinking could not reach by talking to each other. However, that is not quite fair. In England and Holland there were groups of scientists who took their self-imposed responsibilities very seriously. Bill Williams and other British physicists hired a train-carriage that they furnished with leaflets explaining about the nature and dangers of radioactivity from nuclear power and nuclear bombs. This they took across the country trying to teach any who wanted to know what was at stake. In continental Europe national referendums took place in Austria and Switzerland asking a public which was still almost completely ignorant about nuclear energy, what they wanted to be done about nuclear power in their country. It was left to the Dutch to make the essential connection with education. In 1970 their government instituted an eight-year programme of public education in nuclear energy which would culminate in an informed referendum on the subject. Science lecturers from the Free University of Amsterdam led the way and a textbook bearing the name *Physics and Society* was published. It was a significant moment in the history of STS.

Meanwhile in England a group of scientists from universities and polytechnics began a movement called SISCON (Science In a Social CONtext). Somehow they had managed to raise funds, and to get their institutions to sanction courses on the relevant topics. Individually they used the parent body as an academic powerhouse from which to teach each other and to draw out new teaching and learning materials about world resources, nuclear power stations, population expansion, the limits to growth, alternative power for their students. Every year from 1970 to 1979 the SISCON summer school was held at Coleg

Harlech in the middle of Welsh-speaking Wales. The impressive results ranged very widely and made a hesitant but lasting impact on the teaching of science at tertiary level.

Two other points should be noted about this fertile but limited period of tertiary-level education in STS. One was that some of the new topics, like the sociology of science (the trial of Oppenheimer, the nature of public inquiries, etc.), emerged and must have seemed to some to threaten the only other established courses on what John Ziman (1980) calls 'meta-science'. These were quiet and almost dusty courses in the history and philosophy of science (HPS) to be found in many universities. It was an exciting time for the philosophy of science with controversies between Popper and Kuhn, and challenges from Lakatos and Feyerabend. The SISCON constituents plunged enthusiastically into each new topic, which won no plaudits for them from the graver and older community of HPS. The second point was that almost no school teachers (apart from me) were present at the SISCON summer schools where there was so much to be learnt. Both of these factors were to cause trouble for SISCON in the near future.

In 1978 the first of these troubles erupted. The government was presented with a report on meta-science courses in the polytechnics and universities. Almost predictably the author, Alex Cairncross, reported negatively on the innovative and politically conscious STS courses in comparison with the abstract and contextually unchallenging courses in the history and philosophy of science. It was to be the death-knell of tertiary-level SISCON. By 1979 the last organiser of this, Michael Gibbons, presented the only school science teacher at the summer school with a challenge to take these studies down to school level and write new materials, together with the princely sum of just £200 – all that was left in the kitty!

STS begins in schools

Nothing ever starts with a totally clean slate. At the two extremes of age and prestige some new curriculum ideas had already begun to emerge in the schools. The first of these was at the very top of the school and really only concerned with the very bright students in public or grammar schools who had been entered for the competitive Oxford and Cambridge scholarship papers. In addition to tricky and often rather pointless papers full of difficult problems to solve, there was often one on international affairs or general studies, which might contain an issue that was based on contemporary science. While humanities students were usually taught no science at all, science students had compulsory lessons in literature. Charles Snow's Two Cultures were still as different as chalk from cheese! The second innovation was a middle school curriculum where integrated science was just beginning to emerge in the new comprehensive schools. Not only did the curriculum for SCISP (Schools Council Integrated Science Project) mix up the once-proud single sciences but also it included some aspects of social science in a quite unprecedented way.

For the sixth-form students in public schools a new and well-funded project called Science-in-Society which carried over the 'education for leadership' ethos had just emerged. For those in the new and less exclusively academic sixth forms of the comprehensive schools there was to be the new SISCON-in-Schools project. It picked up a democratic thread appropriate to the new situation. The following excerpt from *New Scientist* (8 January 1981) was written while the co-ordinator was still a hard-working school science teacher. It warned against a piecemeal approach to the new STS studies, and set a global/local agenda, without underestimating the problems involved:

> It presupposes the existence of a body of experts full of obscure but objective knowledge, and assumes that all a judge, journalist or concerned citizen need do is to prise out the facts by relentless questioning and then use them to put matters right. This omits any feeling for the varied needs of society. Everyone should know by now that fossil fuels are running out; the important question is how prepared we are to adapt our ways of living . . . how do people in the Third World perceive their own population problems?

This article outlined the nine teaching units, which included:

> War and the Atomic Bomb
> Space-flight and Science Fiction
> Evolution and Human Population
> How can We be Sure (nature of science)?
> Technology, Invention and Industry
> Health, Food and Population
> Energy; the power to work

Despite the confidence and speed with which these units were produced, there was no hiding the new approach to democracy that this course pursued. It stated quite explicitly that it was not the task of schools to wrap its students in a politically sterile cocoon until the minimum voting age was reached:

> A typical comprehensive sixth form spans a wide range of subjects and pupils, from the very bright who are coping easily with three or four A levels, to the one-year hopefuls who are still trying to scrape together a few O levels. But far from presenting a teaching problem this variety provides a splendid basis for that class discussion that must incorporate the other 'thread in the STS braid' the social and political dimensions.
>
> (Solomon, 1981)

When Fensham drew up his well-known eight categories of STS courses he included the SISCON-in-Schools project amongst those where priority is given to systematic learning (Fensham, 1988a). He wrote that as much or more weight is given to the study of the relevant societal knowledge as there is to what he called the 'knowledge of worth', meaning traditional topics in disciplinary science education.

During the 1980s public examinations were prepared at several levels to make sure that credit would be given for good work in this new subject of STS. The lowest level was CSE, an examination with enough freedom for teachers to design their own syllabuses and have them accredited by the examination boards. This I take to be another example of the democracy of the times. At the highest level there was an STS curriculum equivalent to A-level (university entrance) but only equivalent to half a subject because it had less content and could be taught in just one year, as opposed to the two years generally prescribed. What was really memorable about this syllabus was the way in which it was divided into three fundamental compulsory sections to match its title: 'The nature of science, The nature of technology, and The nature of social decision-making in science and technology'. It was the third part that was designed to make a connection between the young citizen's place in society and the values to be associated with the uses of the new science and technology. Dewey's ideas came as close here to the reality of science education, as it was to do for several years to come.

This is a good place to explore the work of science teachers at this energetic time of curriculum reform. Writing about science education in the 1960s when it was commonplace, at least in USA, to boast openly that some new development was 'teacher-proof', Fensham (1988b) claimed that some at least of the new curricula of the 1980s were no longer divisible into 'teaching' and 'science' in such a simplistic way. Some university-based researchers were engaging the teachers as colleagues in their developments, and in the UK it is fair to say that the teachers themselves were achieving new levels of innovation (e.g. the School Science Curriculum Review), as they also did in the SISCON project. In the SSCR project this was done by networking the teachers by region, providing regional organisers and claiming that it was a 'Periphery to Centre' model (Ebbutt, 1985). The SISCON-in-Schools project operated on a small scale as befitted its leaner purse but the networking was similar. (Only a month or two ago I met a teacher from those times who remarked that we had last met in my London kitchen fifteen years ago, where indeed all the early work was done!)

This first phase of STS was like an explosion. As John Ziman wrote *in Teaching and Learning about Science and Society* (1980), 'The STS movement belongs to our own times, and to our own form of civilisation'. It was a reaction to what has been likened to a passing meteorite which changed the environment for science education in a way that even the third dangerous phase of educational change was unable to reverse completely.

The Darwinian analogy

Teacher innovation is a very powerful method in curriculum reform. It is similar to the general learning method that Donald Campbell (1960) claimed was like Darwinian evolution. He called it 'Blind Variation and Selective Retention', or BVSR. In biology one could speak of a kind of 'learning' on the part of the organism which takes place by means of random variation through genetic mutation, followed by the brutal process of selective survival of some, or none, of the mutant individuals. The learning about, for example, what structure of limbs favours a quick turn of speed, or how to glide from one branch of a tree to another by means of a membrane of skin stretched from wrist to torso, is produced by the mechanism of BVSR. This is similar to the success or failure of engineering artefacts, like the shape of aeroplanes' wings that are tried out in the environment of wind tunnels (Vincenti, 1990), or to what might be called 'the struggle of conjectures' to succeed in solving problems within an open learning environment (Popper, 1972).

Campbell was at pains to insist that BVSR was a quite general learning theory which could be used whenever there were possible variations in a system which might make it fit better or worse into the surroundings. He wrote of BVSR that it was 'fundamental to . . . all genuine increases in knowledge, to all increases in fit of system to the environment'. Biological evolution can be described as a process which proceeds in a series of 'breakouts' from the limits of what has been known before, and is then accumulated in a bank of accessible new strategies.

In the case of changes to the processes of education the teaching breakouts may have a very short shelf-life. They are strategies which worked once but were quickly superseded by others. However, if this variation is acted upon by the teacher's reflection on how they worked out in the classroom, there may be a useful selection and modification process which together produce a better style of teaching and learning. The enthusiasm of the teachers to whom the innovation belongs is the fuel for new invention and hence yet more variation in styles of learning.

The Darwinian analogy is useful in describing the kind of healthy and busy environment for science education that existed in England, Australia, and the USA during the first half of the 1980s. In the SISCON-in-Schools project, later to be joined by the SATIS project, the curriculum review of SSCR, and the Children's Learning in Science Project (CLISP) set up by Rosalind Driver in 1983, there was a very healthy involvement of teachers. Peter Fensham (1988b), writing about new directions in science education, looked at this kind of curriculum innovation with a great deal of optimism:

> A common feature of some of these approaches is networking of classroom teachers. This particular reconceptualization of curriculum development is an encouraging development as it does suggest that its proponents are heeding the effects of the divorce, so apparent in the 1960s reforms,

between the development of a curriculum and its materials, and its implementation subsequently in classrooms. . . . Networking implies that groups
of science teachers need to be brought into association with each other, and
with the curriculum developers for the sharing of ideas, information and
experiences.

(p. 24)

The third-phase stage: a bad time for education and STS

Whenever the UK becomes anxious about its 'educational competitiveness',
which happened under the Thatcher government of the 1980s, it always
tends to succumb to a severe inspection system coupled with crude 'payment
by results'. This has been referred to as a 'market system' of education but, as
we shall see later, this is not really a good analogy. Schools are clearly social
institutions and it could be said that under Mrs Thatcher and her Secretaries
of State for Education they became the new organisms to be put under the
microscope. Some were pronounced 'failing schools', named and shamed in
public, and finally closed down. This represented a new wave of Darwinism,
more like social Darwinism than the real thing because it was driven by the
belief that competition between schools, made public through published
league tables of examination results, coupled with complete freedom for parents
to choose the schools, and with money following the numbers of pupils
enrolled, would improve standards of education. Like all other forms of
social Darwinism it aimed to help the forces of selection with a heavy hand.

This selectionist ideology mentioned at the start of this chapter by Carr and
Hartnett (1996), used by the British Conservative Party and later copied by
'New Labour' when it came to power, supposed that 'the struggle to survive'
would stimulate each school to improve the pupils' examination grades in order
to attract more funding. As Gillian Sheppard, Secretary of State for Education in
the last Conservative government, stated in Parliament in 1996, as though the
proposition was quite self-evident: 'The existence of a range of different schools
drives up standards for all our children.' New research has shown that, in reality,
this did not happen. Where there was a choice of schools data proves that the
improvement of examination grades was actually a little less than where there
was no realistic choice because of local geography. A report by Levacic
(1996) showed that the quasi-market competition did not affect school
performance as intended. On average over the whole country, examination
performance rose as teachers and pupils became familiar with the kind of
answers required, even while school budgets declined. It was in socially
deprived environments where previous policy had always tried to compensate
for disadvantage that standards remained low, there was a net loss of pupils, and
a drop in schools' funds. The Grant-Maintained – 'opted out' – schools were
more favourably funded but they were shown not to have attracted any
more pupils when other environmental factors were taken into account. The

author concluded in a valuable and memorable phrase, 'This suggests that successful adaptive changes for schools are not based on surface changes to image' (p. 324).

It would be satisfying to believe that it was other features of the schools – their teaching about democracy, citizenship, and social responsibility, or their encouragement of creativity, not to mention their relationship with the community – about which parents might want to express choice. However, there is sadly little evidence that this was the case. In 1983 the then Secretary of State for Education had ruled that there should be 'no teaching about the social and economic issues in science'. At that time statements of this kind had little power to effect change. So, before the whole inspection system was put into place, STS lessons did continue for a little while, but they were against the climate of the times. Mrs Thatcher herself once memorably announced that there was 'no such thing as society, only people'. This is reminiscent of a pile of salt whose individual grains cannot hold together in any shape other than the unstable cone from which small cascades of grains scuttle down the sides when the system is jolted. That is inevitable, although hard on those 'grains' to whom this rejection process happens. One could almost say that there is no 'hand' held out to help them. Indeed, this was the Prime Minister who rechristened the welfare state, of which the 1945 originators were so proud, as 'The Nanny State'.

In general one could hardly imagine a pronouncement less likely to encourage teaching about citizenship in any part of the curriculum. Once the whole repressive competitive system was in place teacher anxiety about the published inspection reports on their work ensured that there would be much more multiple-choice testable material that would be taught than any other. So the casualties in science of the new educational system included descriptive practical work, mostly in biology and environmental studies, and any discussion of topical scientific issues which might affect society.

New stirrings: citizenship and ethics

After the great revolutions of the eighteenth century in France and America it must have appeared that democracy had, to a greater of lesser extent, won the final victory. Now it could only be a matter of time before equality would pervade all nations. This was allied to a movement advancing from the French enlightenment that aimed to collect and build upon all knowledge for which a proof in logic or a practical demonstration could be provided. That seemed to be victory for science and a mortal blow to poetry or religion. However, none of these 'final victories' turned out to be really final. Religions worldwide are now growing new fundamentalist factions, and science itself has had to swallow postmodernism so that in some ways it becomes more like poetry and less like linear logic with each passing year.

What has happened to democracy is more subtle. When the French enthusiast for democracy, Alexis de Tocqueville, visited the newly independent states of America what he saw disturbed him considerably. It was a form of democracy, but not at all what he had expected. Here in the energetic 'Land of the Free' where science and invention were so highly regarded – Dewey would certainly have approved of that – everyone of the right pigmentation was indeed free but, like a nightmare of Thatcherism and enterprise, it added up to a collection of individuals (worse even than a pile of sand grains) rather than a community. This is how de Tocqueville saw it:

> Individualism at first only saps the virtues of public life: but in the long run it attacks and destroys all others, and is at length absorbed in downright selfishness. . . . Those who went before are soon forgotten: of those who will come after no-one has any idea: the interest of man is confined to those in close propinquity to himself. . . . [People] expect nothing from any man . . . and are apt to imagine that their whole destiny is in their own hands.
>
> (De Tocqueville, 1835. Quoted in Midgley, 2001, p. 15)

My point in quoting that passage at some length is to indicate that democracy urgently needs to be wedded to the community and to community action if it is to exhibit caring qualities to counteract the potentially selfish 'enterprise' character of individualism. Even within the political manifestations of democracy it has, by now, appeared that the individualised action of marking a cross in the darkness of the polling booth is not enough to distinguish democracy from social responsibility which, on the smaller scale of science, was where the whole STS movement began.

One new feature of science and society, but usually called 'the public' in this context, began in 1985 in the UK. The Royal Society launched a report entitled *The Public Understanding of Science*. There was nothing at all postmodern about its pronouncements. The underlying text was that science was clever (as in the days of the 1960s Nuffield projects) and that clever scientists should help members of the public to understand it, by making it all a little easier. The authors of the report did not give much attention to what the public might do with this knowledge, apart from supporting their research. Even the democratic incentive of deciding about issues, which had inspired the early Dutch programme for learning about nuclear energy, was absent.

However, the research programme which followed this report produced some interesting results. It seemed that farmers judged scientific advice against their own agricultural knowledge (Wynne, 1992), and 17-year-old school students judged the ethics of scientific controversies on the television by their own experience of how people behave (Solomon, 1992). Although no one mentioned this at the time, it did seem that postmodernism had struck at last! There was no special respect to be accorded to scientific knowledge by farmers or school students who would certainly not have agreed that scientific knowledge was a meta-narrative (Lyotard, 1984), had they any idea of what that meant, but behaved as though it was all very little different from 'Mother's Maxims'.

Meanwhile the old world order had begun to change and the Soviet Union ceased to be a superpower. In the words of Gorbachev it needed to be 'restructured', as also did education. In the 1970s and 1980s, alongside the rise of STS and yet completely dissociated from it, the educationalist Malcolm Skilbeck had been examining the aims of school curricula in a series of books and articles, and had proposed that one of the two fundamental aims of all education was to provide the next generation with skills for critiquing their own culture, and transforming it. It was quite like Gorbachev's aim of national and cultural reconstruction:

> [H]istory, geography, politics, sociology and morality may be presented as problematic, controversial and many-sided, or as so much settled knowledge to be learnt and reproduced according to the conventions of the essay and the examination question. A curriculum plan in a school can aim to foster critical reflective thinking; it can stimulate and provide opportunities for participation in practical projects by which the community betters itself: it can encourage pupils to see themselves as the organisers of their own society.
>
> (Skilbeck, 1975, p. 34)

Skilbeck rarely if ever mentioned science but developed a concept of education as a preparation for social reconstruction, which clearly encompassed citizens' decisions about new technology.

And so it came about that by 1997 when the new Labour government came to power, the science curriculum began to show changes related to the kind of 'caring cement' which might hold a democratic society together rather than allowing enterprising individuals entirely free range. First, in 1997, pupils were to 'be taught to consider the ethical implications' of new scientific and technological issues. Then, in 2001–2, the science curriculum included considering how the skills of citizenship could best be linked up with an understanding of science. The Minister of Education demonstrated that he accepted the function of concerned groups within a 'civil society' and STS began to wake up to a new age.

Towards the end of their analysis of the struggle for democracy within education, from which a damning quotation was lifted at the very beginning of this chapter, Carr and Hartnett answered their own question – 'How should educational policy be determined?' – in the following way:

> A distinctive feature of a democratic society is that it accepts that no single image of the good society can be theoretically justified to an extent that would allow it to be put beyond rational dispute, and that arguments

and disagreements to which such disputes give rise ought not to be concealed or repressed.

(Carr and Hartnett, 1996, p. 187)

The pendulum is, very, very slowly, beginning to swing back.

References

Bernal, J.D. (1954) *Science in History*, London: Watts.

Campbell, D. (1960) 'Blind variation and selective retention in creative thought as in other knowledge processes', *Psychological Review* 67: 380–400.

Carr, W. and Hartnett, A. (1996) *Education and the Struggle for Democracy*, Buckingham: Open University Press.

Dewey, J. (1916) *Democracy and Education*, New York: Free Press.

Ebbutt, D. (1985) 'Evaluation and the secondary science curriculum review – setting the scene', *School Science Review* 66: 645–50.

Fensham, P. (1983) 'A research base for new objectives of science teaching', *Science Education* 67: 3–12.

Fensham, P. (1988a) 'Approaches to the teaching of STS in science education', *International Journal of Science Education* 10: 346–50.

Fensham, P. (1988b) 'Familiar but different: some dilemmas and new directions in science education', in P. Fensham (ed.) *Development and Dilemmas in Science Education*, London: Falmer Press, pp. 1–26.

Fensham, P. (1992) 'Science and Technology', in P.W. Jackson (ed.) *Handbook of Research on Curriculum*, New York: Macmillan, pp. 789–829.

Hogben, L. (1938) *Science for the Citizen*, London: George Allen and Unwin.

Jenkins, E. (1979) *From Armstrong to Nuffield*, London: Murray.

Levacic, R. (1996) 'Competing for resources: the impact of social disadvantage and other factors on English secondary schools' financial performance', *Oxford Review of Education* 24: 303–28.

Lyotard, J.-F. (1984) *The Postmodern Condition*, Manchester: Manchester University Press.

Midgley, M. (2001) *Science and Poetry*, London and New York: Routledge.

Popper, K. (1972) *Objective Knowledge*, Oxford: Clarendon Press.

Shamos, M. (1995) *The Myth of Scientific Literacy*, New Brunswick, NJ: Rutgers University Press.

Skilbeck, M. (1975) 'The school and cultural development', in M. Golby, J. Greenwald, and R. West (eds) *Curriculum Design*, Milton Keynes: Open University Press, pp. 7–19.

Solomon, J. (1981) 'STS for school children', *New Scientist* 8 January: 77–8.

Solomon, J. (1992) 'The classroom discussion of science-based social issues presented on television: knowledge, attitudes and values', *International Journal of Science Education* 14: 431–44.

Touraine, A. (1997) *What is Democracy?*, trans. David Macey, Boulder, CO: West Press.

Vincenti, W. (1990) *What Engineers Know and How They Know It*, Baltimore, MD: Johns Hopkins University Press.

Wolpert, L. (1993) *The Unnatural Nature of Science*, London: Faber and Faber.

Wynne, B. (1992) 'Misunderstood misunderstanding: social identities and the uptake of science', *Public Understanding of Science* 1: 281–304.

Ziman, J. (1980) *Teaching and Learning about Science and Society*, Cambridge: Cambridge University Press.

Part IV

Gender in science teaching

7 Science for all? Science for girls? Which girls?

Nancy Brickhouse

In the 1980s, Fensham found an intriguing anomaly. He and his colleagues found a case where girls were participating and achieving in science at high levels! In the same era, most of the researchers who were interested in the differences between boys' and girls' participation in science studied the size of the gap and attempted to interpret the participation gap in terms of differences in achievement or attitude, and the variety of factors that might influence achievement and attitude. Girls had generally fared poorly. International studies found that in nineteen countries boys outperformed girls in the physical sciences (Comber and Keeves, 1973).

Fensham (1986), however, discovered that in Thailand this generalisation did not hold. Girls participated in the physical sciences as much as boys, and scored similarly on achievement tests. He and his colleagues systematically investigated these findings to try and understand the reasons why girls in Thailand seemed to fare better in comparison with boys than girls in other countries (Klainin and Fensham, 1987; Klainin *et al.*, 1989). They concluded that a relevant factor was the way in which science courses were organised in Thailand. Girls must take physical sciences throughout secondary school, whereas in many Western countries, girls can choose to take biology as their science course, and thus opt out of the physical sciences. In Thailand, staying in school requires staying engaged in the physical sciences. Furthermore, whereas chemistry and physics teachers in many countries are most frequently male, this is not the case in Thailand. At least at the time of Fensham's research, 80 per cent of the chemistry teachers were female whereas 50 per cent of the physics teachers were female. In chemistry classes throughout Thailand, girls sit at the front of the room, allowing for greater interaction with the teacher. Students reported that they viewed chemistry as related to women and physics as related to men. Girls scored higher than boys on a variety of different kinds of chemistry examinations and at about the same level in physics. Although this research was carried out over a decade ago, the trends found then appear to hold today. Based on recent comparative studies, girls and boys in Thailand continue to score quite similarly on international examinations, including physical science test items (Martin *et al.*, 2001). Furthermore, the positive effect that delaying the choice of area of study has on girls' participation in science was also found in Scotland in the 1980s (Masson, 1995).

In the USA, the landscape has changed considerably over the last two decades. There are no longer sex differences in course taking in the sciences in high school (Campbell *et al.*, 2000). Although it is still the case that many students do not take physics or chemistry courses in high school, of those who do, the sex distribution is quite even. This may be related to the fact that girls are as likely to have collegiate aspirations as boys. The physical science courses are generally regarded as required for admission to competitive colleges and universities in the USA. Boys do outscore girls on the physical science portion of the National Assessment of Educational Progress (NAEP) (Campbell *et al.*, 2000). Globally, the gender gap in science achievement in high school persists in earth science, physics, and chemistry (Martin *et al.*, 2001). Girls continue to express less confidence in their scientific abilities and less positive attitudes (Martin *et al.*, 2001). The greatest concern regarding girls and science in the USA is now focused on the post-secondary years, and in particular in areas such as engineering and computer science where the participation of girls is astonishingly low (National Science Foundation, 1999). Furthermore, there is concern that girls from poor and/or minority backgrounds continue not to participate and achieve as well as middle-class white girls (National Science Foundation, 1999; American Association of University Women, 2000).

Fensham's research has been important because a case of success such as the one he found in Thailand provides considerable explanatory difficulty for those who would naturalise girls' failures in the sciences. In other words, it is more difficult to claim that girls do poorly in the sciences owing to an innate sex difference if there are circumstances under which girls do as well as boys. It provides us with reasons to believe that what we do in shaping policy may well make a difference in how well girls will fare in the sciences. His research is also suggestive of the kinds of structural changes that ought to be considered in order to advance girls' achievement. His suggestion that we might reduce or eradicate sex differences in achievement by either not allowing girls to opt out of the physical sciences, or at least providing real incentives for staying in (e.g. admission to good colleges), is a claim that merits continued study. At least in the USA we have reached parity in course taking. Perhaps parity in achievement and attitude is on its way, but we are not there yet (Campbell *et al.*, 2000).

What I would like to do next is to situate these empirical findings in a contemporary feminist theoretical framework. How might we think about Fensham's gender work if we look at learning as a process of identity formation?

Identity formation and acquisition of scientific discourses

Perspectives from situated cognition suggest that learning ought to be thought of as a process of identity formation (Lave, 1992). As students decide what kind of person they are and what they aspire to be, they acquire what is needed for participation in relevant communities of practice. Competence is acquired through participation and with the help of mediators whose own affiliations help students move across communities, for example from school communities into scientifically oriented communities (Wenger, 1998).

Feminist approaches to learning often find the perspectives of situated cognition to be particularly useful because understanding identity formation requires a consideration that identities are gendered (Brickhouse, 2001). Any complete understanding of identity must take into account that performances of individuals usually tell us about what kind of girl or boy one aspires to be. For example, some girls may identify strongly with intellectual/scientific cultures and perform a role that would allow them to be recognised as such an intellectual. Other girls may desire an identity of an environmentally sensitive girl and thus acquire the knowledge of nature and the naturalistic dress of an environmentalist. But in most cases, these identities would be different if they were boys; both in terms of what identities are likely to be attractive as well as the particulars of the performance.

Another reason situated cognition offers useful resources for feminists is that situated cognition and feminism have overlapping histories and epistemologies (Brickhouse, 2001). Like feminist epistemologies, theories of situated cognition also work against the dichotomies of mind/body, objectivity/subjectivity, masculine/feminine (Lave, 1988).

Identities are not in-born traits, identities are enacted (Gee, 1999). They speak as much to what kind of person we want to be as to our own personal history. When girls acquire scientific knowledge they may do so because of a desire to be a good student or perhaps to be recognised as literate, or to be successful in solving a particular problem. They may engage in scientific practices because they want others to recognise their scientific identities or they may choose not to engage in scientific practices because they do not want to be seen in undesirable ways by their friends. For some girls and women full participation in some scientific communities may be desired but be too costly in terms of the time and energy that would be required to gain the competencies that accompany community membership (Eisenhart and Finkel, 1998).

Gee (1999) described what is learned and recognised in this process of identity formation as a discourse, a way of thinking, talking, acting, and valuing. Different communities have different kinds of discourses that must be acquired in order for someone to be recognised as a member of that community. In order to be seen as a good physics student, a girl must be recognised by others as competent in manipulating certain kinds of equipment, writing certain kinds of laboratory reports, and in participating in classroom discussions in certain ways etc. Of course, much of the activity in a science classroom may have little or nothing to do with science. Some students may enact a discourse of the model student who consistently completes science-related work in science class, yet understands little about how science functions as a social institution outside school. The contextual features of the school or school system also influence the nature of the discourses enacted. While there may be some similarity in discourses enacted in science classrooms across the globe, one would also expect variation as well (Stigler and Hiebert, 1999).

The fact that people have differential access to identities is the central problem of social inequality (Gee, 1999). Throughout history women have been denied access to schools where students were engaged in the practices that could eventually lead to scientific careers. At other times women have engaged in scientific practices but were not recognised by others as 'scientific'. I have argued that this understanding of identity formation is important for feminists who seek to understand the ways in which gender plays a role in science learning (Brickhouse, 2001). Feminist scholars have also argued that young women may refuse to participate in scientific activities that are incongruent with their gendered identities (Carlone, 1999), or may look for non-traditional ways to participate in science that are consistent with their gendered identities (Eisenhart and Finkel, 1998).

It may be the case that a student will decide that she has no desire to be a part of the communities at school that are engaged in school science. Perhaps she finds what they do to be boring or irrelevant to her concerns. Or perhaps she finds the other members of the community to be simply obnoxious (Seymour and Hewitt, 1997). She chooses disengagement and ignorance in the process of deciding that she does not desire membership in school science communities. The decision to disengage, resist, and ignore is the other important side of engagement and learning. Understanding ignorance is important in understanding learning as identity formation. Wenger describes this eloquently:

> But in a complex world we must find a livable identity, ignorance is never simply ignorance, and knowing is not just a matter of information. In practice, understanding is always straddling the known and the unknown in a subtle dance of the self. It is a delicate balance. Whoever we are, understanding in practice is the art of choosing what to know and what to ignore in order to proceed with our lives.
>
> (Wenger, 1998, p. 41)

Interpreting achievement in science as identity formation

So what is it that girls are really up to when they engage in science – particularly at school? My research in US schools (Brickhouse *et al.*, 2000), examining middle school girls' identities, indicates that often success in science is nothing more than an expression of a desire to be seen as a good girl student. Often the girls who are most successful in a science class exhibit behaviours that are no different than would be seen in other classes: they follow school rules, hand in work on time, and learn enough science words and procedures to score reasonably well on examinations (Brickhouse *et al.*, 2000; Costa, 1997; Page, 1999). The girls who are placed in non-academic tracks are not necessarily the girls who understand science less well. The non-academic tracks are filled with girls (and boys) who do not fit the ideal image of a good student

(Eckert, 1989; Oakes, 1985). Perhaps the most tragic consequence of this is that being tracked low in US schools often means that school provides little or no access to a science (Gilbert and Yerrick, 2001; Oakes, 1985). The quality of the science instruction in these lower track classes is poor, but consistent with the low expectations for student learning.

In my own research the girls from poor and/or minority backgrounds who exhibited strong scientific competencies and interests in middle school were tracked out of academic science by the tenth grade. While this research is based on a very small number of girls and should not be over-generalised, it at least indicates what can happen to girls who may be competent in science, yet their identities do not fit with school-sanctioned norms. They never reach the chemistry and physics courses that were the focus of study by Fensham and his colleagues.

As students progress in their studies, classrooms become increasingly male dominated. Both teachers and students are more likely to be male. But perhaps more importantly, by the time girls reach college, classrooms take on an overall environment similar to a rite-of-passage into adulthood:

> The essential [male/female] opposition between two categories embedded in the traditional gender-role system has consequences for all students and faculty. It occurs when a relatively small number of inexperienced young women are encouraged . . . to venture into an institutionalized national (possibly international) teaching and learning system which has evolved over a long period as an approved way to induct young men into the adult fraternities of science, mathematics and engineering. Most young white men seem able to recognise and respond to the unwritten rules of this adult male social system. The rules are familiar because they are con-sistent with, and are an extension of, traditional male norms that were established by parents, and which have been reinforced by male adults and peers throughout their formal education, sports, and social life.
>
> (Seymour and Hewitt, 1997, p. 259)

Under these conditions, when women 'talk about leaving', they also talk about the difficulty of finding a livable identity as a scientist in a community where they simply do not fit in.

It is ironic that the girls who are most likely to achieve in school science (at least through middle school) are those who take on conventional gendered identities. Girls of colour who are 'loud', who question their teachers, or behave in ways that are perceived as overly aggressive (for a girl), are likely to be placed in non-academic science classrooms and are thus tracked out of a potential future as a scientist. Yet when one reads the literature on women who excel in the sciences (Etzkowitz *et al.*, 2000; Gornick, 1983), they have done so only because they were willing and able to break with conventional expectations of womanhood. Overwhelmingly, the data suggest that the scientifically educated woman who takes on conventional identities of wife and mother is far more likely to leave science than is the woman whose life outside of science looks similar to male scientists (Etzkowitz *et al.*, 2000). In other words, the conventional gender identities that work well for girls in middle school, work against their participation in science in later years.

The case of Thailand

So how do we think about learning as identity formation in a country that has structured science education in ways that retain girls who achieve at high levels? When societal structures are changed, new identity possibilities emerge. Thus in Thailand, the discourse of chemistry is not perceived by students as being masculine, and girls perform well in all the sciences. Perhaps being a good student in the physical sciences does not conflict with other gendered identities the girls enact. All girls who are students are, by requirement, physics students. Thus, the possibility that girls would choose ignorance rather than engagement with science is considerably reduced.

This research leaves us with other questions about how girls (who become women) in Thailand participate in the physical sciences. Science is seen to be a masculine enterprise (Harding, 1986; Keller, 1985). So how do these girls create livable identities for themselves? Are sex roles sufficiently flexible that girls do not experience a conflict between feminine identities and scientific ones? Or does their forced participation in the physical sciences ultimately make their participation easier by changing the culture of the classroom that more easily accommodates diverse identities? Or perhaps little has changed. Girls do well in the physical sciences because they have to do well to be a good student. As soon as other options are available, do they opt out of the physical sciences?

'Science for All'?

Fensham has long advocated 'Science for All'. His use of this slogan has generally been intended to claim that science classes must address the needs of all students, not just the ones who take up identities as professional scientists. Millar and Osborne (1998) concur with Fensham's long-standing concern that science classes have been too strongly influenced by the needs of the few students who will go on to become professional, qualified scientists. The needs of the majority are largely overlooked.

Of course, the problem with slogans such as 'Science for All' is that they can be taken to mean many different things. In the USA, for example, 'Science for All' has been part of the rationale for national and state standards-based reform efforts. There is recognition that we cannot be solely focused on the production of professional scientists since the large majority of students do not have such aspirations. Persistent gaps in achievement between boys and girls and between racial/ethnic groups fuelled much of the reform efforts (American Association for the Advancement of Science, 1989; National Research Council, 1996). The dual goals of equity and excellence are key principles of the National Science Education Standards (National Research Council, 1996). The problem that many students are harmed by low expectations in science achievement is addressed by claiming that all students are expected to reach the same high standards. Egalitarian rhetoric is a central feature of the reform. However, although there is less difference between the achievement of boys and girls, thus far, the achievement gap between racial and economic groups persists (Campbell *et al.*, 2000).

One concern of this particular reform effort is that in our effort to raise expectations for girls, students of colour, and students living in poverty 'Science for All' has unfortunately been interpreted by some as 'one size fits all' (Lemke, 2001; Lynch, 2001). All students are expected to take on uniform identities as good science students. Expectations for what students should know and be able to do in science class are the same for all. Even expectations for science-related values and attitudes are the same for all. In the state where I live all K-8 public school students use identical curriculum materials at each grade level. While this may be preferable to the expectation and realisation of failure in science, it is unlikely to address adequately the diversity of identities desired by school–age children.

In the UK, Millar and Osborne (1998, p. 3) have argued that we must attend to the diverse needs of kids: 'There is a lack of choice post-14 and, as a consequence, a science curriculum which fails to take adequate account of the diversity of interests and aptitudes of young people of this age.' What is too often missing is an understanding of the need for students to populate the content of science with their own purposes, thus taking on science-related identities that are meaningful and desirable to them (Wells, 1995). A 'forced march' through a standard science curriculum that is the same for everyone cannot meet the needs of students who are not all the same.

Choice, however, can be dangerous. Fensham has already pointed out that part of the problem in many Western countries is that we have allowed girls to opt out of the physical sciences. Today, in the USA, we allow students in high school to choose between science courses of varying degrees of difficulty. However, the choice is different in degree, not in kind. The lower track curriculum is the same science, but less demanding (Oakes, 1985). Choosing the low-track science class is actually not much better than taking none at all.

But this does not mean we ought not to explore other ways of structuring the curriculum that allows for choice without allowing opting out. In order to provide for diversity the choices must be good ones. Thus we might have engineering as a major theme in physics and chemistry courses. Girls who have a strong interest in history might take science courses with a strong historical theme. Science fiction enthusiasts might choose physics courses that examine the cosmology and technology embedded in some of the great works of science fiction, including feminist science fiction writers. Girls concerned with problems of farming could take biology courses that also deal directly with the problem of modern-day farming. The list of options could get quite large. The point is to find ways in which science can be taken up as a useful part of the identity students are creating for themselves.

Fensham's challenge of creating 'Science for All' will be an ongoing struggle. If we are to meet his challenge we must attend to the diversity of girls for whom we want to take up science as a part of their identity. This means we must no longer rely on easy stereotypes of what appeals to girls, but to offer a range of ways in which science can be a part of many different identities girls find useful and desirable.

References

American Association for the Advancement of Science (1989) *Science for All Americans*, Washington, DC: American Association for the Advancement of Science.

American Association of University Women (2000) *Tech-Savvy*, Washington, DC: American Association of University of Women Educational Foundation.

Brickhouse, N.W. (2001) 'Embodying science: a feminist perspective on learning', *Journal of Research in Science Teaching* 38: 282–95.

Brickhouse, N.W., Lowery, P., and Schultz, K. (2000) 'What kind of a girl does science? The construction of school science identities', *Journal of Research in Science Teaching* 37: 441–58.

Campbell, J.R., Hombo, C.M., and Mazzeo, J. (2000) *NAEP 1999 Trends in Academic Progress: three decades of student performance*, Washington, DC: US Department of Education Office of Educational Research and Improvement, National Center for Educational Statistics.

Carlone, H. (1999) 'Identifying and expanding the meanings of "scientist" in school science: implications for the participation of girls', Paper presented at the annual meeting of the American Educational Research Association, Montreal, April 1999.

Comber, L.C. and Keeves, J.P. (1973) *Science Education in Nineteen Countries: an Empirical Study*, New York: John Wiley.

Costa, V.B. (1997) 'Honours chemistry: high-status knowledge of knowledge about high status?', *Journal of Curriculum Studies* 29: 289–313.

Eckert, P. (1989) *Jocks and Burnouts: social categories and identity in the high school*, New York: Teachers College Press.

Eisenhart, M. and Finkel, E. (1998) *Women's Science*, Chicago: University of Chicago Press.

Etzkowtiz, H., Kemelgor, C., and Uzzi, B. (2000) *Athena Unbound*, New York: Cambridge University Press.

Fensham, P.J. (1986) 'Lessons from science education in Thailand: a case study of gender and learning in the physical sciences', *Research in Science Education* 16: 92–100.

Gee, J.P. (1999) *An Introduction to Discourse Analysis*, New York: Routledge.

Gilbert, A. and Yerrick, R. (2001) 'Same school, separate worlds: a sociocultural study of identity, resistance, and negotiation in a rural, lower track science classroom', *Journal of Research in Science Teaching* 38: 574–98.

Gornick, V. (1983) *Women in Science*, New York: Simon and Schuster.

Harding, S.G. (1986) *The Science Question in Feminism*, Ithaca, NY: Cornell University Press.

Keller, E.F. (1985) *Reflections on Gender and Science*, New Haven, CT: Yale University Press.

Klainin, S. and Fensham, P.J. (1987) 'Learning achievement in upper secondary school chemistry in Thailand: some remarkable sex reversals', *International Journal of Science Education* 9: 217–27.

Klainin, S., Fensham, P.J. and West, L.H.T. (1989) 'Successful achievement by girls in physics learning', *International Journal of Science Education* 11: 101–12.

Lave, J. (1988) *Cognition in Practice*, New York: Cambridge University Press.

Lave, J. (1992) 'Learning as participation in communities of practice', Paper presented at the annual meeting of the American Educational Research Association, San Francisco, April 1992.

Lemke, J.L. (2001) 'Articulating communities: sociocultural perspectives on science education', *Journal for Research in Science Teaching* 38: 296–316.

Lynch, S. (2001) '"Science for All" is not equal to "One Size Fits All": linguistic and cultural diversity and science education reform', *Journal of Research in Science Teaching* 38: 622–7.

Martin, M.O., Mullis, I.V.S., Gonzalez, E.J., O'Connor, K.M., Chrostowski, S.J., Gregory, K.D., Smith, T.A., and Garden, R.A. (2001) *Science Benchmarking Report: 1999 – TIMSS eighth grade*, Chestnut Hill, MA: International Association for the Evaluation of Educational Achievement, http://www.timss.org (accessed 2001).

Masson, M.R. (1995) 'Sex differences in the study of science in Scotland and England', in R. Clair (ed.) *The Scientific Education of Girls: education beyond reproach?*, Paris: UNESCO, pp. 163–7.

Millar, R. and Osborne, J. (eds) (1998) 'Beyond 2000: science education for the future', Report of a seminar series founded by the Nuffield Foundation, London (available from http://www.kcl.ac.uk/education).

National Research Council (1996) *National Science Education Standards*, Washington, DC: National Academy Press.

National Science Foundation (1999) *Women, Minorities, and Persons with Disabilities in Science and Engineering: 1998 (NSF 99–338)*, Arlington, VA: National Science Foundation.

Oakes, J. (1985) *Keeping Track: how schools structure inequality*, New Haven, CT: Yale University Press.

Page, R. (1999) 'The uncertain value of school knowledge: the case of Westridge High', *Teachers College Record* 100: 554–601.

Seymour, E. and Hewitt, N.M. (1997) *Talking About Leaving: why undergraduates leave the sciences*, Boulder, CO: Westview Press.

Stigler, J.W. and Hiebert, J. (1999) *The Teaching Gap: best ideas from the world's teachers for improving education in the classroom*, New York: Free Press.

Wells, G. (1995) 'Language and the inquiry-oriented curriculum', *Curriculum Inquiry* 25: 233–69.

Wenger, E. (1998) *Communities of Practice: learning, meaning and identity*, New York: Cambridge University Press.

8 Understanding gender differences in science education

Peter Fensham's contribution

Léonie Rennie

In 1986, I made my first presentation to the American Education Research Association (AERA) held in San Francisco. Apart from the excitement of visiting the USA for the first time, and the wonderment that people were having 'earthquake parties' to celebrate the eightieth anniversary of the 18 April 1906 earthquake that virtually destroyed the city, I have two abiding memories. One is bumping into Peter Fensham as he hurried to the Mosconi Center to present his keynote address at AERA on 'Science for All'. He hardly knew me, and I was both surprised and pleased to have this friendly Australian take the time to stop and greet me. The other memory is giving my first paper at a large international conference. It reported research with colleagues Lesley Parker and Pauline Hutchinson using teacher in-service to promote gender-inclusive teaching about electricity to Year 5 students (Rennie *et al.*, 1985). Findings of importance in the climate of that time were that in the experimental group girls participated in, and performed as well in, the activities as did boys. Further, the effectiveness of children doing activities in groups depended more on how comfortable the children were working with each other than on whether the groups were of the same sex or not (Rennie and Parker, 1987). Boys and girls could work very well together, provided that they were used to doing so. Despite my nervousness I managed to get through the paper without stumbling over too many words. However, I soon discovered that although my presentation was well practised, I wasn't well prepared for the question which followed! 'Why did you focus on learning science through doing activities?' called out a voice, 'What's so special about doing activities?' I was nonplussed. It had not occurred to me that anyone could question the importance of 'doing' in science at school. I simply had no answer and stood there speechless, wondering what on earth I could say. Fortunately, I didn't have to say anything, because another voice from the audience said, 'Well, that's a silly question!' and went on to explain why. No doubt Peter Fensham does not remember saving me from embarrassment that day, but I shall always be grateful.

These personal anecdotes say two important things about Peter Fensham. First, like any real scientist, he is observant and he thinks about what he sees, hears, and reads. He takes notice of everything, people, research, what ideas are current, and he knows what ideas will come next. This is why he was one of the first male science educators to realise the importance of gender as a source of inequality in science (and mathematics) education. Second, he is not afraid to 'tell it like it is'. Few people will tell another person that their question is silly and then explain why in a logical, reasoned way, rather than simply provide an alternative opinion. Fensham's contribution to the issue of gender in science education was topical in the early 1980s and also significant, because he was a male writing things that others, including many females, found confronting.

In this chapter I will pursue two themes. The first relates to Fensham's (mostly joint) publications concerning gender and science achievement in Thailand. These papers capture much of the empirical research he reported and they attracted interest because the results were contrary to accepted international trends. The second theme relates to Fensham's other contributions to the gender issue: some involved writing, but more involved action to promote awareness and understanding of gender, particularly in Australia.

Gender differences in physical science in Thailand

The cluster of articles by Fensham, Klainin, and West, based on data collected in Thailand by Sunee Klainin for her doctoral work, has received considerable attention. The data was quite comprehensive for both physics and chemistry. In the chemistry study (Klainin and Fensham, 1987) in 1983–4, data was collected from samples of over 700 boys and 700 girls in Years 10, 11, and 12, the three senior secondary years of schooling in Thailand, where all students in the science stream studied chemistry, physics, and biology. Two classes at each year level in two single-sex boys' schools, two single-sex girls' schools, and two co-educational schools in Bangkok formed the sample. For the physics study (Klainin et al., 1989), which began in the second half of 1985, one of the two classes at each level in six other schools of the same composition was randomly selected, so the sample was about half as large, totalling nearly 800 students. In the two studies, students completed a common battery of tests – two practical tests measuring manipulative skills and problem solving, and three pen-and-paper tests about knowledge in physics or chemistry, sources of evidence, and scientific attitudes (the chemistry study also included a test of observational skills and one about linking theory to practice). In sum, the outcomes showed that (1) girls performed as well as boys in physics and better than boys in chemistry, (2) in laboratory-related outcomes (manipulative skills and problem solving) girls performed better than boys in both chemistry and physics, and (3) there were differences in results between single-sex and co-educational schools. Girls in single-sex schools performed best on all pen-and-paper tests in chemistry, but girls in co-educational schools performed best on practical tests. In physics, girls in single-sex schools performed best on the practical tests (see later for explanations of these apparently inconsistent differences).

These results were interesting because they went against the generally accepted principles that, internationally, boys did better than girls in physical science, especially physics, and that sex differences increased with grade level. These principles were well supported by the First International Science Study (FISS) conducted in 1970–1 (Comber and Keeves, 1973), and the Second International Science Study (SISS) conducted in 1983–4 (Postlethwaite and Wiley, 1991) by the International Association for the Evaluation of Educational Achievement (IEA). Further, at that time there was evidence in various countries of persistent sex differences in performance in large-scale national studies (such as the National Assessment of Educational Progress), and even greater differences in participation, with girls tending to opt out of physical science. Despite contemporary research offering reasonable explanations for these differences, especially with regard to gender-stereotyped sex differences in science-related experiences and the need to look very carefully at how achievement was measured (see, for example, Kahle and Lakes (1983) in the USA, Johnson and Murphy (1986) and Kelly (1985) in the UK, Parker and Offer (1987) and Parker and Rennie (1986) in Australia), in the 1980s there remained firmly entrenched views of the inferiority of girls' performance in physical science compared with that of boys, and a lingering suggestion that biological factors were the cause. Consequently, the Thai results were, as the title of one paper (Klainin and Fensham, 1987, p. 94) suggested, quite remarkable, and they certainly lay to rest the idea of biological difference as a cause of differential achievement. However, there was a tendency to discount these results because they came from a developing country, and as Fensham (1986) himself reported, science educators from at least one developed Western country exhibited 'dismissive incredulity' when he tried to present the achievements of Thai science education at conferences.

I also experienced a dismissal of the interesting Thai results when I asked a researcher involved with the IEA studies why the Klainin–Fensham results were so different from those of the SISS and FISS. 'Biased sample; not representative; they're wrong', I was told. In this context, it is interesting to compare the sex differences in achievement in the SISS and FISS results for Thailand with those reported by Klainin and Fensham. In a selection of results reported by Keeves and Kotte (1996, p. 79) in their study of sex differences across ten countries involved in the FISS and SISS, the effect sizes for Thailand and the mean effect sizes over countries for chemistry and physics were reported for the 14-year-old level and the upper secondary level (the last year of secondary schooling), which are the populations of closest interest to this discussion.

As shown by Keeves and Kotte, the mean results across the countries involved (including Thailand, the only developing country) show clear differences in favour of boys in chemistry and physics for both the 14-year-old level and the upper secondary level. For Thailand, however, the differences are much less, except for the SISS at the 14-year-old level. In fact the Thai result for chemistry of -0.09 in the FISS for 14-year-olds was the only result for chemistry which favoured girls in the ten countries reported at three age levels (Keeves and Kotte do not report results for 10-year-olds, the other population studied), and the effect size for physics at this level was the smallest of all countries. At the upper secondary level, the effect size for physics (0.29) was the smallest (less than half of the second smallest), and for chemistry (0.34), it was the third smallest. In the SISS, the Thai results are less dramatic, but still noteworthy. The effect sizes for both chemistry and physics are the smallest among countries for the upper secondary level but for the 14-year-old population, the effect size for physics is about average, and chemistry among the largest. The very low results in the FISS for 14-year-olds in Thailand caused some concern. In their full reporting of the FISS, Comber and Keeves (1973, p. 143) noted 'the result for Thailand is so striking that it suggests that some bias may have occurred in the sampling or that the tests were very difficult for substantial proportions of both sexes'. Concern about bias seemed to increase over time, for in 1996, Keeves and Kotte reported of the FISS results that 'in Thailand, the sample employed at this (14-year-old) level was known to be biased seriously' (p. 78). No such concern was expressed for the upper secondary sample for either population, even though their results were also strikingly low in contrast with other countries, perhaps because they did at least show the expected direction of sex difference. The results from the Third International Mathematics and Science Study (TIMSS) conducted in 1994–5 add further intrigue. Sex differences in Thailand for overall science achievement are negative (favouring girls) and trivial for both the 10-year-old (Martin *et al.*, 1997, Table 1.6) and 14-year-old populations (Beaton *et al.*, 1996, Table 1.6), but it is reported that the sampling procedures at the classroom level were unapproved for Thailand! Results for the upper secondary level do not include Thailand.

Clearly, these two sets of Thai results are contradictory, especially for the SISS data, which was collected at about the same time as the Klainin–Fensham data. It is not sensible to ask 'who was "right": Klainin and Fensham or the IEA studies?' Better questions are: 'how can we explain these differences?' and 'what can we learn from them?' The answer to the first question is straightforward; the differences occur because the samples are different and the testing battery was different. The IEA studies pay careful attention to sampling because their purpose is one of comparison between countries. Sampling usually employs a two-stage stratified probability process: schools are selected with a probability proportional to the size of the school, and then students are selected within schools. Provided the process is carried out to specifications then the sample should be nationally representative. The testing battery also is used internationally; it is translated into many languages, and may not always match the curriculum of particular countries. Klainin's data was collected from a total of twelve schools in Bangkok. Schools were stratified by their sex composition (single-sex or co-educational) and selected randomly, although there was some replacement if a school was unable to be involved in the study (Klainin and Fensham, 2002). We do not know where the SISS data came from, but probably a large portion came from Bangkok. Certainly, Klainin and Fensham do not claim national representativeness, but they report data from large samples collected with test batteries carefully selected to match the science curricula and it deserves to be viewed with credibility.

The answer to the second question is quite extensive. First, it must be emphasised that Thailand is rather special among the countries referred to as 'developing'. Unlike most developing countries, including its South East Asian neighbours, Thailand has not been colonised by a foreign country or wracked by wars of independence, and it is culturally homogeneous with about 95 per cent of its people of Buddhist religion. It was the first developing country to close the 'gender gap' in participation in secondary schooling (Knodel, 1997), and as many boys as girls complete secondary schooling, although more boys than girls select the vocational stream. Thus, Keeves and Kotte (1996, Table III) report that 47 per cent of the science stream in the upper secondary level sample in the SISS (1983–4) were male in biology, chemistry, and physics. Klainin *et al.* (1987) report around 48 per cent males in their two samples. In particular, the Thai government has invested significantly in science over several decades, establishing the Institute for Promotion of Teaching Science and Technology (IPST) in 1970 which rewrote the science curriculum to integrate practical work with theoretical work in a learner-centred programme. Thus, practical work is an essential component of the science curriculum, and Klainin *et al.* (1987) report that two out of five classes weekly are devoted to practical work in small groups. The results for Thailand are based on curricula that were very forward thinking for their time.

The results did, as Klainin and Fensham proclaimed, negate the argument of the biological cause of sex differences in achievement. Synthesis studies, such as that by Linn and Hyde (1989), show conclusively that over the years well-accepted sex differences in a range of science- and mathematics-related variables have decreased as boys and girls have more equal opportunities for participation in relevant activities. In fact, sex differences in participation and in attitudes about physical science were the practically significant differences remaining during the 1980s, despite the prevalent perception of a difference in achievement. For example, Steinkamp and Maehr (1984), in reporting findings from their large meta-analysis of gender differences in school-level science (including effect sizes from the FISS), concluded that 'sex differences in . . . achievement in science are smaller than is assumed generally' (p. 56). Importantly, the students in the Klainin and Fensham studies had similar backgrounds in science courses taken, and all students were taking biology, chemistry, and physics. This is unusual compared with most Western countries, where the science selections made by students result in quite different patterns of participation for boys and girls. When students take the same courses, sex differences usually are trivial. For example, Rennie and Parker (1993) examined the academic results of the entire population of Year 10 students (15-year-olds) in Western Australia and found differences over the three years of data that were either trivial or favoured girls.

Klainin and Fensham had solid background information to explain their surprising results, explanations entirely in tune with a range of socio-cultural explanations for the sex differences that did exist at the time. Contemporary accounts of thinking in this area can be found in the contributions and proceedings of the 1981, 1983, 1985, and 1987 Gender and Science and Technology (GASAT) Conferences held in The Netherlands (Raat *et al.*, 1981), Norway (Sjøberg, 1983), the UK (Harding, 1985) and the USA (Daniels and Kahle, 1987; Daniels *et al.*, 1987). Syntheses are provided by Sjøberg and Imsen (1988) and Kahle (1988), both chapters in Fensham (1988).

Klainin *et al.* (1987) outlined the explanations for their results in a paper presented at the Fourth GASAT Conference. A major argument in socio-cultural explanations for sex differences in attitudes towards, and participation in, science, especially physical sciences, is the masculine image of science. In her seminal paper, Kelly (1985) elucidates the factors contributing to the perception that science is masculine, and how this perception is perpetuated in schooling. In the physics study, Klainin collected data about students' perceptions of whether physics and chemistry were more suitable for boys or girls, or suitable for both. The latter view was the majority opinion; that is, physics and chemistry are suitable for both sexes. Those who did not agree were more likely to perceive physics as more suitable for boys and chemistry for girls. In the case of chemistry, practical work was perceived as similar to kitchen tasks, explaining why students perceived the experimental tasks in chemistry as matching women's tasks (except for use of the mortar and pestle, as the grinding of herbs and spices for making curry paste is one of very few kitchen tasks undertaken by males in Thailand). The effects of these perceptions are best illustrated by comparison of the results of the studies in single-sex and co-educational schools. In co-educational schools, girls performed better on the practical tests in chemistry because they did more of the practical work (boys were observed to stand back because it was perceived to be women's work). But in physics, girls were observed to stand back and allow the boys to do the activities while they recorded and wrote reports. In single-sex schools, girls did all of the work; thus they outperformed other groups on a number of scales, especially practical work in physics. In addition, another socio-culturally based argument often espoused with regard to gender is role-modelling. In the case of the Klainin–Fensham studies it is worth noting that thirty-two out of thirty-five chemistry teachers were female, and there were equal numbers of male and female teachers of physics in the studies.

In sum then, and as emphasised by Harding *et al.* (1988), the Klainin–Fensham findings of either girls' superior performance, or no sex differences over a range of measures in chemistry and physics, are important because they come from a system where the socio-cultural factors differ from those in the majority of Western countries where sex differences in performance have been found. In Thailand at the senior secondary level all students study science with a teaching approach that explicitly linked theory and practical work. Students perceived chemistry tasks as women's work and science itself does not appear to have a masculine image (although Klainin *et al.* (1987) point out that the textbooks used tended to be gender biased just as they were in Western countries at this time). Further, Harding *et al.* (1988) point out that teachers and parents expect boys and girls to possess equal capacities to learn science, and in Thailand, as in many developing countries, science and technology are highly valued. Women as well as men work in a variety of science-related fields and are well paid. Harding *et al.* concluded: 'these factors encourage girls to choose science in schools and their success refutes any theory of an innate lesser ability' (p. 191). Fensham recognised this point but he consistently argued another point as well, to his Australian colleagues (Fensham, 1986), internationally (Fensham, 1988; 1992), and at the 1999 annual meeting of the National Association for Research in Science Teaching, when he accepted its highest accolade, the Distinguished Contribution to Science Education Through Research Award (Fensham, 1999). This second point relates to what we as Westerners can learn from developing countries such as Thailand. Certainly the curriculum developers at IPST borrowed ideas from curricula originating in the USA and the UK (Klainin, 1988), but they were also able to learn from others' mistakes. They created courses in a system that required boys and girls in the same stream to take the same science classes throughout secondary schooling and enabled girls and boys to achieve well in science.

Promoting awareness and understanding of gender in science education

The Thai research probably influenced Fensham's thinking about gender in science education, but it was not the beginning of his thinking about gender. He reports that working on a project to recognise the twentieth Anniversary of the United Nation's Universal Declaration of Human Rights (made on 10 December 1948) led to his awareness of the gender impact on equality in science education (Fensham, 1999). Thus he was well aware of the issue a decade and a half before Klainin began the doctoral work at Monash University leading to her data collection in 1983.

The decade of the 1980s was very active for gender research in Australia. Following the Commonwealth government's report *Girls, Schools and Society*, in 1975, which outlined, among other things, the effects on later career choice of girls' decisions to opt out of science and mathematics in upper secondary school, considerable funds were invested by State and Commonwealth Ministries and Departments in special projects to address gender bias in the curricular and pedagogical aspects of schooling. In 1987, the Commonwealth Schools Commission published the first National Policy for the Education of Girls in Australian Schools. In the same year, the Commonwealth government allocated $1million over two years to a new programme, The Education of Girls in Mathematics and Science, to produce gender-inclusive materials to support schools. Other Commonwealth-supported projects included the Melbourne-based Gender and Mathematics and Science Teaching (GAMAST) project (Lewis and Davies, 1988) and Getting into Gear (Gianello, 1988) based on the work of the McClintock Collective. (See Rennie *et al.* (1999) for a brief summary of Australian research into gender and science education, and Kenway *et al.* (1998) for an evaluation of some of these gender-based reform efforts.) Fensham was well aware of these developments, and as Deputy Chair, Science, of the Commonwealth's Department of Education, Employment and Training Discipline Review of Teacher Education in Mathematics and Science, he was part of a team that ensured gender was well covered in the review. The thirteen-member Steering Committee included six females and the Report and Recommendations (Speedy *et al.*, 1989, Vol. 1) contains a chapter on equity and access and one on gender, and a discussion paper on gender (Parker and Rennie, 1989) was commissioned for the review.

It was also significant that Fensham included two (of fourteen) chapters on gender in his edited book *Developments and Dilemmas in Science Education* (Fensham, 1988). This truly international offering (the authors represented nine countries) was a genuine attempt to analyse and assess progress in science education over the previous decades and to identify challenges and developments important to progress positively in the future. The book's contribution is discussed in other chapters, but the point of interest here is the clear identification of gender as a major matter in science education. There were other significant volumes devoted to gender and science education published in the 1980s (such as Harding, 1986; Kahle, 1985; Kelly, 1981) but they were entirely gender based, and these edited books included few male authors. Fensham's book placed gender in a volume with significant, international authors, giving it equivalence in importance to other issues such as curriculum structure, language, practical work, and choice of content.

Fensham continued to profile gender. For example, in his foreword to *Science and Technology Education in the Post-Compulsory Years* (Fensham, 1996), he lamented the inadequate treatment of gender in Australia's Curriculum Statement on Science, and he ensured that the role of gender in subject choice in the post-compulsory years was well covered by contributing a section on 'The Gender Dilemma' in his own Chapter 2 as well as in a chapter by Parker (1996). He also invited a chapter on a gender-inclusive teacher education course (Kirkwood *et al.*, 1996).

But it is one thing to highlight the issue of gender and another to understand what it means. In a section entitled 'The Women's Movement' forming part of a major review of the science and technology curriculum, Fensham (1992) discussed a range of efforts to increase girls' participation in science, first, by attempting to remove blatant gender bias in science curriculum materials, second, by changing the ways options and choice to participate in science were built into schooling, and third, by changing the content of science learning, mainly by trying to build on the different attitudes and interests of girls and boys. Importantly, he noted that there is considerable overlap between the interests of girls and boys, a point ignored by many authors at the time. But, Fensham (1992) points out, all of theses approaches 'are essentially a means to an end: to induce girls into a science that is essentially unchanged' (p. 808). And herein lies the crux of the matter. Encouraging more equal participation by girls and boys right to the end of high school and into university science does not change the nature of the science that is practised at this level or in the workplace. Many science educators now take a socially critical perspective, recognising that the practice of science itself maintains the dominant cultural values that, in many countries, tend to be exclusive of females (see Parker *et al.*, 1996).

Elsewhere I have reviewed changes in thinking about gender differences in science education (Rennie, 1998; 2000; 2001), and others will continue to do so in the future, using different perspectives and theoretical referents. The important thing is to realise that gender is not a simple variable, able to be represented by a student's biological sex. It is just one (very complex) variable among the many social categories (including race, religion, ethnicity, and class) that contribute to the construction of gender and science. But it has taken the education community time to realise this. Gender permeates the way curriculum is constructed, how teachers teach, how assessment is implemented, and how choices are made. (So do other social variables, of course, in a multitude of interacting ways.) But even by the 1980s, many educators did not recognise the socio-cultural role of gender. It had to be disembedded to be made visible. Fensham helped that disembedding.

We have come a long way, but there is still far to go. Thinking about gender in terms of biological sex only encourages stereotyping. It stultifies research and disadvantages both boys and girls in schooling. Instead, as Goodrum *et al.* (2000, p. 28) point out in their review of teaching and learning science in Australian schools, 'the bottom line is that a socially just science education occurs only when all students are treated according to their needs as individuals, not according to their membership of a social group such as gender, culture or social background'. I think that as a foremost proponent of science for all, Fensham would agree.

References

Beaton, A.E., Martin, M.O., Mullis, I.V.S., Gonzalez, E.S., Smith, T.A., and Kelly, D.L. (1996) *Science Achievement in the Middle School Years: IEA's Third International Mathematics and Science Study (TIMSS)*, Chestnut Hill, MA: Center for the Study of Testing, Evaluation, and Educational Policy, Boston College.

Comber, L.C. and Keeves, J.P. (1973) *Science Education in Nineteen Countries*, Stockholm: Almqvist and Wiksell.

Daniels, J.Z. and Kahle, J.B. (eds) (1987) *Contributions to the Fourth GASAT Conference* (Vols 1, 2, 3 and Addendum), Ann Arbor, MI: The University of Michigan Press.

Daniels, J.Z., Kahle, J.B. and Harding, J. (eds) (1987) *Proceedings of the Fourth GASAT Conference*, Ann Arbor, MI: The University of Michigan Press.

Fensham, P.J. (1986) 'Lessons from science education in Thailand: a case study of gender and learning in the physical sciences', *Research in Science Education* 16: 92–100.

Fensham, P.J. (ed.) (1988) *Development and Dilemmas in Science Education*, London: Falmer Press.

Fensham, P.J. (1992) 'Science and technology', in P.W. Jackson (ed.) *Handbook of Research on Curriculum*, New York: Macmillan, pp. 789–829.

Fensham, P.J. (ed.) (1996) *Science and Technology Education in the Post-Compulsory Years*, Melbourne: Australian Council for Educational Research.

Fensham, P.J. (1999) 'International perspectives', *NARST News* 42(2): 4.

Gianello, L. (1988) *Getting into Gear–Gender-Inclusive Teaching Strategies*, Canberra: Curriculum Development Centre.

Goodrum, G., Hackling, M., and Rennie, L. (2000) *The Status and Quality of Teaching and Learning of Science in Australian Schools*, Canberra: Department of Education, Training and Youth Affairs.

Harding, J. (ed.) (1985) *Contributions to the Third GASAT Conference* (Vols. 1 and 2), London: Chelsea College, University of London.

Harding, J. (ed.) (1986) *Perspectives on Gender and Science*, London: Falmer Press.

Harding, J., Hildebrand, G., and Klainin, S. (1988) 'International concerns in gender and science/technology', *Educational Review* 40: 185–93.

Johnson, S. and Murphy, P. (1986) *Girls and Physics*, London: Department of Education and Science.

Kahle, J.B. (ed.) (1985) *Women in Science: a report from the field*, Philadelphia, PA: Falmer Press.

Kahle, J.B. (1988) 'Gender and science education II', in P.J. Fensham (ed.) *Development and Dilemmas in Science Education*, London: Falmer Press, pp. 249–65.

Kahle, J.B. and Lakes, M.K. (1983) 'The myth of equality in science classrooms', *Journal of Research in Science Teaching* 20: 131–40.

Keeves, J.P. and Kotte, D. (1996) 'Patterns of science achievement: international comparisons', in L.H. Parker, L.J. Rennie, and B.J. Fraser (eds) *Gender, Science and Mathematics: shortening the shadow*, Dordrecht: Kluwer Academic Publishers, pp. 77–93.

Kelly, A. (ed.) (1981) *The Missing Half: girls and science education*, Manchester: Manchester University Press.

Kelly, A. (1985) 'The construction of masculine science', *British Journal of Sociology of Education* 6: 133–53.

Kenway, J., Willis, S., with Blackmore, J. and Rennie, L. (1998) *Answering Back: Girls, Boys and Feminism in Schools*, London: Routledge.

Kirkwood, V., Bearlin, M., and Hardy, T. (1996) 'A gender-sensitive science and technology program in primary teacher professional development', in P.J. Fensham (ed.) *Science and Technology Education in the Post-Compulsory Years*, Melbourne: Australian Council for Educational Research, pp. 291–316.

Klainin, S. (1988) 'Practical work and science education I', in P.J. Fensham (ed.) *Development and Dilemmas in Science Education*, London: Falmer Press, pp. 169–80.

Klainin, S. and Fensham, P.J. (1987) 'Learning achievement in upper secondary school chemistry in Thailand: some remarkable sex reversals', *International Journal of Science Education* 9: 217–27.

Klainin, S. and Fensham, P. (2002) Personal communication, January.

Klainin, S., Fensham, P.J., and West, L.H.T. (1987) 'Some remarkable gender findings about learning the physical sciences in Thailand', in J.Z. Daniels and J.B. Kahle (eds), *Contributions to the Fourth GASAT Conference* (Vol. 2), pp. 66–87, Ann Arbor, MI: The University of Michigan Press.

Klainin, S., Fensham, P.J., and West, L.H.T. (1989) 'Successful achievement by girls in physics learning', *International Journal of Science Education* 11: 101–12.

Knodel, J. (1997) 'The closing of the gender gap in schooling: the case of Thailand', *Comparative Education* 33: 61–86.

Lewis, S. and Davies, A. (1988) *GAMAST Professional Development Manual–Gender Equity in Mathematics and Science*, Canberra: Curriculum Development Corporation.

Linn, M.C. and Hyde, J.S. (1989) 'Gender, mathematics and science', *Educational Researcher* 18(8): 17–19, 22–7.

Martin, M.O., Mullis, I.V.S., Beaton, A.E., Gonzalez, E.J., Smith, T.A., and Kelly, D.L. (1997) *Science Achievement in the Primary School Years: IEA's third international mathematics and science study (TIMSS)*, Chestnut Hill, MA: Center for the Study of Testing, Evaluation, and Educational Policy, Boston College.

Parker, L.H. (1996) 'System-wide curriculum design: its significance for science studies', in P.J. Fensham (ed.) *Science and Technology Education in the Post-Compulsory Years*, Melbourne: Australian Council for Educational Research, pp. 77–96.

Parker, L.H. and Offer, J.A. (1987) 'School science achievement: conditions for equality', *European Journal of Science Education* 9: 263–9.

Parker, L.H. and Rennie, L.J. (1986) 'Sex-stereotyped attitudes about science: can they be changed?', *European Journal of Science Education* 8: 173–83.

Parker, L.J. and Rennie, L.J. (1989) 'Gender issues in science education with special reference to teacher education', in G. Speedy, C. Annice, and P. Fensham (eds) *Discipline Review in Teacher Education in Mathematics and Science* (Vol. 3), Canberra: Department of Employment, Education and Training, pp. 230–47.

Parker, L.H., Rennie, L.J., and Fraser, B.J. (eds) (1996) *Gender, Science and Mathematics: shortening the shadow*, Dordrecht: Kluwer Academic Publishers.

Postlethwaite, T.N. and Wiley, D.E. (1991) *The IEA Study in Science II: science achievement in 21 countries*, Oxford: Pergamon Press.

Raat, J., Harding, J., and Mottier, I. (eds) (1981) *Girls and Science and Technology. Congress book GASAT Conference 1981*, Eindhoven: Eindhoven University Press.

Rennie, L.J. (1998) 'Gender equity: toward clarification and a research direction for science teacher education', *Journal of Research in Science Teaching* 35: 951–61.

Rennie, L.J. (2000) 'Equity in science education: gender is just one variable: reply to Atwater', *Journal of Research in Science Teaching* 38: 391–3.

Rennie, L. (2001) 'Gender equity and science teacher preparation', in D. Lavoie and W.-M. Roth (eds) *Models of Science Teacher Preparation: theory into practice*, Dordrecht: Kluwer Academic Publishers, pp. 127–47.

Rennie, L.J. and Parker, L.H. (1987) 'Detecting and accounting for gender differences in mixed-sex and single-sex groupings in science lessons', *Educational Review* 39: 65–73.

Rennie, L.J. and Parker, L.H. (1993) 'Curriculum reform and choice of science: consequences for balanced and equitable participation and achievement', *Journal of Research in Science Teaching* 30: 1017–28.

Rennie, L.J., Parker, L.H., and Hutchinson, P.E. (1985) *The Effect of Inservice Training on Teacher Attitudes and Primary School Science Classroom Climates* (Research Report

No. 12), Perth: The University of Western Australia, Measurement and Statistics Laboratory, Department of Education. ED 280 867.

Rennie, L.J., Fraser, B.F., and Treagust, D.F. (1999) 'Research in science education', in J.P. Keeves and K. Marjoribanks (eds) *Australian Education: review of research 1965–1998*, Melbourne: Australian Council for Educational Research, pp. 171–203.

Sjøberg, S. (ed.) (1983) *Contributions to the Second GASAT Conference*, Oslo: University of Oslo, Centre for Science Education.

Sjøberg, S. and Imsen, G. (1988) 'Gender and science education I', in P.J. Fensham (ed.) *Development and Dilemmas in Science Education*, London: Falmer Press, pp. 218–48.

Speedy, G., Annice, C., and Fensham, P. (eds) (1989) *Discipline Review in Teacher Education in Mathematics and Science* (Vol. 1), Canberra: Department of Employment, Education and Training.

Steinkamp, M.W. and Maehr, M.L. (1984) 'Gender differences in motivational orientation toward achievement in school science: a quantitative synthesis, *American Educational Research Journal* 21: 39–59.

Part V

The theory and practice of science teaching

9   Fensham's lodestar criterion

James Wandersee

Thesis

A lodestar is 'a star to steer by'. Over time, this navigational term has come to connote 'the focus or aim of one's'. In this chapter I seek to demonstrate that a major research contribution of Peter J. Fensham, with respect to the theory and practice of science teaching, is as follows:

> Lodestar Criterion: Is the science teaching under consideration 'of actual use' to the targeted student group in affectively synchronistic, real-world contexts that its members confront on a daily basis?

Although this criterion is emergent and thus only partially detectable in many of his prior published works, the kernel of this idea surfaces rather clearly and concisely in Fensham's chapter on 'beginning to teach chemistry' (Fensham, 1994). In that chapter's conclusion, he credits Robin Millar who, in 1990, articulated the startling insight that 'kinetic theory is of almost no use to learners' early in their study of chemistry (Fensham, 1994, p. 24) – counter-intuitive as that may be. However, one senses that this is just an instance of a general conjecture Fensham himself had been harbouring for quite some time. Consider the thorough way he clarifies the 'of no use' statement with this explanation: 'By "no use" he [Millar] meant both the operational or functional sense of the words and also the cognitive/affective sense that could be associated with an improved understanding of matters of interest.' Thus, for the purposes of understanding a component of Fensham's 'Lodestar Criterion', 'of no use' has both an operational, practical-use, skills-oriented definition and a cognitive efficiency definition – which speaks to the sequencing of content during instruction.

Peter Fensham's sustained interest in using student-appropriate personal, societal, and technological applications of science to teach science in under-standable ways indicates that he has long weighed science teaching outcomes on a 'usefulness to students' balance. Many of his research studies can be viewed as investigations intent on informing the construction of better science curricula and/or improving science instruction that maintain scientific integrity while ensuring utilitarian value for students. He remains sceptical of 'one size fits all' research findings and national recommendations, and perhaps this is because he values the importance of context in science teaching and learning. He has demonstrated a keen awareness and concern that, in the past, science teaching has differentially benefited some students, while failing to meet the practical needs of many other students.

It may also be noted that Fensham's humanitarian and egalitarian values resonate strongly with today's 'Science for All' concept that rose to prominence in the second half of the twentieth century. Therefore, Fensham the chemist (with all the rigour that appellation entails) is nevertheless able to step out of his research chemist's lab coat to empathise with science students from various target groups, especially disadvantaged ones – rather than join fellow scientists in bemoaning the decline in preparation and interest of today's science students. (*Editor's note*: The reader should consult Chapter 1 to discover a reason for Peter Fensham's ability to set aside his chemist's 'lab coat'.) Indeed, it may be argued that it is Fensham's student focus and his boldness in ferreting out gaps in (and challenging) outdated but entrenched traditions of science education practice that ultimately enable him to help shape science education theory.

Some contributory principles

The following principles, each representative of one or more aspects of Fensham's 'Lodestar Criterion' (a term proposed by this author, and not by PJF), are both illustrative and emblematic of this repetitive pattern interwoven within the fabric of his science education research programme and writings: his extensive international network of research collaborators, and his intuitive ability to frame important research questions that, when answered, are highly likely to spur progress in science educational theory by spearheading changes in practice. These have led to the representative set of 'Fenshamian' principles presented here.

The 'dual impact of prior knowledge' principle

In 1974, West and Fensham reviewed David Ausubel's theory of meaningful learning and plumbed its implications for science teaching. Both authors brought a wealth of knowledge and experience to bear on the topic. Consider the fact that a key learning variable, according to Ausubel's theory, is the quality and quantity of the learner's prior knowledge. West and Fensham were likely the first science educators to lucidly partition the potential learning influences of a student's prior knowledge into: (1) the determinant 'of what further (science) learning can occur' and (2) the influence on 'the process whereby this (science) learning occurs' (p. 62).

The two considered Gagne's 'prerequisite knowledge' theory to be a work-able model of the first aspect of prior knowledge. They then assigned Ausubel's theory as a complementary model of the second type of influence:

> We will see that various evidence exists which supports this theory as a 'useful' theory – by 'useful' we mean both that it raises questions for further research to answer, and that it has implications – that can be translated into real possibilities for the classroom.
>
> (West and Fensham, 1974, p. 62)

The two authors highlight the fact that Ausubel is the kind of theorist whose 'constant focus is the real classroom (science) situation where teachers and learners are grappling with complex but highly verbal meaningful material' (p. 63).

West and Fensham wisely counsel science educators that identifying par-ticular clusters of science concepts students hold prior to instruction is not the same as identifying the set of potential subsuming concepts they hold for that topic prior to instruction – the latter facilitate psychological ordering (rather than the logical analysis) of material to match the cognitive process of learning. In contrast to what often happens in science education during inter-pretation, West and Fensham seem to make every effort to be faithful to the theorist's ideas, to compare and contrast the theoretical stance with other compatible ones, and to unpack and test the claims without misrepresenting them.

To one who has co-edited and co-authored three recent science education textbooks showing how the human constructivist theory applies to the mean-ingful learning of science (Fisher *et al.*, 2000; Mintzes *et al.*, 1998; 2000), even today West and Fensham's 1974 article has currency. It not only offers a vital cache of helpful science teaching ideas, but also suggests potential lines of research and theory building areas worthy of pursuit today. In addition, it fore-shadows the thousands of misconceptions/alternative conceptions studies that have been completed worldwide, and which now undergird much of today's constructivist science teaching (Wandersee *et al.*, 1994). More importantly for the purposes of this chapter, it explicitly values the careful study and elabora-tion of instruction that may prove 'useful' for the learner.

The 'hands' principle for curriculum design

In a 1981 'think piece' article published in *The Australian Science Teachers Journal* Fensham sets forth his view that neither an intellect-oriented, sequen-tial, 'head' science approach to science teaching nor a positive-affect-driven, non-sequential, 'heart' science approach will 'yield' the scientifically literate graduate, the 'holy grail' of contemporary science education.

Autobiographically, Fensham admits that he is troubled by the fact that he is constantly confronted with scientific/technical situations in his own non-professional life for which he finds that he lacks practical skills – regardless of his own vast, accumulated store of chemistry, mathematics, and physics knowledge (p. 55). As a solution to this dilemma, he proposes a model for designing 'hands'-type science courses which first develops student skills, and then teaches students the science knowledge on which the skills are based, until the student ends up with a set of mastered skills. He finds this approach as uniting head, heart, and hands in a more powerful way than the 'head'-alone and 'heart'-alone approaches mentioned earlier. In his 1981 article, PJF reflects on his own science education, from youth to cutting-edge chemist, and finds that only a tiny fraction of what he has learned has been of practical use to him!

He speculates that the learning of social responsibility can also be enhanced by introducing meaningful practical skills into science curricula and eschewing what he calls 'unreal activities'. His diagram illustrating 'the socialization of science teachers away from reality and from the "activities of science"' helps pinpoint the main problems in today's science teacher education programmes, and his concise distillation of curricular alternatives makes this article a true gem. In my opinion, it represents a significant contribution to science education thought, and, because of its richly integrated verbal–visual content, it is the uncontested favourite of this author and rewards multiple readings and reconsiderations.

Abandoning the *tabula rasa*: the principle of recognising 'children's science'

We now know that science students are not *tabula rasa*, and that treating them as if they were results in minimal, inert, or conflicted science learning. In their 1982 article Gilbert, Osborne, and Fensham examine the nature and consequences of 'children's science' – namely, the conceptual structures that a child constructs from his/her everyday experiences and which serve as a sensible way to explain the world from a child's viewpoint.

After a brief but thorough review of related research, the researchers propose that mixed outcomes, rather than unified scientific outcomes, are the norm when classroom science collides with children's science. The powerful and learning-insightful claim is made that 'teachers need to be aware of children's science and encourage students to express their views . . . it is only against that background of sensitivity and perception that we can decide what to do, and how to do it' (Gilbert *et al.*, p. 631). The importance of this principle lies in the fact that science educators need to recognise (but have not until now) that children's science exists apart from scientists' science, that the nature of its thought also differs, and that they must first value what children bring to their science lessons from their everyday lives if they are to teach them effectively and usefully.

The principle of expanding horizons: fostering awareness that some ideas are useful to scientists

In Fensham and Marton's 1992 analysis of the role of intuition in science education, Fensham revisits an idea he first proposed in 1982, namely:

> Science educators should, for some topics, be content with the modest goal of making students aware that scientists often find it *useful* to hold different conceptions from everyday ones many students hold . . . [acknowledging that] the 'wait' for the scientists' *truths* to be taken on board personally by school students may have to be until after they have made the decision to study to become a professional scientist.
>
> (p. 120)

In my opinion, for particular controversial or highly abstract topics, Fensham's principle of 'first expanding their scientific horizons' before expecting students to master and adopt the current scientific explanations of such topics is eminently sensible. It also shows how he wants science education to respect students' personal choices, while avoiding authoritarianism, scientism, and dogmatism in the approach to teaching science.

Based upon some of my conversations with my students from past science courses during more than three decades of biology teaching, not all-conceptual change occurs within the science course calendar or by the time of the final course examination. Sometimes a science concept that was merely 'visited' by the learner, barely considered because it challenged knowledge gained in other domains, and thus obviously not adopted by the learner during a science course taken years ago, required a perturbing later-life event to be recalled, appreciated, and integrated into the learner's current conceptual framework. Once triggered, learning may be postponed but still occur. Such affective/cognitive delay of conceptual change has implications for the conclusions that science educators reach about a student's learning achievement after the completion of a unit or a course. It also supports Fensham's principle that we not gauge science teaching success by a 'yes–no; all or none' definition of accepted, contemporary science content learning. While digital representation of variables may currently be superior in electronics, analogue variable representation remains more appropriate for science learning.

Indeed, in his 1994 book chapter on beginning to teach the content of chemistry, Fensham reveals that: 'recently, there has been a very strong international interest in developing the curricula of the school sciences like chemistry so that they can be studied by much wider cross sections of students than has been the case hitherto' (p. 26). He surmises that

> An introductory study of chemistry in which concepts are given meaning by contexts that make sense to learners (the chemistry of everyday things; the industrial, technological, economic, and social implications of the

content of chemistry) should have advantages for teachers wishing to take a constructivist approach.

While the content of science is undeniably important to Fensham, science teaching that respects, allows, and even promotes variations in different science learners' journeys towards skills, appreciations, and understandings is even more important to him.

A reasonable goal: the principle of promoting movement towards scientific thought

In a 1983 article in *Science Education*, Fensham points out that, in the 1960s and 1970s, science teachers were largely unaware that student inputs could 'swamp' instructional inputs, and thus divert intended learning outcomes. He illustrates this by citing persuasive research indicating that Third World immigrant children and children in the non-industrial world often hold differing, and often more holistic, worldviews of natural phenomena than their First World counterparts. He points out that: 'Acknowledgment of the world views science students bring to their science classrooms is a major basis for new types of objectives for science education' (p. 6). He then suggests six new research-based objectives for science education – a *tour de force* of Fensham's integrative capabilities. A coherent set, all of these highlight and then contrast the differences between how scientists see and think about the world, and how students see and think about the world. Therefore, these divergent viewpoints require new styles of pedagogical interaction – he contends. Fensham aptly demonstrates that current instruction often teaches and tests 'algorithmic' performance rather than challenging students' existing worldviews, or strengthening and extending them.

In his conclusion, he revamps the famous 1960 Brunerian dictum to reflect science education's changing understanding of the learning process: 'The child studying science at school should become aware, in a number of instances, of how scientists look at the world and how this view is useful and satisfying to them' (p. 11). He gives the children who are studying science permission either to change their own worldviews towards science or essentially to retain or partially modify the ones which they bring with them when they arrive at the science classroom. To do otherwise, he says, may be overly ambitious and arrogant. Such is Fensham's respect for the learner's right to make value decisions. He likes Osborne's phrase: move them in the direction of science. The standards and accountability movement of today would likely cringe and call this a concession, but the teachers in classrooms worldwide will know that Fensham's proposal correlates with what actually happens in real classrooms with increasingly diverse populations of learners, even when science teachers make every effort to effect total conceptual change and the adoption of current scientific understandings.

The principle of collaborative reflection

In 1991, Baird *et al.* published a research report on their three-year naturalistic case study which aimed to find out if collaborative reflection could improve the teaching and learning of science for Australian students in Grades 8 to 11. At Monash University, Fensham found and attracted supportive and stimulating colleagues who shared and sparked his own research interests. In the afore-mentioned three-year study, 'the preservice component involved 13 student teachers and teacher educators; the in-service component involved 14 novice and experienced science teachers and 350 of their students' (p. 163).

Foundational to the 1991 study were the ideas that 'constructivism com-plements metacognition in effecting personal change' (p. 164) and that both personal and professional reflection on the processes and outcomes of science teaching are vital (p. 165). Baird and Mitchell's (1986) long-running study (known as the 'PEEL Project' – Project for Enhancing Effective Learning) had already shown that development of science teachers' metacognition must precede that of their students, and that collaborative action research can catalyse teachers' own conceptual change.

The 1991 researchers (Baird *et al.*) found that the regular, long-term, system-atically gathered phenomenological reflections of teachers and students could be stimulated by a set of carefully designed questions presented on phenomen-ology forms (which are included in the 1991 article), and that the subjective data they gathered was often corroborated by teachers or students.

The regular personal and professional reflections for enhancing meta-cognition led to improvements in science teaching and learning within the classrooms that were impacted by the treatment. In addition, these reflections were shown to be facilitated through collaboration, and both types of reflection appeared to be necessary for classroom success.

When situated in a constructivist classroom context where 'the pursuit of concrete goals important to the participants, and the clear indications of progress (or lack of it)' were valued, the study showed that such a systematic programme of collaborative reflective activities clearly enhanced science teach-ing and learning. Initially, many students seemed to have no idea why they were studying a particular science topic. Without integrated reflection and metacognition components in their instructional programmes, learning had been construed by students in the study as the acquisition of content without knowing why they were doing what they were doing in the lesson.

What was the insightful 'bottom line' of the study as far as improving science learning for various types of students? 'Conceptions of the nature of successful teaching as law-governed and generalizable need to change to ones which view it as developing in a constructivist manner through a process of individual reflection on personal life experiences (i.e., phenomenological reflection)' (Baird *et al.*, p. 181), and '*collaboration* fosters reflection by providing a means of exchange of information and resources, and provision of support during the demanding and unsettling change process' (p. 182).

The principle of implicit perception of the total problem: ideas, acts, and capabilities

In a 1992 article co-authored with Ference Marton, Peter Fensham encourages instruction that fosters students' scientific intuition (implicit perception of the total problem in a scientific context). This research paper stems from the authors' keen detection that, of the four key themes of the famous 1957 science education reform and renewal conference held at Woods Hole, Massachusetts, the fourth theme, the nature of intuition, was largely neglected by researchers in the years following the meeting. Why might this be? Perhaps scientists and science educators were reluctant to dethrone logic as the king of scientific problem solving. Sensing this might be so, the two authors provocatively assert that 'Scientific research is much messier than is often supposed' (p. 115). Then in a brilliantly designed probe of the value of intuition, they chose to use interview data drawn from a group of scientists their colleagues could not easily dismiss. The 1993 study of eighty-three Nobel laureates by Marton, Fensham, and Chaitlin found that 87 per cent of these top scientists thought scientific intuition was important in doing science, and the researchers found that the laureates used the term *intuition* in three ways: to denote outcomes (ideas, thoughts, answers) or experiences (acts, events) or individual capabilities. Those Nobel laureates who commented on its human origin were most likely to attribute its development in a given scientist to possession of a wealth of prior knowledge and relevant experiences.

Having demonstrated its consensual importance, Fensham and Marton (1992, p. 120) note, paradoxically: 'Probably only a few science teachers model intuition to their students or could recognize intuition in their students . . . so far research studies that could assist teachers in these matters seem not to have begun.' They also point out that the Nobel laureates reported using intuition mainly in problem-solving situations where there was a plethora of information that muddied decision making – something unlikely to be experienced first-hand by science students until personal computers became common in school and society. Thus, more than ever, today's science curricula need to teach and test scientific intuition if they are to serve their target students well. Once again, Fensham and his colleagues have opened up important new lines of research – and these student-focused lines have become increasingly relevant and viable over time. Fensham's radar-like problem-posing sense is one of the hallmarks of his research style, and can serve as a model for all science education researchers to study. Another hallmark of his work is: always ask, what are the implications of these findings for promoting useful science learning?

Fensham's advice for finding successful science education researchers

In the Foreword of his 1988 edited book, *Development and Dilemmas in Science Education*, Peter J. Fensham sets forth his own criteria for identifying successful science education researchers (pp. ix–xiii): (1) interact with persons who have important things to say in science education; (2) choose leaders who take the content of science seriously, see learners as active constructors of scientific meaning, and recognise the importance of social context; and (3) seek ideas from science education researchers in a range of national contexts.

Fensham writes (1988, p. ix)

> [i]n my own numerous contacts with science educators from both indus-
> trialized and less industrialized countries I have been increasingly aware
> in the 1980s that some of the best organization, effective practice, and
> most original insights and innovations are occurring in some of the latter
> countries.

In the first chapter of his 1988 book, a chapter entitled 'Familiar but different: some dilemmas and new directions in science education', he points out that science education is now possible, for the first time, for the masses as well as the elite. In many nations, there persists a gender bias in favour of boys in science education, as well as unequal learning opportunities for the poor, Fensham warns. The increasingly multicultural nature of school populations in First World nations is also recognised – presenting new challenges and opportunities for science educators.

Later in that chapter, Fensham draws attention to: (1) the emphasis on rote learning of science facts, concepts, and algorithms that are not obviously socially useful; (2) the lack of 'experiencing the scientific usefulness' of concepts; (3) the emphasis on high levels of abstraction in concept learning without pointing out their consequent limitations in real situations; (4) the pedagogical sequence of moving from scientific abstractions to real-world examples rather than from life experiences to scientific explanations and social applications; (5) the failure to use practical work, not only to support concept learning, but also to learn essential skills and apply science to real-world problems; (6) the rush to and over-valuing of the quantitative aspects of science at the expense of conceptual understanding; (7) leaving to higher education or employment, the remediation of points 1–6; (8) the emphasis on teaching increasingly abstract science content that is preparatory for further study in the sciences at the expense of personal life and society's needs. These would all seem to be potentially fruitful areas of science education research, in Fensham's view, and still of relevance today.

Closing with a fable

Two science teachers went out in the forest to chop firewood to use in heating their homes for the coming winter. One worked hard the entire day – never stopping to rest, and gulping down a hearty noon lunch in a scant ten minutes! The other took several breaks, and even managed a short nap, after a much more leisurely lunch. At day's end, the teacher who had been working twice as hard was quite irritated to see that the other teacher had actually cut more wood. He said, 'I just don't understand – every time I glanced over at you, you were sitting down, yet, in the end, you chopped more wood than I did!' In reply, his companion said, 'Did you happen to notice that while I was sitting down, I was sharpening my axe?'

Likewise, while other science education researchers were chopping away frantically at science education's multiplying problems, Fensham took time to reflect before proceeding, took time to sharpen his investigative axe, and thus made every swing count. Ultimately, his reflections on his own research progress, on his collaborative research efforts, and on the published findings of the field's leading researchers have made a huge difference in the quality of his work for improving theory and practice in science education. Those entering the field today and looking for a role-model can do no better than turn to the research studies and science education policy writings of Peter Fensham. His 'Lodestar Criterion': is the science teaching under consideration 'of actual use' to the targeted student group in affectively synchronistic, real-world contexts that its members confront on a daily basis? This is but one example of his leadership for and influence on sailing the waters that lie between science education theory and practice.

References

Baird, J.R. and Mitchell, I.J. (eds) (1986) *Improving the Quality of Teaching and Learning: an Australian case study – the PEEL project*, Melbourne: Monash University.

Baird, J.R., Fensham, P.J., Gunstone, R.F., and White, R.T. (1991) 'The importance of reflection in improving science teaching and learning', *Journal of Research in Science Teaching* 28: 163–82.

Fensham, P.J. (1981) 'Heads, hearts and hands – future alternatives for science education', *The Australian Science Teachers Journal* 27: 53–60.

Fensham, P.J. (1983) 'A research base for new objectives of science teaching', *Science Education* 67: 3–12.

Fensham, P.J. (ed.) (1988) *Development and Dilemmas in Science Education*, London: Falmer Press.

Fensham, P.J. (1994) 'Beginning to teach chemistry', in P.J. Fensham, R.F. Gunstone, and R.T. White (eds) *The Content of Science: a constructivist approach to its teaching and learning*, London: Falmer Press, pp. 14–28.

Fensham, P.J. and Marton, F. (1992) 'What has happened to intuition in science education?', *Research in Science Education* 22: 114–22.

Fisher, K.M., Wandersee, J.H., and Moody, D.E. (2000) *Mapping Biology Knowledge*, Dordrecht: Kluwer Academic Publishers.

Gilbert, J.K., Osborne, R.J., and Fensham, P.J. (1982) 'Children's science and its consequences for teaching', *Science Education* 66: 623–33.

Marton, F., Fensham, P.J., and Chaitlin, S. (1993) 'A Nobel's eye view of scientific intuition', *International Journal of Science Education* 16: 457–73.

Mintzes, J.J., Wandersee, J.H., and Novak, J.D. (1998) *Teaching Science for Understanding: a human constructivist view*, San Diego: Academic Press.

Mintzes, J.J., Wandersee, J.H., and Novak, J.D. (2000) *Assessing Science Understanding: a human constructivist view*, San Diego: Academic Press.

Wandersee, J.H., Mintzes, J.J., and Novak, J.D. (1994) 'Research on alternative conceptions in science', in D. Gabel (ed.) *Handbook of Research on Science Teaching and Learning: a project of the National Science Teachers Association*, New York: Macmillan, pp. 177–210.

West, L.H.T. and Fensham, P.J. (1974) 'Prior knowledge and the learning of science: a review of Ausubel's theory of this process', *Studies in Science Education* 1: 61–81.

Part VI

Politics of the science curriculum

10 Partners or opponents

The role of academic scientists in secondary science education

Harrie Eijkelhof

During his long career as science educator Peter Fensham has struggled with academic scientists in his efforts to introduce innovations in secondary science education (Fensham, 1993; 1998). In the state of Victoria, where he lives, he has experienced academic scientists exerting a major influence on what happens in school science, especially in senior secondary schools. From their side he encountered opposition to proposed innovations such as the inclusion of social, economic, and environmental implications, the use of contexts while introducing concepts, and the use of activities to reflect on the personal learning process. Using Roberts's classification scheme of curriculum emphases (1982) he concludes that the priorities of academic scientists are with 'solid foundation', 'correct explanations', and, to a lesser extent, 'scientific skill development' (Fensham, 1998, p. 189). This is in conflict with trends in science education in which other emphases are receiving more attention (see below for examples).

Fensham's experiences are not unique. Panwar and Hoddinott (1995) and Blades (1997) describe, in different ways, the influence of academic scientists and technologists on the renewal of Alberta's secondary science curriculum – a story well known to Peter (1995a; 1999). In this Canadian case, teachers also played an important role in the debate, alongside other stakeholders such as parents, industry, and professional organisations. In other countries the role of the government has been all important (Donnelly and Jenkins, 2001), and I am sure that Peter will agree that also science educators, like himself, are often key players in the field of innovation of science education.

It would be too ambitious to outline in this short chapter the role of all these stakeholders. I prefer to focus on that of academic scientists, partly to follow up Peter's work, and partly to share with the readers my own experiences in this field during the last twenty-five years as a science educator within two physics faculties at Dutch universities. I will also try to incorporate experiences reported by others and to offer some ideas on why it is important to involve academic scientists in secondary science education.

Experiences in The Netherlands

Before 1930 no national programme for secondary physics education existed in The Netherlands. The first programme was written in 1927 by a committee set up by the Dutch Physical Society, comprised mainly of university physicists. In the remaining part of the twentieth century a new programme was written almost every decade. Until 1980, the majority of the members of these committees were academic scientists. I would agree with Peter that the programmes proposed by these committees emphasised the 'correct explanations' and 'solid foundation' perspectives. However, two committees, in the 1980s and 1990s, consisted mainly of teachers and science educators, some of whom had experience with the PLON project (Eijkelhof and Kortland, 1988; Lijnse *et al.*, 1990). In the PLON project physics was presented in a variety of contexts, chosen from daily life (bridges, traffic, the home), socio-scientific issues (choice of energy sources, risk of radiation), and technological and scientific innovations (medical technology, electronics, particle physics). The new physics curricula proposed by these committees put more emphasis on 'everyday coping', 'science, technology and decisions', 'science in making', 'science in applications', the last two categories added by Peter (Fensham, 1995b) to Roberts's scheme of curriculum emphases. It is difficult to judge what caused the lack of opposition from academic circles towards the changes in the new physics programmes. I suggest several factors might have been of influence:

- a rather stable influx of physics students at universities until 1990, so there was not much to worry about;
- a number of developments (budget cuts, reorganisations, increased competition) within the universities kept academic scientists occupied;
- the gap between universities and secondary schools with a limited number of contacts between the staff of these institutions;
- the view of some university educators that it does not matter so much which topics are covered in secondary schools as long as students develop some scientific thinking and mathematical skills and do not develop too many misconceptions;
- the trust in the standards of the national examination, a system with some inertia.

During the last decade the situation has been changing. Science faculties of the universities are taking more initiatives towards secondary schools and schools are making more use of the services offered by universities. The following factors are probably of influence:

- The number of first-year physics students is decreasing annually, so faculties are worried, and become more active to recruit students: they offer master classes, guest lectures, science days, and practical work opportunities to secondary school students and involve secondary school teachers in university teaching.

- Some recently implemented radical changes in senior secondary schools (emphasis on self-supported learning and a much broader set of subjects) have been debated in the national press; beginning in September 2001 students who followed the new curricula will enter the universities and this forces universities to adapt their first-year programmes.
- Innovations have become more visible in the national examinations. Some prominent physicists have been shocked by the emphasis on contexts, the extensive use of language, and the decrease in use of mathematics in examination questions. In May 2000 they published their complaints in the national press; in the following discussions they argued that their worries concerned not so much the examination questions but the teaching of physics, which they hoped to be able to influence through their criticism of the examination questions. They argued that contexts make physics too difficult (for a similar argument used in Australia, see Fensham, 1998, pp. 187–8), impossible for language-weak students with non-Dutch backgrounds, and unattractive for more abstract-oriented potential physics students.
- Radical changes in the university system (introduction of bachelor–master system) require a new study of the link with secondary education.

The physics community as a whole is again becoming more active towards secondary education. For instance, the Dutch Physical Society, the Foundation for Physics Research, and the physics faculties of nine universities are investing in a large website for secondary students and teachers to start in 2002, in order to offer a more up-to-date view on physics.

Another experience with academic influence relates to the introduction of a new science subject ANW (*Algemene NatuurWetenschappen*), focusing on the nature, limitations, history, and implications of science – it is obligatory for all senior secondary students in the country (De Vos and Reiding, 1999; Eijkelhof and Kapteijn, 2000). The main emphases are on 'self as explainer', 'science in making', and 'science, technology and decisions'. During the development of the course and the writing of textbooks many scientists were consulted. However, after the introduction in schools, the textbooks were criticised in the national press from several quarters: from a medical scientist for the attention given to alternative medicine, from an evolution specialist for mistakes in the presentation of theories, from two historians of science for the simplifications of discoveries, from an astrophysicist for the failure to use astronomy as a coherent factor between the topics Life, Biosphere, and Matter, and from an earth scientist for lack of attention to earth science. On the other hand, when in December 1999 the subject was almost eliminated by the Secretary of State for Education (Eijkelhof and Kapteijn, 2000), under pressure from students who felt overloaded with schoolwork, strong support came from the Royal Academy of Science, the Institutes of Biology and

Chemistry, and a number of prominent individual scientists. The Royal Academy of Science appointed a committee to evaluate the ANW textbooks; it concluded that although the books could be improved on several topics, they also contained a large amount of interesting information. The subject was seen as important and several suggestions were given for improvement. Since the introduction of ANW a lot of support has been given to it by life scientists and astronomers, through lectures to teachers and students, and by science centres, museums, and astronomy centres through educational activities in their buildings and through their websites. It appears to me that many academic scientists are seeing the subject as a window to science as it is practised now and as means to develop an appreciation of science.

Experiences in Europe

Not only in The Netherlands but also elsewhere in Europe contacts between academic scientists and science teachers at secondary schools are being intensified. An example is the European-wide programme called Physics on Stage. Its main aims are to assess the current situation in physics education and to raise the public awareness of physics and related sciences. The main initiators are CERN (European Centre for Nuclear Research), ESA (European Space Agency), and ESO (European Southern Observatory), in cooperation with the European Commission, the European Physical Society, and the European Association for Astronomy Education. Topics discussed at its first five-day festival (November 2000) were, among others, curriculum development and the potential contributions of European science organisations to physics education. Recommendations of a working group on the last issue included the proposal to reserve 1 per cent of research project funds for education and outreach activities and to set up a system of teachers-in-residence to allow in-service training (ESA, 2001). In science education circles there was some criticism (Sjøberg, 2000) of some of the claims voiced when the programme was launched, for example 'a frightening decline of interest in physics and technology among Europe's citizens, especially school children', and 'a progressively deteriorating state of physics literacy among the European population at all levels', neither of which are based on firm evidence but may illustrate the way academic scientists view the world.

In the UK, the Institute of Physics has launched the 'Post-16 Initiative', announced as a 'radical, forward looking initiative' to shape and develop physics for all involved in post-16 education. It started from the fact that physics A-level enrolment in the UK has declined, both absolutely and relative to the age cohort. To counterbalance this decline a new physics curriculum for A-level has been developed in order to bring physics teaching up to date, to respect the technical, and to give a better picture of the way physics is used in a variety of careers. The course was devised in close cooperation with the subject groups of the Institute of Physics consisting of academic physicists. Consensus was sought with teachers and professional groups on radical steps to be taken.

The books produced (Ogborn and Whitehouse, 2000; 2001) indeed contain some topics that are not common in physics textbooks, such as imaging, modelling, designing materials, quantum physics, cosmology, and matter in extremes. Practice should show if the right balance has been found between 'simplicity' and 'truthfulness', important for all efforts to teach new topics to students.

Another innovative approach has been taken by the University of York Science Education Group to develop a new A-level physics course based on contexts, called Salters Horners Advanced Physics (Science Education Group, 2000; 2001). Here it is not modern physics that has been the main focus but rather physics in everyday use, touching a wide variety of contexts, including the food industry, sports, music, and rail traffic. Here wide use was made of the expertise of physicists working in a variety of fields.

Also in the UK the physics community runs a number of service schemes for schools (i.e. the Institute of Physics), including school affiliation, lecture tours, exhibitions (Physics at Work, Physics in Action), and competitions (Paperclip Physics).

In Portugal the programme Ciencia Viva was initiated in 1996 by the Ministry of Science and Technology to promote scientific and technological culture in Portuguese society. Science and technology professionals were invited to participate in partnership with educational communities. Activities include inviting hundreds of students to scientific institutes during the holidays. They are given an opportunity to get closer to the reality of research work in a laboratory. Also the twinning of schools and scientific institutions is supported. The largest part of the programme is formed by more than 1,000 projects in over 2,000 schools to promote the experimental teaching of science in schools. In these projects many scientific societies, university departments, and state research centres are involved.

The importance of partnerships between education and science

Of course, these are only examples, chosen from my own experience, and I suppose many more activities are carried out elsewhere in fruitful cooperation between academic scientists and education professionals – even at the primary level (Fiolhais and Pessoa, 2001). They represent the positive side of academic influence on science education.

It cannot be denied that there have been negative experiences. In the introduction, I referred to Peter's experiences in Victoria, and the case of Alberta. In my own contacts with academic physicists I also have the impression that their main interest is not in public education in science as such, but in the education of the talented students whom they often see as opting for non-science studies. Also, their respect for science teachers is not always at a desired level: some scientists see science teachers mainly as 'failed researchers'.

In my view these negative experiences should not lead to a situation in which scientists and educators either battle or avoid each other. Let us consider why they might need each other:

1   Science education has to incorporate new developments in science in order to remain up to date: active scientists are essential collaborators in this respect as they know what is important in view of the development of the subject area.
2   Science education needs academic scientists to tame the influence of general educators who often do not appreciate the position of science education in schools. Some argue that education should focus strongly on skills, as if skills such as problem solving, knowledge management, and research skills could be learned, and used isolated from content. Others do not see the specific nature of scientific knowledge because of its relation with a reality outside human beings and believe scientific knowledge is just ideas in the heads of scientists.
3   Science education needs academic scientists in order to validate science teaching materials. Teachers and science educators tend to overestimate their scientific knowledge as they are often not in a position to be corrected.
4   Academic scientists need science education to recruit science students: science education can contribute by making talented students enthusiastic for a science or technology career.
5   Academic scientists need science education to gain public interest and support: it can expose the relevance of science for modern society and the utility of having some basic scientific knowledge in order to cope with daily life and to participate in debates about socio-scientific issues.
6   Academic scientists involved in university teaching might benefit from knowledge and insights that have been collected over decades of research and curriculum development in science education.

In my view, instead of battling or avoiding academic scientists, professionals in science education should join forces with them to improve continuously and support science education. Lederman speaks of 'marrying education with science' (Fiolhais and Pessoa, 2001). This will, I believe, benefit students in schools, and also make the profession of science teaching more attractive by destroying the image that teaching science means repeating the same lessons for many years. Teachers and curriculum developers will profit from the co-operation by being able to talk with experts about conceptually difficult topics and become familiar with new developments in science and higher education. Also, academic scientists will benefit by becoming more familiar with the reality of school life, which has changed since they left school, and with the knowledge and interest base of today's young people. They will be challenged to show the attractiveness of their subject area and possibly by learning ways of effective teaching from secondary school teachers.

I expect that academic scientists who have been involved in such collaborative activities would be able to play a useful role in cases of conflict about the contents of new curricula. Within their societies and institutions they might be able to promote mutual respect with colleagues who did not have the opportunity to cooperate within the science education area.

Of course developing such a system of cooperation takes time, and it may not be very effective where radical curricular changes are at hand. But maybe we, as science educators, should be more patient: the next new curriculum is not our final destination but a stepping stone towards better science education in the future.

References

Blades, D.W. (1997) *Procedures of Power and Curriculum Change: Foucault and the quest for possibilities in science education*, New York: Peter Lang Publishing.

De Vos, W. and Reiding, J. (1999) 'Public understanding of science as a separate subject in secondary schools in The Netherlands', *International Journal of Science Education* 21: 711–19.

Donnelly, J.F. and Jenkins, E.W. (2001) *Science Education. Policy, Professionalism and Change*, London: Paul Chapman Publishing.

Eijkelhof, H. and Kapteijn, M. (2000) 'Algemene Natuurwetenschappen (ANW): a new course on public understanding of science for senior general secondary education in the Netherlands', in R.T. Cross and P.J. Fensham (eds) *Science and the Citizen: for educators and the public*, Melbourne: Arena Publications, pp. 189–99.

Eijkelhof, H.M.C. and Kortland, J. (1988) 'Broadening the aims of physics education', in P. Fensham (ed.) *Development and Dilemmas in Science Education*, London: Falmer Press, pp 282–305.

ESA (2001) *Physics on Stage. Executive Summary 2000*, Noordwijk: ESA Publications Division.

Fensham, P.J. (1993) 'Academic influence on school science curricula', *Journal of Curriculum Studies* 25: 53–64.

Fensham, P.J. (1995a) 'Editorial policy and science education', *International Journal of Science Education* 17: 411–12.

Fensham, P.J. (1995b) 'One step forward', *Australian Science Teachers Journal* 41: 24–9.

Fensham, P.J. (1998) 'The politics of legitimating and marginalizing companion meanings: three Australian case stories', in D. Roberts and L. Ostman (eds) *Problems of Meaning in Science Curriculum*, New York: Teachers College Press, pp. 178–98.

Fensham, P.J. (1999) 'Book review of Blades (1997)', *Australian Journal of Education*, 43: 215–18.

Fiolhais, C. and Pessoa, C. (2001) 'Marrying education with science: an interview with Leon Lederman', *Europhysics News* July/August: 145–7.

Institute of Physics, http://post16.iop.org/initiative/ (accessed September 2001).

Lijnse, P.L., Kortland, J., Eijkelhof, H.M.C., van Genderen, D., and Hooymayers, H.P. (1990) 'A thematic physics curriculum: a balance between contradictory curriculum forces', *Science Education* 74: 95–103.

Ministry of Science and Technology, www.ucv.mct.pt (accessed September 2001).

Ogborn, J. and Whitehouse, M. (2000) *Advancing Physics AS*, Bristol: Institute of Physics Publishing.

Ogborn, J. and Whitehouse, M. (2001) *Advancing Physics A2*, Bristol: Institute of Physics Publishing.

Panwar, R. and Hoddinott, J. (1995) 'The influence of academic scientists and technologists on Alberta's secondary science curriculum policy and programme', *International Journal of Science Education* 17: 505–18.

Roberts, D. (1982) 'Developing the concept of "curriculum emphases" in science education', *Science Education* 66: 243–60.

Science Education Group, University of York (2000) *Salters Horners Advanced Physics AS Level, student book*, Oxford: Heinemann Educational Publishers.

Science Education Group, University of York (2001) *Salters Horners Advanced Physics A2 Level, student book*, Oxford: Heinemann Educational Publishers.

Sjøberg, S. (2000) *Falling enrolment: yes! illiteracy: no.* E-mail message to ESERA members, 20 December 2000.

11 Perspectives and possibilities in the politics of science curriculum

Jim Gaskell

As a tireless promoter for the reform of science education, Peter Fensham has had ample opportunity for experiencing, reflecting on, and working the politics of school science. He has been at the centre of efforts to change the school science curriculum in his home state of Victoria, in Australia as a whole, and internationally. He understood that changing the science curriculum required more than developing new materials, convincing teachers that the materials were good, and giving teachers the skills to implement them. There were limits to the autonomy of science teachers, especially in upper secondary levels (Fensham, 1980a). There were many actors inside and outside the classroom who had an interest in the science curriculum. In the period of Cold War competition in the 1960s, for example, governments invested heavily in science curriculum development on the assumption that new curricula would lead to an increased number of scientists who, in turn, would contribute to the economy and military defence as well as develop students' intellect and scientific literacy. Working in different countries, Fensham understood firsthand that change was not a technical process; the actors shaping the curriculum had to be sensitive to different cultural traditions as they did the political work of change (Fensham, 1980b).

As the limits of the 1960s' curriculum reform movement became apparent, as our understanding of teaching and learning grew (again with significant contributions from Peter Fensham – see below), and as pressures for more inclusive science education became more insistent, Fensham became heavily involved in policy and development work around 'Science for All' and science–technology–society (STS) curricula, as discussed later. These more socially relevant curricula provided significant challenges to school science based on the preparation of future scientists that had been promoted by the academic scientists who were centrally involved in the reforms of the 1960s. With this new direction, the heady days of the 1960s when science educators, science teachers, and scientists worked collaboratively to enact reforms came to an end. The academic scientists with the support of most senior science teachers now worked to block or limit efforts to redraw the boundaries of school science (Fensham, 1993; 1997; 1998). The academic scientists seemed to prevail despite their minority status on curriculum committees and despite evidence of students' positive attitudes to the more socially relevant curricula. Student voices, despite their interests as future citizens in a complex world, were not part of the dialogue. Fensham, following Layton (1973), talks of the academic scientists as 'guardians of the disciplines'. But what and against whom are they guarding? And why are the boundaries of physics and chemistry policed more diligently than biology? And why, if university bridging courses can prepare students as well as or better than traditional secondary science courses (Fensham, 1996), is there so much pressure to maintain the purity of school science? Fensham (1998) despairs that change is not a process of laying bare the competing claims and needs and of meeting them with a rational compromise. Are we stuck, then, with the tyranny of the few? In this chapter, I will provide some perspectives on this issue and argue that if we step outside the usual cast of actors in our plots we might be able to construct a rationale for change. This might be persuasive because of the size and strength of the interests that it encompasses.

This resistance of academic scientists to broadening the school curriculum has a long history. David Layton has commented that '[a]ttempts to make the school curriculum more practical, more related to productive industry and more relevant to the perceived needs of pupils, parents and employers are as old as state-supported schooling' (Layton, 1984b, p. 21). A major impetus for state support for the introduction of science into the school curriculum in England in the middle of the nineteenth century was the government's concern about the ability of England to meet economic and technological competition from other nations that already had well-developed school science programmes (Layton, 1973). Science began in the elementary school as a community-related 'science of common things' designed to develop students' interests and intellects through investigations of relevant objects in their everyday environment. Influential scientists, however, were opposed to the teaching of applied science in the context of general education. They were concerned that such an emphasis would be 'prejudicial to the future welfare of scientific inquiry' (Layton, 1973, p. 159). A curriculum based on practical topics would, it was argued, emphasise the application of existing knowledge and downplay the importance of science discovering new truths that would advance civilisation. These ideas, combined with the prevailing ideas of faculty psychology and of general education as a humanising agent that should seek to bridge divisions in society, led to the replacement of the science of common things with a common curriculum based on systemic botany that would train the mind and lead children to an appreciation of nature.

Similarly, in the elite secondary schools, pressure to introduce science into the curriculum initially came from the introduction of competitive examinations to gain entrance to the Civil Service and army (Layton, 1984a; Meadows and Brock, 1975). The two major military officer training colleges of Sandhurst and Woolwich in the UK required science subjects and this meant that the elite schools had to make provision for boys contemplating military careers as officers. In this sense science was early on tied to a vocation other than becoming a professional scientist. Security and status in the curriculum of these elite secondary schools, however, only came when cogent arguments were made that science was a necessary part of a liberal education and when it became a secure subject of study at Oxford and Cambridge (Meadows and Brock, 1975). Scientists, as they developed their own respectability and influence during the mid-nineteenth century, argued that science was necessary to train areas of the mind left untouched by the classics. The focus on developing liberally educated gentlemen again entailed a move away from practicality and towards topics that would have a humanising and academic emphasis.

Governments and science education

Governments across the political spectrum have lamented the narrow nature of school science education but even when rhetorically supported by industry spokespeople they have had little success in making long-term changes in the face of pressure from university scientists and science teachers and in the face of internal division over the audience for, and precise goals of, the proposed changes. As McCulloch *et al.* (1985) describe in their history of school science and technology in England and Wales after 1945, in the 1960s and 1970s under the Labour governments of Harold Wilson and James Callaghan efforts were made to create a more practical science education to meet the changing needs of industry. In the 1980s, the Conservative Margaret Thatcher responded to similar pressures and concerns by instituting the Technical and Vocational Education Initiative (TVEI) with funding from outside the Department of Education and Science. While it was possible, with large infusions of money, to create some interesting curriculum projects very little long-term change has been effected.

Probably the most dramatic changes in the curriculum occurred during the 1960s and early 1970s in the USA when the interests of governments and scientists coincided and governments poured millions of dollars into curriculum development projects sponsored by the National Science Foundation. Behind this confluence of interests were two assumptions that scientists have worked hard to establish. One assumption is that the support of pure science will pay off in future applications that will benefit the material and physical health of the population through new inventions and medical advances (Daniels, 1967). The second is that the advancement of science is best encouraged and protected from distortion by letting scientists decide which research proposals should be funded irrespective of political priorities. In the context of these assumptions, the promotion of curricula stressing 'science for science's sake' and the production of more scientists could be seen to fulfil the 'useful' interests of the state and the academic interests of the scientists. The reforms of the 1960s had two broad goals. One was to reform teaching to encourage more laboratory-based enquiry supposedly as performed by scientists and the second was to reform the curriculum to emphasise the structure of the discipline as defined by academic scientists. The first encountered heavy going in the school system and was not supported by similar reforms in university-level classes. The second goal was widely achieved through the writing and adoption of new textbooks that came from, or were influenced by, the large projects (Jackson, 1983).

The relative consensus of the 1960s' curriculum projects was not to last, however. Issues of gender and racial inequality and poverty were pushed into the political arena by a new generation of political activists. Public concerns about environmental degradation began to increase and the environmental movement began to take off. Science began to lose some of its cachet as *The Greening of America* (Reich, 1970) became a new mantra. Concerns for the long-term health of science began to increase as the public support necessary for continued high levels of funding began to weaken. Organisations responsible for the health of science as an institution began to worry and a variety of reports were produced. In 1980, for example, a report to the US President was issued by Shirley Hufstedler, the Secretary of Education, and Donald Langenberg, the Acting Director of the National Science Foundation (1980). They pointed out that the health of science (and therefore the country's security and prosperity) depended not only on an adequate supply of scientists but also on a public willing to pay the taxes needed to support a large science establishment. The existing academic science curricula developed during the 1960s, while good for future scientists, did not do enough to address personal or societal problems involving science and technology; nor did they have vocational relevance except for the chosen few. A different kind of science was needed. Within this context, STS became a major curriculum goal in state curriculum documents under the banner of science for all and scientific literacy.

The Canadian situation

In Canada, the Science Council of Canada charged with providing advice on maintaining the health of Canadian science became alarmed at the trends and instituted its first and only study of pre-university science education. In the final report of the study, titled *Science for Every Student* (Science Council of Canada, 1984), the Science Council endorsed the concept of 'Science for All' (p. 10) and recommended a renewal of science education through presenting a more authentic view of science, emphasising the STS connection, setting science education in a Canadian context, and introducing technology education. The prestige of the Science Council facilitated the rapid adoption of STS curriculum goals by provincial Ministries of Education.

In 1988, the Royal Society of Canada held a conference and issued a report, *Science and the Public* (Neale, 1988), designed to provide guidelines to officers and members of scientific and engineering societies in their efforts to enhance the public appreciation of science and technology. An important element was to encourage individual scientists to view their work in its social context and to recognise their obligations to explain it to the public.

These reports indicate that at a national policy level there appeared to be considerable support from the scientific community for a broadening of the science curriculum and a movement away from a focus just on the education of future scientists. Despite, however, support from national science groups, educators, and science educators, the actual classroom use of STS curriculum resources and textbooks was marginal (Bybee, 1991; Gaskell, 2001). One of the few exceptions was in Saskatchewan where Glen Aikenhead's (1991) *Logical Reasoning in Science and Technology* was adopted for use in Grade 10.

The resistance to making a more socially relevant science in school classrooms seems to come from scientists working on specific course curriculum committees. The scientists working and teaching in local universities are more focused on the preparation of secondary students for university science courses than on the needs of students who will not take further science in university, even if these students may be involved in making political decisions about levels of science funding later on.

The power of local scientists in Canada

Understanding how local scientists come to be seen to have the power to block progressive changes to the science curriculum is important if we are to think about how to act politically to achieve a different result. Blades (1997) in his description of what happened in Alberta when the Ministry of Education tried to bring in a new science curriculum with a significant STS emphasis talks about the ability of the scientists to rally a variety of science-based professional organisations to their cause. In a province heavily dependent on the oil and gas industry these groups argued that the 'radical' changes being proposed would lead to a severe shortage of competent engineers, geologists, and scientists and even, according to the Alberta Medical Association, threaten the long-term future of Medicare. The discourse used to back up these claims was that the new courses represented a 'dumbing down' that would lead to the 'death of science in Alberta' – it was 'social science masquerading as science', 'pop science', 'Reader's Digest science curriculum'. The assumptions on which such arguments are made may be shaky but they were sufficient to persuade the Ministry of Education to back off and to revamp the curriculum proposals to reinstate the study of the separate sciences within a general science framework. But why did the Ministry listen to these groups? Part of the answer, it seems, is the absence of support from the audience for whom the original STS curriculum proposals were intended. Where were the voices of students and parents who are supposed to be not well served by the traditional science curriculum? They were absent.

One of the key moves in the struggle over the new science curriculum in Alberta was made by the University of Alberta when it declared that

Science 30 was unacceptable for admission to science courses in its faculty. This declaration destroyed the academic acceptability of Science 30 at the University of Alberta. If the academic credibility of the course is destroyed at a university, it is also destroyed for the parents and students. Their interests are in courses that are acceptable for entrance to the university. A university education represents, in general, the best route to higher incomes and secure employment and with an increasing demand for skilled workers, the financial returns on a university education are increasing (Berryman, 1993). Local scientists have an interest in having students well prepared for the courses that the scientists will teach in university. From the scientists' point of view, having students discuss social issues related to science topics takes time away from learning more science. Only a small percentage of students may go to university, but most will want to keep the doors open to that possibility as long as possible.

The strong link between university entrance and the boundaries of school science partially explains why the universities are more concerned about senior secondary science courses and are prepared to be more flexible with junior secondary courses. Physics and chemistry are often seen as more important to future scientists than biology. At the University of British Columbia, for example, Grade 11 physics and chemistry are required for entrance to the Faculty of Science but not Grade 11 biology.

Of course, it might be possible for the government to exert control over the state-supported universities and to insist on the acceptability of the new secondary school curriculum as being in the best interests of the students and society in general because, it might be argued, the students would become more adept at engaging in and making decisions about complex socio-scientific issues that are common in a modern society. A study by Rafea (1999) illustrates the additional resources that local scientists can draw on when faced by a determined government. As a member of the Ministry of Education in a small, Middle Eastern authoritarian country, Rafea had been used to having the power to set the physics curriculum. What he wrote became the new curriculum. During his doctoral studies, however, he became interested in broadening the boundaries of the traditional physics curriculum through introducing some STS, or PTS (Physics, Technology, and Society), elements into the secondary physics curriculum. For his study he translated some relevant units from the Dutch PLON project (Eijkelhof and Lijnse, 1988) and showed them to representatives of various stakeholder groups in his country. The groups included physics teachers, students, university physicists, university physics educators, industrialists, Ministry of Education officials, and first-year university science and engineering students. Not surprisingly, the university physicists were the most strongly opposed. They argued that if such a curriculum were implemented secondary school students would not be properly prepared for university physics courses either in their own country or in any foreign country. The international community would see that the standards of the country's education system were lacking. They emphasised that their view of what constituted proper physics was not idiosyncratic; it was shared by a vast network of other physicists around the world, especially and most importantly, physicists in the most prestigious institutions in the world. As one physicist said:

> So yes, the secondary physics curriculum has a given perspective or format, and this is not set by me, as you know. It is a universal one. Whether in Bahrain or the Arab world, Europe or America. Everywhere.
>
> (Cited in Rafea, 1999, p. 97)

As they were challenged and presented with the views of other stakeholders, the physicists became more adamant about the importance of their control over the curriculum:

> So between you and I, the final say has to come from physicists . . . because we are talking about the student who will specialize in physics. So, we have the final say and we see how we can compromise. I don't care about educators, industry, students or others.
>
> (Cited in Rafea, 1999, p. 119)

Interestingly, in Rafea's study the responses of the industrialists he interviewed were more ambiguous. Initially, given that they had never been asked before, they assumed that the traditional view of physics was the most appropriate one. It had served to sort out the able students that they had then hired and trained within their companies. As they thought more about the proposals, though, they came to appreciate the possibilities of a curriculum that focused on science in a context that would also encourage practical problem solving, teamwork, communication skills, decision making, integration of knowledge, etc. However, given the strength of the physicists' opposition and their ability to mobilise local and international networks of support, and the more ambiguous, weaker response of industry, the Ministry of Education decided that the proposed changes to the physics curriculum should proceed slowly and through a series of pilot studies. This was the first time that pilot studies had been used in the process of science curriculum change in this country – there were, after all, limits to the authority of the state in the face of possibilities that the credibility of the country's academic institutions might be challenged not only locally but internationally. The few local scientists were well connected into far-flung international networks of scientists who influenced pathways to further education that might be of interest to local students and parents.

Rafea's study also illustrates a useful perspective on power. Until the controversy was settled, the situation was fluid. The different actors manoeuvred to line up other actors, both human and non-human, to back up their interests. For example, some physicists worked to enrol God on their side:

> We should not select from science what is useful to us and say that something else is not useful. . . . God created us and bestowed upon us the ability

to think and find out, so that ultimately we become believers, to ultimately have faith in God.

(Cited in Rafea, 1999, p. 101)

Other physicists suggested that the promotion of a PTS curriculum was associated with an alien, Western, materialistic society: 'We live in a different society, we are governed by religious and moral values, not materialistic' (Rafea, 1999, p. 102). Power was not something that could be seen to be possessed in advance in measurable amounts so that the outcome of the controversy could be forecast. The power of the university physicists was an effect of the actions of others – ministry bureaucrats, parents, students, industrialists, etc., not something physicists possessed. The students and bureaucrats were operating rationally within a material and social world, making choices such that their interests were aligned with those of the physicists in this particular curriculum dispute. This perspective is consistent with Foucault's (1979; 1980) concept of power as strategies, tactics, and manoeuvres exercised within a network of relations. Rafea, following Latour (1986), Callon (1986), and Law (1991), extends Foucault's focus on social relations to the idea of actor–networks encompassing both human and non-human elements.

If we accept that local academic scientists do not 'possess' power over the science curriculum but that the power they appear to have is an effect of the actions of many other actors, then it is possible to conceive of the construction of alternative actor–networks encompassing alternative conceptions of school science.

Possibilities

It is possible to find examples in Western countries of reasonably stable, systemic reform in the science-based curriculum. The introduction of problem-based learning (PBL) in university professional education is an interesting example (Boud and Feletti, 1997a). In medicine (Barrows and Tamblyn, 1980) and architecture (Maitland, 1997), for example, there have been significant moves towards PBL models of professional education that are explicitly designed to develop sound academic knowledge in the context of working on practice-based problems. PBL is a way of conceiving of the curriculum as being centred upon key problems in professional practice. It is not simply an addition of problem-solving activities to an otherwise discipline-centred curriculum. PBL courses move students towards the acquisition of knowledge and skills through a staged sequence of problems presented in context, together with associated learning materials and support from teachers (Boud and Feletti, 1997b). The problem-based approach is a significant challenge to traditional models of university-based professional education, which emphasise the initial acquisition of basic knowledge followed by an internship in which students learn to 'apply' the knowledge. An emphasis on learning through occupationally realistic problems does not entail a neglect of basic science. The issue is how it is learned so that it is accessible to doctors carrying out their primary mission to evaluate and manage health problems competently.

The rapid spread of PBL is related to strong support from the professional bodies that regulate entrance to the professions. These groups have argued that graduates from traditional programmes are not well equipped to begin their professional practices. In order to ensure continued accreditation of their programmes, for example, medical schools had to show how their curricula included opportunities for students to engage in self-directed learning. PBL came to be seen as the most acceptable way of accomplishing this. By articulating and acting on new criteria for accreditation, the professions through their regulatory bodies provide clear guidelines for medical schools (Hunt, 1991). Students will not enrol in programmes that are not accredited.

Are there lessons to be learned from the example of the spread of PBL in professional education for efforts to challenge traditional notions of scientific knowledge in the schools? Where might we find the equivalent of the professional bodies that acted as a counterweight to the traditional notions of the separation of pure and applied knowledge found in university faculties of arts and science?

The responses of the industrialists in Rafea's (1999) study provide some clues. When presented with a choice, they saw the PTS curriculum as encouraging students to engage in the kinds of collaborative, technology-based, problem-solving activities that would be beneficial to them as workers in their industries. As Hurd (1989; 1998) points out, similar arguments are being made by industrialists in North America. Industrialists have made these argument before, but the kinds of technological and structural changes that are taking place in industry make these arguments more urgent in the context of global competition. The fundamental requirements of industrial work – bodily exertion, manual dexterity, and endurance – have been increasingly displaced by the requirements for rapid perception, attentiveness, and the ability to analyse problems and make decisions (Casey, 1999). This applies both to shopfloor workers and to supervisors and managers (Berryman, 1993). Piore and Sable (1984) argue that the flatter management structures of today's industry along with the need to be responsive to local contexts around the globe create a need for 'flexible specialisation'. Designers must be so broadly qualified that they can envision product and production together – something not learnt by book learning alone. Production workers must be so broadly skilled that they are able to collaborate with designers to solve the problems that inevitably arise in production. Joe Kincheloe (1995), from a critical theory perspective, argues that these changes require 'smart workers' who are able to integrate academic and vocational knowledge. School curricula need to be reorganised to reflect these needs. Kincheloe's argument is reinforced by Michael F.D. Young (1998) in his book *The Curriculum of the Future: from the 'new sociology of education' to a critical theory of learning*. Young's equivalent to Piore and Sable's flexible specialisation is connective specialisation. Connective specialists need to see specific subjects such as science from the point of view of the curriculum whereas divisive specialists see the curriculum from the point of view of their subjects. Young's concept of critical vocationalism gives priority to the ways that young people can relate to work and knowledge and how they can draw on both subject knowledge and their experience and understanding of work in developing their ideas about the future.

These arguments suggest the potential of enlisting industry as an actor in constructing an alternative science education – one that would move away from the assumption of the academic scientists that students must first learn decontextualised basic science before they can apply it. Despite the arguments of Kincheloe and Young, many will view such alliances with scepticism and as being antithetical to the development of critical citizens able to challenge the prevailing status quo. But the establishment of close links between education and work, as mentioned previously, has been advocated by groups across the political spectrum. The integration of mental and manual labour and academic and vocational education were central principles of educational reform in the former Soviet Union and countries such as Cuba and China (McFadden, 1980). Because industry groups have adopted this rhetoric at the moment should not mean that science educators interested in social reform should automatically abandon the territory. It should be possible to reclaim the rhetoric and to hold industrial spokespeople to their claims about the need to prepare workers who are able to solve problems, think critically, and act morally. Getting industry on side supporting a science education that looks at the interaction of science and technology in the social context of workplaces may be one way of challenging the hegemony of the universities over the narrowly academic definition of school science. In the high-stakes game of educational policy and practice, it is important to have powerful allies.

It was with the support of industry and labour unions that the British Columbia Ministry of Education was able to introduce a programme of 'applied academics' based on the idea of integrating academic and occupational education in secondary schools (Gaskell and Hepburn, 1997; 1998). Principles of physics were to be developed through analysing workplace contexts. The programme was intended to create pathways to further education in universities and community colleges and pathways directly to the workplace. Needless to say, the academic community has not been supportive of these developments as they threaten the traditional academic definitions of school subjects. Even though the courses are provincially examinable, the universities are not accepting them on par with regular courses for initial admission. Although industry lobbied hard to set up the programme with the support of organised labour, it did not follow up that work by promoting well-paid, secure jobs for people who took the courses and it did not encourage public lobbying of the universities to change their admission criteria by offering to give preferential hiring to graduates admitted through those programmes. Under the circumstances, students and parents were wary of the courses and even in a demonstration district that has committed funds and administrative support to promoting the new programme, it is not doing well (Gaskell and Tsai, 2000).

Within the various sites, however, there are indications of the importance of alternative pathways to student choice. The programme began, for instance, in a heavily industrial community where new advances in automation, instrumentation, and process control had made increased educational standards and higher levels of training essential, even for entry-level production jobs. After some negotiation with industry, the school system agreed to develop a new science and technology sequence for students not normally interested in taking advanced academic courses. The courses would give the students a sense of how mathematics and physics related to the jobs that they might obtain in local industry. The courses did well as long as industry maintained a commitment to give preferential hiring to graduates of the programme. When industry backed away from this commitment, the programme folded.

Building an alternative science education can be seen as parallel to the construction of a fact or artefact (Gaskell and Hepburn, 1998). Building support for it can be seen as a process of interesting credible actors in a curriculum. These actors are likely to include people inside and outside the classroom such as students, parents, industry, board and ministry officials as well as non-human actors such as curriculum materials, economic resources, assessment technologies, etc. As with the development of a scientific fact, the process of interesting additional actors in a curriculum artefact will require transformations of the original idea as work is done to create a stable network of course materials, financial resources, pedagogy, and assessment strategies tied to interested teachers, students, politicians, and industry human resource managers. Today's changing economic and social contexts open up possibilities for transforming traditional academic science education into a critical science and technology education related to economic and occupational challenges. The politics of such a transformation will require convincing industry that long-term curriculum change requires more than lobbying governments for the introduction of new courses. Industry needs to be a part of convincing parents and students that enrolling in such courses will lead to desirable employment. Industry also needs to act like the professional accreditation agencies that lobbied for PBL to convince universities that if they do not accept and provide alternative forms of learning and knowledge then other institutions that do will gradually get more students because those students will get the preferred jobs. Science educators can help this process by providing the research that industry can use to argue for alternative forms of learning and science knowledge and an understanding of the complexities of curriculum change that industry must be attuned to. Science educators must also play an important role in ensuring that the resultant curricula do encourage a critical perspective on the world. Such political work will entail new ways of thinking and acting for science educators, but when even as distinguished a reformer (and ex-fellow scientist – see the start of this chapter) as Peter Fensham finds convincing academic scientists to accept an alternative form of school science constantly frustrating, it is time to try something different.

Acknowledgements

The support of the Social Science and Humanities Research Council of Canada through the Western Research Network in Education and Training is gratefully acknowledged.

References

Aikenhead, G. (1991) *Logical Reasoning in Science and Technology*, Toronto: John Wiley.

Barrows, H.S. and Tamblyn, R.M. (1980) *Problem-Based Learning: an approach to medical education*, New York: Springer.

Berryman, S.E. (1993) 'Learning for the workplace', *Review of Research in Education* 19: 343–401.

Blades, D. (1997) *Procedures of Power and Curriculum Change: Foucault and the quest for possibilities in science education*, New York: Peter Lang.

Boud, D. and Feletti, G. (eds) (1997a) *The Challenge of Problem-Based Learning* (2nd edition), London: Kogan Page.

Boud, D. and Feletti, G. (1997b) 'Changing problem-based learning. Introduction to the second edition', in D. Boud and G. Feletti (eds) *The Challenge of Problem-Based Learning* (2nd edition), London: Kogan Page.

Bybee, R. (1991) 'Science-Technology-Society in science curriculum: the policy-practice gap', *Theory into Practice* 30: 294–302.

Callon, M. (1986) 'Some elements of a sociology of translation: domestication of the scallops and the fishermen of St. Brieuc Bay', in J. Law (ed.) *Power, Action and Belief: a new sociology of knowledge*, London: Routledge & Kegan Paul, pp. 196–233.

Casey, C. (1999) 'The changing contexts of work', in D. Boud and J. Garrick (eds) *Understanding Learning at Work*, London: Routledge.

Daniels, G.H. (1967) 'The pure-science ideal and democratic culture', *Science* 156: 1699–1705.

Eijkelhof, H. and Lijnse, P. (1988) 'The role of research and development to improve STS education: experience from the PLON project', *International Journal of Science Education* 10: 464–74.

Fensham, P. (1980a) 'Constraint and autonomy in Australian secondary science education', *Journal of Curriculum Studies* 12: 189–206.

Fensham, P. (1980b) 'Books, teachers, and committees – a comparative essay on authority in science education', *European Journal of Science Education* 2: 245–52.

Fensham, P. (1993) 'Academic influence on school science curricula', *Journal of Curriculum Studies* 25: 53–64.

Fensham, P. (1996) 'Post-compulsory education and science: dilemmas and opportunities', in P. Fensham (ed.) *Science and Technology Education in the Post-Compulsory Years*, Melbourne: The Australian Council for Educational Research, pp. 9–30.

Fensham, P. (1997) 'School science and its problems with scientific literacy', in R. Levinson and J. Thomas (eds) *Science Today: problem or crisis?*, London: Routledge.

Fensham, P. (1998) 'The politics of legitimating and marginalizing companion meanings: three Australian case stories', in D.A. Roberts and L. Östman (eds) *Problems of Meaning in Science Curriculum*, New York: Teachers College Press, pp. 178–92.

Foucault, M. (1979) *Discipline and Punish: the birth of the prison*, trans. A. Sheridan, New York: Vintage Books.

Foucault, M. (1980) *Power/Knowledge: selected interviews and other writings*, trans. C. Gordon, New York: Pantheon Books.

Gaskell, P.J. (2001) 'STS in a time of economic change: what's love got to do with it?', *Canadian Journal of Science, Mathematics and Technology Education* 1: 385–98.

Gaskell, P.J. and Hepburn, G. (1997) 'Integration of academic and occupational curricula in science and technology education', *Science Education* 81: 469–81.

Gaskell, P.J. and Hepburn, G. (1998) 'The course as token: a construction of/by networks', *Research in Science Education* 28: 65–76.

Gaskell, P.J. and Tsai, L.-L. (2000) 'Education for/through work: issues in a demonstration site. WRNET working paper 00.07', Unpublished manuscript, Vancouver, BC.

Hufstedler, S.M. and Langenberg, D.N. (1980) *Science and Engineering education for the 1980's and Beyond. A report prepared by the National Science Foundation and the Department of Education*, Washington, DC: Government Printing Office.

Hunt, A.D. (1991) *Medical Education, Accreditation, and the Nation's Health: reflections of an atypical dean*, East Lansing, MI: Michigan State University Press.

Hurd, P. (1989) 'Science education and the nation's economy', in A. Champagne, B. Lovitts, and B. Calinger (eds) *Scientific Literacy*, Washington, DC: American Association for the Advancement of Science, pp. 15–40.

Hurd, P. (1998) 'Linking science education to the workplace', *Journal of Science Education and Technology* 7: 329–35.

Jackson, P.W. (1983) 'The reform of science education: a cautionary tale', *Daedalus* 112: 143–66.

Kincheloe, J. (1995) *Toil and Trouble: good work, smart workers, and the integration of academic and vocational education*, New York: Peter Lang.

Latour, B. (1986) 'The powers of association', in J. Law (ed.) *Power, Action, and Belief: a new sociology of knowledge*, London: Routledge & Kegan Paul.

Law, J. (1991) 'Power, discretion and strategy', in J. Law (ed.) *A Sociology of Monsters*, London: Routledge, pp. 165–91.

Layton, D. (1973) *Science for the People: the origins of the school science curriculum in England*, London: George Allen and Unwin.

Layton, D. (1984a) *Interpreters of Science: a history of the Association for Science Education*, London: John Murray.

Layton, D. (1984b) 'The secondary school science curriculum and the alternative road', in D. Layton (ed.) *The Alternative Road: the rehabilitation of the practical*, Leeds: Centre for Studies in Science and Mathematics Education, University of Leeds, pp. 21–35.

Maitland, B. (1997) 'Problem-based learning for architecture and construction management', in D. Boud and G. Feletti (eds) *The Challenge of Problem-Based Learning* (2nd edition), London: Kogan Page.

McCulloch, G., Jenkins, E., and Layton, D. (1985) *Technological Revolution? The politics of school science and technology in England and Wales since 1945*, London: Falmer Press.

McFadden, C. (ed.) (1980) *World Trends in Science Education*, Halifax, Nova Scotia: Atlantic Institute of Education.

Meadows, A.J. and Brock, W.H. (1975) 'Topics fit for gentlemen: the problem of science in the public school curriculum', in B. Simon and I. Bradley (eds) *The Victorian Public School: Studies in the development of an educational institution*, Dublin: Gill and Macmillan.

Neale, E.R. (1988) *Science and the Public*, Ottawa: Royal Society of Canada.

Piore, M. and Sabel, C. (1984) *The Second Industrial Divide: possibilities for prosperity*, New York: Basic Books.

Rafea, A.M. (1999) 'Power, curriculum making and actor–network theory: the case of physics, technology and society curriculum in Bahrain', Unpublished doctoral dissertation, University of British Columbia, Vancouver.

Reich, C.A. (1970) *The Greening of America*, New York: Random House.

Science Council of Canada (1984) *Science for Every Student: educating Canadians for tomorrow's world (Report No. 36)*, Ottawa: The Science Council of Canada.

Young, M.F.D. (1998) *The Curriculum of the Future: from the 'new sociology of education' to a critical theory of learning*, London: Falmer Press.

Part VII

Peter Fensham's reform agenda

The 'vision thing'

12 Visions, research, and school practice

Reinders Duit

> Science for All is a vision splendid. Like any worthwhile vision it recurs to lift the spirits of those who have become depressed with what they and others are achieving with current ways of doing things.
>
> (Fensham, 1985, p. 435)
>
> Without vision the people perish.
>
> (Fensham, 1996, p. 10)

In this chapter I will address Peter Fensham's visions for a science education that encourages all students to learn science, and to experience the excitement of knowing science. However, I will not discuss his visions as such. This is done in a number of other contributions to this book. My major concern is how his visions for science education might become the hopes for the future for teachers, and to what extent they could be implemented by teachers.

Visions are clearly a necessary condition for any progress (Fullan, 1993). Therefore, visions always have to be ahead of the status quo. However, there is always also the danger that they are so far ahead of the actual views and practices that they fail to change the actual state. With regard to the many facets of Peter Fensham's ideas embedded in 'Science for All' (Fensham, 1985) Richard White (Chapter 13) asks whether it is possible for teachers to master such extensive and diverse knowledge, skills, and applications, and then inevitably these ideas will fail.

I will deal with the issue of the problem of improving educational practice by visions and research. It appears that there is a tendency within the academic culture of science education research (and of research on teaching and learning other domains also) towards alienation from what is possible in school practice.

Scientific literacy

Visions and ideals

The 1990s saw an intensive debate about scientific literacy inspired by concerns about the educational demands of the twenty-first century (Gräber and Bolte, 1997). Later in the 1990s these discussions were further fuelled by the results of the TIMSS project (Third International Mathematics and Science Studies) that uncovered striking deficiencies in the state of scientific literacy in many countries.

In the UK, the Nuffield Foundation supported the project 'Beyond 2000: science education for the future' (Millar and Osborne, 1998). Driver and Osborne (1998) summarised the major results of this project in the following four arguments for the need to improve scientific literacy: (1) the economic argument – modern societies need scientifically and technologically literate workforces to maintain their competencies; (2) the utility argument – individuals need some basic understanding of science and technology to function effectively as individuals and consumers; (3) the cultural argument – science is a great human achievement and it is a major contributor to our culture; (4) the democratic argument – citizens need to be able to reach an informed view on matters of science-related public policies in order to participate in discussions and decision making. It should be added that the 'utility argument' includes two of the core ideas in Peter Fensham's conception of 'Science for All': '(i) The likely usefulness of the learning in the students' everyday life out of school and (ii) the chance that it will produce a response of wonder and curiosity about nature' (Fensham, 2002a, p. 211).

The arguments by Driver and Osborne (1998) focus on developing the understanding of science for various purposes. One issue is missing, or at least not explicitly stated, namely the contribution of learning science to general school education. Here usually the more general intellectual and practical skills (e.g. the cross-curricular competencies of the OECD Programme for International Student Assessment, PISA) play the major role. It may be interesting to note that over the history of science education the contribution of science learning to these cross-curricular competencies was always given particular emphasis when learning science for its own sake was questioned.

Gräber and Nentwig (1999) summarised the broad spectrum of competencies affiliated with scientific literacy as follows:

> What do people know? Subject competence (knowledge, understanding, application); epistemological competence (includes views of the nature of science).
> What can people do? Learning competence; social competence; communicative competence; procedural competence (includes various science and general processes).
> What do people value? Ethical competence.

The levels of scientific literacy proposed by Bybee (1997) have become a reference position in the recent discussion. These are:

> Nominal scientific literacy: Certain names and terms are known; understanding of a particular situation is basically restricted to the level of naive theories.

Functional scientific literacy: Individuals can use scientific vocabulary but the use is confined to a particular activity or need. Knowledge of vocabulary is usually out of context.

Conceptual and procedural scientific literacy: Understanding and application of concepts and processes.

Multidimensional scientific literacy: Includes understanding of the nature of science, the history of science, and the role of science within culture and society.

The extensive contemporary literature on scientific literacy includes a large spectrum of rather extravagant claims (Laugksch, 2000; DeBoer, 2000). However, although there is a substantial common core in which Fensham's conception of 'Science for All' fits nicely, there are two problems with the contemporary debate about scientific literacy. First, there is a tendency to include a large variety of issues based on different ideologies without sufficiently investigating whether they fit together. Second, 'Science for All' has become a major term in the debate of scientific literacy. Sometimes it appears that the meaning of the term has lost the spirit of Fensham's vision of scientific literacy and simply indicates that everybody should learn some science.

The conception of scientific literacy in PISA is a rather focused view of scientific literacy (Fensham and Harlen, 1999; Harlen, 2001). It is seen as the capacity to identify questions and to draw evidence-based conclusions in order to understand and help make decisions about the natural world and the changes made to it through human activity. The foci are the following science processes and cross-curricular competencies:

Science processes:

(1) recognising scientifically investigable questions;
(2) identifying evidence needed in a scientific investigation;
(3) drawing or evaluating conclusions;
(4) communicating valid conclusions;
(5) demonstrating understanding of science concepts.

Cross-curricular competencies:

(a) self-regulated learning;
(b) ability to solve problems;
(c) communication and cooperation.

Peter Fensham is a member of the international 'Functional Expert Group' of PISA 2000 (Harlen, 2001, p. 51). One of his colleagues in this group (Prenzel, 2002) points out that Peter views the PISA concept of scientific literacy as a valuable framework to promote as possible major features of his ideas of 'Science for All', especially to find out to what extent students are able to make use of scientific knowledge and skills in daily life, and in participating in the public debate on science-related issues. According to Prenzel, he also holds that by promoting the PISA features of scientific literacy school science instruction could be substantially improved. In Peter's owns words this issue reads as follows (Fensham, 2002b):

> I have had great fun being part of this project. . . . In different ways they have broken new ground in relation to how science in school might be a much more empowering experience for many more students than it traditionally has been.

Facing reality

As already mentioned, Richard White is sceptical about whether it is possible for teachers to master the variety of issues comprising Peter Fensham's conceptions of 'Science for All'. More generally, there is reason to be sceptical that students are able to achieve the even more widespread competencies described in the scientific literacy literature.

Shamos (1995) argues, for instance, that only about 5 per cent of the students may achieve the highest levels of scientific literacy (like Bybee's level of multidimensional scientific literacy). Miller (1997) concludes, on the basis of an empirical study, that only about 7 per cent of his students could be called scientifically literate. Baumert (1997) in summarising results of TIMSS and other studies in Germany states that the goal of universal scientific literacy seems to be wishful thinking.

In fact, research on teaching and learning science shows that science instruction is usually able to guide students from their everyday conceptions towards the science concepts only to a limited degree and it often results in a significant decrease of students' interests and self-concepts.

It is remarkable that the issue of which level of scientific literacy may be achieved by the students is not often addressed in the recent literature on scientific literacy. It is also notable that the presentation of visions frequently does not include considerations on how the visions may be adopted by the teachers. (For an attempt to address the latter issue, see Gräber and Nentwig, 1999.)

Constructivist research on teaching and learning science

Developments in a fruitful research domain

Research on students' (and teachers') conceptions and their roles in teaching and learning science has been the most important domain of science education research on teaching and learning in the past decades. Briefly outlined, the research began in the 1970s with the investigation of students' pre-instructional conceptions on various science content domains. It became clear that students do not come into science instruction without pre-instructional knowledge, or beliefs, about the phenomena and concepts to be taught – but already hold deeply rooted conceptions and ideas (Driver and Easley, 1978). Usually, their pre-instructional conceptions are not in harmony with the scientific view and may even be in stark contrast to it. Over the years students' pre-instructional conceptions in the major science domains have been investigated (Pfundt and Duit, 2001).

Since the 1980s students' conceptions of the nature of science, and their views of learning (i.e. metacognitive conceptions), have been given considerable attention. It was shown that students' conceptions here are also limited and naive. It became evident that many teachers also hold limited views of the nature of science and the nature of the teaching and learning process. Indeed many teachers are found to hold conceptions on the science content that are very much reminiscent of students' pre-instructional everyday conceptions.

Finally, the 1980s also saw the rapid growth of studies, within the framework of 'conceptual change', investigating the development of students' pre-instructional conceptions towards the intended science concepts (Posner *et al.*, 1982). Although these new conceptual change approaches were embedded in student-oriented pedagogy and were also affiliated with ideas from STS (Science–Technology–Society), it is surprising to see that the emphasis was mainly on changing the methods of science instruction. The science content taught was mainly the old traditional set of concepts and principles. Peter Fensham (2001) has convincingly argued that traditional science concepts should be seen as problematic. He points out two major concerns. First, traditional science content is only suited to a limited degree to address the core issues of 'Science for All'. Making use of science knowledge and skills in daily life, and participating in the public debate on science-related issues, are likely only if the science content learned is relevant for these purposes. Second, research has shown that traditional content is often not intrinsically attractive for students. Hence, traditional content should be embedded within contexts that are attractive to more students.

Research on the role of pre-instructional conceptions has developed from a focus on students' conceptions of science content issues towards a rather complex system of students' and teachers' conceptions that influence science teaching and learning. This development is affiliated with the development towards multiperspective theoretical frameworks (Duit and Treagust, 1998). Initially, in the 1970s, Piagetian ideas and ideas of early theories of cognitive psychology were adopted. In the 1980s constructivist views developed merging various approaches with a focus on viewing knowledge as constructed (like Piagetian interplay of assimilation and accommodation, Kuhnian ideas of theory change in the history of science, and radical constructivist ideas). It turned out that the initial constructivist frameworks of teaching and learning were limited at least in two respects. First, there was a strong focus on the individual, with the result of neglecting issues of social construction of knowledge. Second, there was an emphasis on cognitive issues of the construction process with a tendency to neglect affective features of the learning environment. Hence, the initial constructivist frameworks were further developed by including issues of social constructivist origin and by viewing conceptual change as being embedded within 'conceptual change supporting' learning environments like the 'multidimensional framework of conceptual change' by Tyson *et al.* (1997).

Briefly summarised, multiperspective frameworks have to be employed in order to address adequately the complexity of the teaching and learning processes. There appear to be the following major developments towards multi-perspective views of science learning and instruction. (1) Towards multiple conceptual changes. Conceptual change at the content level has to be closely linked to changes at meta-levels such as views about the nature of science knowledge and metacognitive views about learning. (2) Towards merging cognitive and affective domains. There is much research evidence that cognitive and affective domains are closely linked. Interests, for instance, mediate effective learning. It should be an important aim of science instruction to develop interests in much the same way as to develop students' pre-instructional conceptions towards the intended science concepts. (3) Towards merging moderate and social constructivist views of learning. Studies on learning (science) were mostly oriented at views of learning that are monistic to a certain extent. However, the complex phenomenon we call learning may only be adequately addressed by pluralistic epistemological frameworks (Greeno *et al.*, 1997). Further only multiperspective views appear to be suited to address the ambitious levels of scientific literacy outlined above. (4) Towards bringing science content issues, views of scientific literacy, and students' perspectives and needs into balance. As outlined above, science content should be seen as problematic (Fensham, 2001). Kattmann *et al.* (1995; 1997) have developed a 'Model of Educational Reconstruction' in order to allow the construction of a content structure for instruction that addresses key elementary ideas of the particular science content, the particular features of scientific literacy addressed, and students' conceptions, views, interests, and needs. The model is based on the German Didaktik tradition. This tradition holds that science content for instruction has nothing 'given', but has to be reconstructed for educational purposes.

Facing the reality of science classrooms

Constructivist research provides a powerful means to improve science teaching and learning. However, it appears that the perspectives developed are far ahead of the views of most science teachers. Taking into account what is known about the (limited) views many science teachers hold about teaching and learning in general and teaching and learning science in particular, it seems to be rather difficult for science teachers to adopt major new research findings.

Impact of research in school practice

It appears that educational research in general is in danger of being viewed as irrelevant by many teachers. Kennedy (1997), for instance, argued that the 'awful reputation of educational research' (Kaestle, 1993) is due to the domination of basic research by cognitive psychology. Such studies are usually carried out in laboratory settings in order to allow strict control of variables. The price to be paid for a large degree of experimental 'cleanness' is that the results often do not inform the actual practice of teaching and learning. Wright (1993) provided similar arguments to explain that science education research is frequently viewed as irrelevant by policy makers, curriculum developers, and science teachers. He also claims that most science education researchers have little interest in putting into practice what is known. My main point here is that every research community develops a particular research culture that defines what counts as good research. What counts as good research in such a community may not be in accordance with what teachers expect and need. Hence, there is always a tendency for the research culture to alienate teachers.

As outlined above, this appears to be also true for constructivist research although the epistemological orientation of research is substantially different from the basic research that Kennedy (1997) attacked. In fact, research in science education in the constructivist camp has been more of an applied research type from the very start. It is most fortunate that there has also been a turn towards cognitive psychology during the 1990s and towards addressing the needs of educational practice in this kind of research (Vosniadou, 1996).

With regard to possibilities to set the visions of scientific literacy into practice there is substantial research available. Anderson and Helms (2001) provide a most valuable review of research findings available and research that is still needed. They discuss the National Science Education Standards (National Research Council, 1996) in the USA. They are of the opinion that this document presents a vision for science education that is both exciting and viable, but they also describe the problems facing its implementation:

> Research potentially can assist in the process of implementing the National Science Education Standards (National Research Council, 1996). Existing research shows that changes called for in the Standards are difficult to put into practice, create dilemmas for teachers, require significant changes in teachers' values and beliefs, are fostered when change is pursued within departments within schools, are influenced powerfully by teacher collaboration in the work context, are often resisted strongly by parents, and often demand new student roles and different student work. The results of research on reform do not give a definitive picture of the most productive roles for students, the nature of the desired student work, how teachers can best be engaged in reassessing values and beliefs and taking responsibility for acquiring new professional competencies, how to realize 'science for all', and the most effective ways of involving parents.
>
> (Anderson and Helms, 2001, p. 3)

Among the major dilemmas teachers experience is the tension between 'ideal' and 'reality': they think that the ideals such as those portrayed in the standards and what they perceive to be realities of their classroom do not fit. Anderson and Helms argue that implementation of new standards and research should go hand in hand. They close their article in stating: 'There is a clear need for collaboration of another kind – collaboration between action oriented reformers who are working 'in the trenches' and skilled researchers who are prepared to conduct their research in these settings' (p. 14).

In summarising the contributions of a special issue of the *Journal of Research in Science Teaching*, Lynch (2001) addresses another important issue of changes towards 'Science for All'. She argues that the linguistic and cultural diversity in science classes needs to be taken into account and claims that 'Science for All' does not necessarily mean that 'one size fits all'.

Although there is much research on attempts to change school practice, studies on the impact of research on normal school practice appear to be rare. More recent video studies like the TIMSS video study on mathematics instruction in the USA, Japan, and Germany (Stigler *et al.*, 1999) or the TIMSS-R video studies on science (Roth *et al.*, 2001) are beginning to fill this gap. In order to find out which teaching and learning scripts are dominating German physics instruction we carried out such a video study comprising a sample of fourteen teachers. Data sources included video documents of about ninety lessons on the introduction to electric circuits and the force concept, indepth interviews with every teacher (including stimulated recall), and various student questionnaires. Only preliminary results are available so far (Prenzel *et al.*, 2001a). However, with regard to the impact of visions of scientific literacy, contemporary constructivist views of teaching and learning, and conceptual change strategies, it turns out that most of our teachers are not familiar with these issues of the science education literature. Their views of the aims of physics instruction are rather limited. It also appears that most of them do not hold explicit theories about the teaching and learning process. Their view of learning seems to be transmissive rather than constructivist. It is particularly remarkable that most of the teachers are not even familiar with the kind of students' pre-instructional conceptions that have to be taken into account when the concepts of the electric circuits and force are introduced. Their views about dealing with pre-instructional conceptions are not informed by conceptual change ideas. The dominating way of thinking about teaching physics may be called subject specific. They have a quite substantial and well-organised repertoire of the kind of experiments available and of how to introduce a certain concept. But this subject-specific thinking is only rather loosely based on more general views of good science teaching.

Briefly summarised, the impact of more recent research ideas and research findings on teachers' views and classroom actions appears to be rather limited in our study. Of course, the small sample we have investigated may not be representative for German physics teachers as a whole. However, all teachers are members of teams within a national quality development programme. In a second phase of our project, we will include a larger sample of about fifty randomly selected teachers in order to find out whether the preliminary findings are of more general significance for physics instruction in Germany.

Quality development projects

Improving scientific literacy was a major concern of science education research and development during the 1990s. Public awareness about the urgent need for a sufficient level of scientific literacy has proven a most powerful driving force. In a number of countries the disappointing results of students in TIMSS has alarmed a broader public, as well as politicians and school administrators, who demand that school science instruction become more effective. Quite frequently, discussion in the mass media has focused on the idea of making schools more effective in a narrow sense. It is, however, most fortunate that actual projects have addressed the major issues of scientific literacy for all as outlined above.

Quality development projects are large-scale attempts that include a sub-stantial number of schools (e.g. Beeth, 2001; Prenzel and Duit, 2000; Tytler and Conley, 2001; Wickman, 2001). They share a conception of 'Science for All' and the following characteristics (Duit and Tytler, 2001): (1) Supporting schools and teachers to rethink the representation of science in the curriculum. (Hence, they address Peter Fensham's (2001) issue that science content should be viewed as problematic.) (2) Enlarging the repertoire of tasks, experiments, and teaching and learning strategies and resources. (3) Promoting strategies and resources that attempt to increase students' engagement and interest. (4) Setting constructivist principle into practice. On the teachers' side, the reflective practitioner with a non-transmissive view of teaching and learning; on the students' side, the active, self-responsible, cooperative, and self-reflective learner. (5) Attention to principles of teacher development. (6) Atten-tion to principles of systemic change. (7) Development of methods to monitor the change process for groups of teachers, and the overall impact on student learning and achieving major issues of scientific literacy. On the organisational side, a major common feature of these projects is a researcher–teacher partner-ship which gives teachers a strong voice in the process of improving practice. The project settings hence need to adopt the key ideas of action research.

In order to provide an example, the German project 'Increasing the efficiency of science and mathematics instruction' (Prenzel and Duit, 2000) will be briefly outlined. German students did not do as well as expected in the TIMSS studies. Their results in science and mathematics were just mediocre. What was even more worrying, however, was the fact that relatively large numbers of German students had problems solving the more demanding tasks, especially those requiring conceptual understanding. From a longitudinal point of view these results showed relatively limited increases in competency in the course of compulsory education in Germany. These results clearly indicate that science and mathematics education in Germany is far less successful than expected, and then what is necessary to guarantee a minimum of scientific and mathematics literacy. The German students' deficiencies have been hotly debated, not only among the educational specialists and those responsible for science and mathematics education in the Ministries of Education, but also by the broader public. This prepared the ground for joint action to increase the quality of science and mathematics instruction in Germany.

Based on an analysis of the major deficiencies in science and mathematics education in Germany a nation-wide project was developed and funded by the German Board of Education. The Ministries of Education and Culture in Germany's sixteen states control this board. The goal of the programme is to stimulate, promote, and scientifically guide processes that are aimed at optimising the quality of teaching and learning in mathematics and science in an inter-state network of schools.

In all, 180 schools are participating, with thirty sets of six schools each. Each school set had the opportunity to select its subjects according to its particular needs and interests from a list of eleven modules. These modules provide the framework for the work in the sets. They address the following needs of German science and mathematics instruction as identified by a group of experts: (1) Further development of the task culture. (2) Towards more adequate views of scientific work and experiments. (3) Learning from mistakes – and admitting that mistakes are not just impediments of learning. (4) Towards securing basic knowledge – meaningful learning at different levels. (5) Making students aware of their increase of competence – cumulative learning. (6) Making students aware of the limited view of a particular subject – towards integrative features of instruction. (7) Promoting the learning of both girls and boys. (8) Developing tasks for cooperative learning. (9) Strengthening students' responsibility for their learning. (10) Assessment: measuring and feedback of progress of competencies. (11) Quality development within and across schools.

At first sight, this list of modules appears to address quite traditional issues. However, a vision of constructivist science instruction forms the framework for these modules. Further, the basic idea of the innovation strategy is to start from where the teachers are and to approach the vision and the needs step by step.

The project organisers provide summaries of research findings and further information that may support the work in the sets by means of an Internet server. They also organise meetings of the sets at the national and local levels. A number of science and mathematics education researchers are engaged in the work of the sets. There are empirical studies on the implementation of the programme (Prenzel *et al.*, 2001b). An initial study focuses on the acceptance of the programme by teachers. A subsequent study will investigate more fully the development towards the programme goals in a number of sets. The programme schools participated in an additional national PISA sample in 2000 and will also participate in the PISA studies of 2003 and 2006. Data will then be available to identify characteristics of the schools in the programme in comparison with other German schools.

Experience gained so far displays the problems of improving quality as described by Anderson and Helms (2001). There are exciting developments in a number of school sets but there are also many difficulties of change processes. Clearly, there will be substantial changes for a number of teachers over the five years the programme runs. However, in other cases the progress achieved will be less than expected. Another problem is the dissemination of progress achieved among the participating teachers to the large number of teachers outside the programme. Simple dissemination of products and ideas developed in the sets will not lead to the change that is necessary. Therefore, there will be a subsequent project on dissemination. The results of PISA 2000 (Baumert *et al.*, 2001) again revealed severe deficiencies in German science and mathematics education. According to the data available it appears that the German school system in general has to undergo major changes. Hence, it has proven to be absolutely necessary to disseminate the findings of the above quality development project.

Elsewhere there are a number of other initiatives to bridge the gap between research and school practice on a somewhat smaller scale. Embedded within the 'Teaching and Learning Research Programme' of the UK's 'Economic and Social Research Council', for instance, there are two projects dealing with 'using research to improve practice in science education' (Leach *et al.*, 2001; Millar and Hames, 2001). The basic idea here is to use a partnership of researchers and teachers. New means of assessment and new teaching sequences are designed in close cooperation with 'normal' classroom teachers. There is no doubt that the materials developed will be of substantial quality and will be suited to initiate changes towards improving scientific literacy. However, it will be as difficult as in other such partnership frameworks to disseminate the results to the teachers outside the teacher–researcher partnership group.

Briefly summarised, there are several attempts around the world to improve scientific literacy. Regarding such attempts in the USA, Lynch (2001) states: 'Unfortunately, the reform has not significantly reduced achievement gaps overall in the U.S. (although there has been progress in some specific locations).' It appears that this also holds for other quality development attempts. Change can only be achieved to a limited degree in the short time such programmes are running. Further, the expectations about the effectiveness of science instruction often seem to be beyond what is possible.

Bridging the gap

'Science for All' is a splendid vision. Visions like this are the key for any progress towards a level of scientific literacy that allows students to deal adequately with the demands of the future, and to participate in public decisions on future technologies. It is absolutely necessary to keep the discussion on scientific literacy going. But it is also necessary to be sceptical, to ask whether the visions can be put into practice. In Peter Fensham's work we find a fine balance of vision and practicality. However, much research still needs to be carried out on two major issues: (1) The level of scientific literacy which may be achieved by students. To achieve all of the many facets of scientific literacy as described in the literature appears to be impossible – at least for the large majority of students. (2) The way science classrooms have to become different to allow achievement of the goals. Here more research is necessary on the actual state of science instruction and on the possibilities to change teachers' and students' scripts of good science teaching. Without visions, science education research and development will lead nowhere – without facing the reality of science classes, research and development will fail. Facing reality includes avoiding further alienation of research from school practice. It is time to bridge the gap.

Regarding the results of PISA 2000, Peter Fensham (2002c) argues

> that 15 year olds in a number of countries in different continents did score remarkably well on the PISA tests, exceeding the gloomy predictions that were made early in the project that would simply show that students every-where could not deal with such questions.

Is the PISA concept of scientific literacy a first fruitful step to bridge the gap? At least it appears that it will be most valuable to analyse further the data gained in that project.

References

Anderson, R.D. and Helms, J.V. (2001) 'The ideal of standards and the reality of schools: needed research', *Journal of Research in Science Teaching* 38: 3–16.

Baumert, J. (1997) 'Scientific literacy a German perspective', in W. Gräber and K. Bolte (eds) *Scientific Literacy*, Kiel: Leibniz-Institute for Science Education (IPN), pp. 167–80.

Baumert, J., Klieme, E., Neubrand, M., Prenzel, M., Schiefele, U., Schneider, W., Stanat, P., Tillmann, K.J., and Weiß, M. (eds) (2001) *PISA 2000 Basiskompetenzen von Schülerinnen und Schülern im internationalen Vergleich (PISA 2000 Students' Basic Competencies in International Comparison)*, Opladen: Leske & Budrich.

Beeth, M. (2001) 'Systemic reform in mathematics and science education in Ohio (USA): 1991–2000', in D. Psillos, P. Kariotoglou, V. Tselfes, G. Bisdikian, G. Fas-soulopoulos, E. Hatzikraniotis, and M. Kallery (eds) *Proceedings of the Third Inter-national Conference on Science Education Research in the Knowledge Based Society, Vol. 1*, Thessaloniki: Aristotle University of Thessaloniki, pp. 198–200.

Bybee, R. (1997) *Achieving Scientific Literacy: from purposes to practices*, Portsmouth, NH: Heinemann Publishing.

DeBoer, G. E. (2000) 'Scientific literacy: another look at its historical and contempor-ary meanings and its relationship to science education reform', *Journal of Research in Science Teaching* 37: 582–601.

Driver, R. and Easley, J. (1978) 'Pupils and paradigms: a review of the literature related to concept development in adolescent science students', *Studies in Science Education* 5: 61–84.

Driver, R. and Osborne, J. (1998) 'Reappraising science education for scientific literacy', Paper presented at the annual meeting of the National Association for Research in Science Teaching (NARST), San Diego, CA, April 1998.

Duit, R. and Treagust, D. (1998) 'Learning in science – from behaviourism towards social constructivism and beyond', in B. Fraser and K. Tobin (eds) *International Handbook of Science Education*, Dordrecht: Kluwer Academic Publishers, pp. 3–26.

Duit, R. and Tytler, R. (2001) 'Quality development programmes in science education', in D. Psillos, P. Kariotoglou, V. Tselfes, G. Bisdikian, G. Fassoulopoulos, E. Hatzikraniotis, and M. Kallery (eds) *Proceedings of the Third International Conference on Science Education Research in the Knowledge Based Society, Vol. 1*, Thessaloniki: Aristotle University of Thessaloniki, pp. 3–26.

Fensham, P. (1985) 'Science for all: a reflective essay', *Journal of Curriculum Studies* 17: 415–35.

Fensham, P. (1996) 'Education without a vision: the aftermath of the National Curriculum Project', *Education Alternatives* 5(3): 10–11.

Fensham, P. (2001) 'Science content as problematic – issues for research', in H. Behrendt, H. Dahncke, R. Duit, W. Gräber, M. Komorek, A. Kross, and P. Reiska, (eds) *Research in Science Education – past, present, and future*, Dordrecht: Kluwer Academic Publishers, pp. 27–41.

Fensham, P. (2002a) 'Surviving science lessons is not scientific literacy', in J. Wallace and W. Louden (eds) *Dilemmas of Science Teaching – perspectives on problems of practice*, London and New York: RoutledgeFalmer, pp. 209–12.

Fensham, P. (2002b) Personal communication.

Fensham, P. (2002c) Personal communication.

Fensham, P. and Harlen, W. (1999) 'School science and public understanding of science', *International Journal of Science Education* 21: 755–63.

Fullan, M.G. (1993) *Force Changes: probing the depths of educational reform*, London: Falmer Press.

Gräber, W. and Bolte, K. (eds) (1997) *Scientific Literacy*, Kiel: Leibniz-Institute for Science Education (IPN).

Gräber, W. and Nentwig, P. (1999) 'Scientific literacy: bridging the gap between theory and practice', in W. Gräber and P. Nentwig (eds) *Proceedings of the 2nd International IPN Symposium on Scientific Literacy*, Kiel: Leibniz-Institute for Science Education (IPN) (CD-ROM; http://www.ipn.uni-kiel.de).

Greeno, J.G., Collins, A.M., and Resnick, L.B. (1997) 'Cognition and learning', in D.C. Berliner and R.C. Calfee (eds) *Handbook of Educational Psychology*, New York: Macmillan, pp. 15–46.

Harlen, W. (2001) 'The assessment of scientific literacy in the OECD/PISA project', in H. Behrendt, H. Dahncke, R. Duit, W. Gräber, M. Komorek, and A. Kross (eds) *Research in Science Education past, present and future*, Dordrecht: Kluwer Academic Publishers, pp. 49–60.

Kaestle, C.F. (1993) 'The awful reputation of educational research', *Educational Researcher* 22(1): 23–31.

Kattmann, U., Duit, R., Gropengießer, H., and Komorek, M. (1995) 'A model of educational reconstruction', Paper presented at the annual meeting of the National Association for Research in Science Teaching (NARST), San Francisco, CA, April 1995.

Kattmann, U., Duit, R., Gropengießer, H,. and Komorek, M. (1997) 'Das Modell der didaktischen Rekonstruktion Ein Rahmen für naturwissenschaftsdidaktische

Forschung und Entwicklung (The model of educational reconstruction a framework for science education research and development)', *Zeitschrift für Didaktik der Naturwissenschaften*, 3(3): 3–18.

Kennedy, M.M. (1997) 'The connection between research and practice', *Educational Researcher* 26(7): 4–12.

Laugksch, R.C. (2000) 'Scientific literacy: a conceptual overview', *Science Education* 84: 71–94.

Leach, J., Hind, A., Lewis, J., and Scott, P. (2001) 'Designing and implementing science teaching drawing upon research evidence about learning', in D. Psillos, P. Kariotoglou, V. Tselfes, G. Bisdikian, G. Fassoulopoulos, E. Hatzikraniotis, and M. Kallery (eds) *Proceedings of the Third International Conference on Science Education Research in the Knowledge Based Society, Vol. 1*, Thessaloniki: Aristotle University of Thessaloniki, pp. 138–40.

Lynch, S. (2001) '"Science for All" is not equal to "One Size Fits All": linguistic and cultural diversity and science education reform', *Journal of Research in Science Teaching* 38: 622–7.

Millar, R. and Hames, V. (2001) 'Using diagnostic assessment to improve students' learning in science', in D. Psillos, P. Kariotoglou, V. Tselfes, G. Bisdikian, G. Fassoulopoulos, E. Hatzikraniotis, and M. Kallery (eds) *Proceedings of the Third International Conference on Science Education Research in the Knowledge Based Society, Vol. 1*, Thessaloniki: Aristotle University of Thessaloniki, pp. 141–3.

Millar, R. and Osborne, J. (1998) *Beyond 2000: science education for the future. The report of a seminar series funded by the Nuffield Foundation*, London: King's College London, School of Education (http://www.kcl.ac.uk/education).

Miller, J.D. (1997) 'Civic scientific literacy in the United States: a developmental analysis from middle-school through adulthood', in W. Gräber and K. Bolte (eds) *Scientific Literacy*, Kiel: Leibniz-Institute for Science Education (IPN), pp. 121–40.

National Research Council (1996) *National Science Education Standards*, Washington, DC: National Academy Press.

Pfundt, H. and Duit, R. (2001) *Bibliography: students alternative frameworks and science education*, Kiel: Leibniz-Institute for Science Education (IPN).

Posner, G.J., Strike, K.A., Hewson, P.W., and Gertzog, W.A. (1982) 'Accommodation of a scientific conception: toward a theory of conceptual change', *Science Education* 66: 211–27.

Prenzel, M. (2002) Personal communication.

Prenzel, M. and Duit, R. (2000) 'Increasing the efficiency of science and mathematics instruction: report of a national quality development programme', Paper presented at the annual meeting of the National Association for Research in Science Teaching (NARST), New Orleans, April, 2000 (http://www.ipn.uni-kiel.de/projekte/blk_sinus).

Prenzel, M., Duit, R., Euler, M., Geiser, H., Hoffmann, L., Lehrke, M., Müller, C., Rimmele, R., Seidel, T., and Widodo, A. (2001a) 'Studies on the interplay of teaching and learning processes in physics instruction', Paper presented at the conference of the European Science Education Research Association (ESERA) in Thessaloniki, August 2001 (http://www.ipn.uni-kiel.de/projekte/video/main16.htm).

Prenzel, M., Ostermeier, C., and Duit, R. (2001b) 'Improving science and mathematics education in Germany the concept of a national quality development programme and findings on its implementation', in D. Psillos, P. Kariotoglou, V. Tselfes,

G. Bisdikian, G. Fassoulopoulos, E. Hatzikraniotis, and M. Kallery (eds) *Proceedings of the Third International Conference on Science Education Research in the Knowledge Based Society, Vol. 1,* Thessaloniki: Aristotle University of Thessaloniki, pp. 201–201.

Roth, K.J., Druker, S., Kawanaka, T., Okamoto, Y., Trubacova, D., Warvi, D., Rasmussen, D., and Gallimore, R. (2001) 'Uses of video-based technology and conceptual tools in research: the case of the TIMSS-R Video Study', Paper presented at the annual meeting of the National Association for Research on Science Teaching (NARST), St Louis, MO, March 2001.

Shamos, M.A. (1995) *The Myth of Scientific Literacy,* New Brunswick, NJ: Rutgers University Press.

Stigler, J.W., Gonzales, P., Kawanaka, T., Knoll, S., and Serrano, A. (1999) *The TIMSS Videotape Classroom Study. Methods and findings from an exploratory research project on eighth-grade mathematics instruction in Germany, Japan, and the United States,* Washington, DC: US Department of Education.

Tyson, L.M., Venville, G.J., Harrison, A.G., and Treagust, D.F. (1997) 'A multi-dimensional framework for interpreting conceptual change in the classroom', *Science Education* 81: 387–404.

Tytler, R. and Conley, H. (2001) 'The science in schools research project: improving science teaching and learning in Australian schools', in D. Psillos, P. Kariotoglou, V. Tselfes, G. Bisdikian, G. Fassoulopoulos, E. Hatzikraniotis, and M. Kallery (eds) *Proceedings of the Third International Conference on Science Education Research in the Knowledge Based Society. Vol. 1,* Thessaloniki: Aristotle University of Thessaloniki, pp. 204–6.

Vosniadou, S. (1996) 'Towards a revised cognitive psychology for new advances in learning and instruction', *Learning and Instruction* 6: 95–109.

Wickman, P.O. (2001) 'NTA – a Swedish school project for science and technology', in D. Psillos, P. Kariotoglou, V. Tselfes, G. Bisdikian, G. Fassoulopoulos, E. Hatzikraniotis, and M. Kallery (eds) *Proceedings of the Third International Conference on Science Education Research in the Knowledge Based Society, Vol. 1,* Thessaloniki: Aristotle University of Thessaloniki, pp. 210–12.

Wright, E. (1993) 'The irrelevancy of science education research: perception or reality?', *NARST News* 35(1): 1–2.

13 Changing the script for science teaching

Richard White

A script is the knowledge of how to behave in a class of situations. Most of us, for instance, have a script for catching a bus, which includes knowing that some sort of sign indicates where to wait for the bus, knowing that on entry we have to pay a fare or show a pass, and knowing where it is socially acceptable to sit. We learn scripts by watching others or by being told how to behave. So we build up a repertoire of scripts for the social situations that we encounter frequently: scripts for entering restaurants, for parties, for family gatherings, for concerts, for being a spectator at sports, for driving in traffic.

We become so accustomed to our scripts that we find it difficult to appreciate that there may be other ways of doing things. When we travel to a foreign land a different way of acting sometimes surprises us. On entering a bus in Melbourne you expect the driver to give you change when you pay the fare, but in San Francisco you have to pay the exact money, and the script is to ask the other passengers to break a ten- or twenty-dollar note for you; their script is to search their wallets or purses to see if they can do that, whereas in Melbourne the script would be to avoid eye contact and ignore the request.

Foreign experience can lead you to revise your scripts. The great ease of travel and spectacular advances in telecommunications in the second half of the twentieth century encouraged much reconsideration of scripts; regional differences diminished, and the world became a more homogeneous place. Globalisation wipes out differences. This has advantages in efficiency, as is evident in companies such as McDonald's where the same script applies everywhere, and in ease of understanding between people from different societies, but also brings the danger of stagnation. Where there is one universal way of doing things, there is no alternative to consider and to learn from, and no model to encourage change.

All of this applies to schooling. We have scripts for how to behave in all matters to do with education. Although each class, each school, and each school system has its own peculiar scripts, one overarching script is so widespread as to dominate behaviour in schools and everything to do with them. This script reflects the belief that schooling is for the acquisition of knowledge, which is needed for two purposes: to equip students for employment, and to prepare them for further study of the same sort of knowledge. The script guides the behaviour of teachers, students, parents, curriculum designers, examiners, administrators, and governments. All accept it. The script is so widespread that it is difficult to find classrooms where it is not directing the behaviour of teacher and students.

The dominant script is open to two criticisms. One is that the resultant teaching and learning fails to satisfy the purposes of preparation for employment or for further study. The other is that it does not address other important goals. Although these criticisms apply for all subjects, discussion here focuses on science.

Preparation for employment and further study

Advances in subtlety of assessment accompanied the replacement of behaviourism by constructivism as the prevailing theory of learning for science. Although multiple-choice and simple completion questions continued to be popular, in the 1970s researchers began to probe students' understanding with the more penetrating tools of interviews (e.g. Za'rour, 1976), prediction–observation–explanation tasks (e.g. Champagne *et al.*, 1980), Venn diagrams (e.g. Gunstone and White, 1986), and drawings (e.g. Novick and Nussbaum, 1978). These sharp probes revealed that students' learning was often shallow, and that despite scoring well on traditional tests students could hold beliefs about the natural world that were at odds with the scientific explanations that they had been taught. Some, of course, did form sound understandings, but the proportion was unsatisfactorily low. Nor was shallow learning a foundation for advanced learning. In any case, it was soon forgotten. Surveys (e.g. Durant *et al.*, 1989) have found public understanding of science to be unsatisfactorily low. Lucas (1987) observed that people who had not taken science courses at school had as good an understanding of biology as those who had studied it. Not only was little learned, but what knowledge was acquired was rigid and not applicable to the new circumstances that arose in employment.

Students who learned without good understanding must have been aware of the sterility of their knowledge of science. This may be why so many turned away from it. Studies showed that although students' interest in science itself remained high, each year spent studying it decreased liking for science as a school subject (Breakwell and Robertson, 2001; Office of Science and Technology and the Wellcome Trust, 2001; Osborne *et al.*, 1997; Simpson and Oliver, 1985; Yager and Penick, 1986). Physics and chemistry were less popular than biology (Havard, 1996). A fatal spiral commenced in advanced countries, in which fewer went on to study physical science at university, so that fewer became science teachers and science teaching in secondary schools became the unwelcome task for more and more people who were not sufficiently qualified. The teaching of science became more mechanical and textbook based, and less inspirational. Baird *et al.* (1991) asked students what they felt about being a science student. A typical response from a Year 7 student was 'just another subject at school that I have to go through. Although I may learn different things in science than in any other subject it is still just a compulsory subject at school that everyone has to do.' In answering another question about what you do in learning science, the student wrote 'answering questions, doing assignments, having class discussions, doing some prac[tical] experiments and finding out things that don't really interest me at all'. Another study, (Baird *et al.*, 1990, p. 13) found that Year 7 students, who had been looking forward to studying science in secondary school, had been disappointed: 'We hardly do anything except copy notes that the teacher has written (not our own words) and do experiments that the teacher does for us.' Poor teaching leads to even fewer students enjoying science, and the spiral accelerates downwards. One outcome has been the decline in departments of physics and chemistry at universities.

There are, then, reasons for disquiet about the dominant script even before considering whether it is effective in attaining goals beyond preparation for employment and further study.

Other goals

Another way of describing scripts is that they are like the rules and procedures that govern behaviour in games or sports. Teachers and students learn to play the game of schooling.

Most games have a single criterion for success: most runs, most points, longest distance, or shortest time. The game of schooling has taken on that characteristic, as highest marks on tests of circumscribed subject matter knowledge have become the criterion. Fensham (1985; 1988), Aikenhead (1994), Solomon (1993), and Ziman (1980) have long argued for a better game, in which there is more than one goal and more than one criterion for success. Their campaign opens two questions: Should we agree with them, and why have they not convinced the players of the game?

Fensham's arguments

In advocating 'Science for All', Fensham (1985) asserts that science curricula overlook important needs. In testing this assertion, we need to be convinced not only that curricula have not met a number of needs but also that those overlooked are important.

Fensham (1988) identifies two groups of demands that science curricula might meet. One concerns political, economic, and subject-maintenance demands, the other cultural, social, and individual demands. He points out that current curricula concentrate on the first group and ignore the second. These curricula are then unbalanced, and leave learners with distorted understandings of science. Teaching scripts fit the first group but not the second.

Why the game of schooling remains narrow

Even under the narrow script, science teaching is demanding, complex, and difficult. In addition to all the tasks that teachers of any subject must complete, science teachers are busy with preparation of materials, plus their acquisition and stocktaking; they must attend to safety in the laboratory, and in biology must be alert to ethical issues with living organisms. The subject matter they are expected to master is exceptionally demanding. It grows at a rapid rate, probably faster than in any other subject. It is already extensive and diverse: the teacher of general science needs some command of physics, chemistry, botany, zoology, earth science, and astronomy. It is difficult to fit all of this knowledge into an undergraduate degree. In the 1950s the University of Melbourne attempted to meet the need by introducing a science degree for teachers which required students to take one or two years on each of a wide range of sciences rather than do a three-year major study of one. Though a sensible idea, academics and students perceived the degree to be inferior to one with specialism in one science, and before long it was discontinued. Lack of confidence in one's knowledge of the subject affects a teacher's performance. An uncertain teacher relies on the textbook, is unwilling to encourage questioning by students or explorations into unknown territory, and sticks closely not only to the predetermined curriculum but also to the traditional script for the classroom.

The subject matter of science is diverse in further ways. Knowledge can be divided into categories of propositions and processes, or 'knowing that' and 'knowing how' (Ryle, 1949). These categories have further divisions. In science, 'knowing that' includes images as well as words. Students acquire mental pictures of gas molecules, chemical bonds, atomic orbitals, cell structures, crystal types, and many others. Such images are learned, and taught, differently from verbal propositions such as 'chlorophyll is necessary for photosynthesis' and 'ceramics are good insulators'. In 'knowing how', the science teacher has to get the students to acquire numerous algorithms, for example balancing chemical equations, substituting in formulae, constructing genetic tables, and deducing chemical properties from place in the periodic table. Knowing how also includes motor skills: pouring liquids, measuring in many forms, preparing microscope sections, connecting up electrical circuits. Also prominent in science learning is 'knowing what', that is being able to recognise members of classes of things: monocotyledons and dicotyledons, metals and non-metals, algae and fungi, vertebrates and invertebrates, reptiles and amphibians. Teaching knowing that, how, and what calls for distinct skills, in each of which the teacher needs at least competence if not mastery. Then there is the further challenge of teaching students: 'knowing why'.

Another form of 'knowing that' that is important in science, and vital for 'knowing why', is recollections of experiences. Gagne and White (1978) term these recollections *episodes*. Science teachers tap students' episodes whenever they ask questions that begin 'Have you ever . . .' or 'Do you remember when . . .'. One of the functions of laboratory work and of demonstrations is to provide students with episodes that will help them to understand a topic. Arranging experiences that lead to useful episodes takes skill, but even greater skill is needed to get students to link an episode with relevant propositions. Mackenzie and White (1982) provide an account of how this can be done with excursions, and show how powerful the effect can be on retention of information. They also show that linking does not occur automatically, but needs management by the teacher.

If these characteristics of science content were not enough challenge, teachers also have to cope with important differences in the nature of topics. Topics vary in the amount of prior knowledge and experience that students bring to them. In force and motion, for instance, they have pushed and pulled and thrown and dropped things, which provides useful foundations on which the teacher can build but also can have led them to form beliefs that are contrary to the scientific explanation. Such topics require different teaching than ones such as atomic theory where students have had little relevant experience. Another dimension on which topics vary is abstractness. Some deal with concepts that are relatively easy to perceive, such as velocity, others with notions such as potential difference that are less obvious. Yet further dimensions are degree of complexity, presence or absence of alternative explanations, relative balances of common and uncommon words, whether principles are demonstrable or arbitrary, degree of social acceptance, and emotive power (see White (1994) for descriptions of dimensions of content). Each of these characteristics can affect how best to teach a topic.

On top of all these demands on the skill of the science teacher, Fensham and other critics of the narrow curriculum want to pile additional responsibilities: teaching science so that it not only meets society's demands for preparation for employment and further study but also to give students appreciation of science as a human endeavour and a significant part of culture, and to assist each individual to grow intellectually. So the curriculum must not only include the transmission of knowledge of the principles and concepts of science, intellectual and motor skills, and the ability to solve problems, but also cover knowledge of applications of science, show that science is not a fixed body of knowledge but an evolving attempt by humans to create a coherent description of the physical universe, give students an understanding of the limitations of science, and foster appreciation of traits and attitudes that are central to science such as 'honesty of observation and reporting and open-mindedness regarding explanation and phenomena' (Fensham, 1985, p. 426).

Is this all too much to ask? Would it be possible for teachers to master such extensive and diverse knowledge, skills, and appreciations? Is it not inevitable that they will fail? One argument is that noble goals are good in themselves, even if only rarely attained. To fall short is not a disaster – religions set goals that few adherents approach. 'Richness is better than narrowness, life itself is not measured against one criterion, diversity is needed for survival.' A counter-argument is that it is better to set goals that are attainable, and that in trying to achieve many things a curriculum will achieve none. Better to be successful in a limited way than to fail across the board.

The counter-argument accepts that the game deals with a fixed sum, so that any time given to one goal is a subtraction from another. Any time spent giving teachers broad knowledge across the sciences is time lost from giving them deep knowledge of one specialism. While this line of thinking may appear realistic, we might question the presumption that the amount of time for teaching or the amount for the training of teachers is fixed. We should also remember that past concentration on the limited goal of good understanding of science has not been markedly successful.

An alternative line, still accepting fixed sum of time, is to offer a choice between curricula with different emphases on goals. This may be attractive in theory but fragile in practice. For several years the Year 12 programmes in Victorian schools included physical science as a subject, alternative to the more established physics and chemistry subjects. Although physical science was innovative and appeared lively and interesting, the numbers of students who enrolled in it remained small. This may have been because the science faculties in the local universities did not accord it the same standing as physics and chemistry. Conservative teachers, comfortable in teaching the separate subjects of physics or chemistry, were another obstacle. Smaller schools could not afford the staff to teach physical science as well as physics and chemistry, and tended to stay with the longer standing pair. These difficulties of relative prestige and shortage of resources are likely to threaten innovations whenever reformers try to insert a new subject alongside existing ones.

If parallel alternatives cannot survive, the remaining option is to replace the present science curriculum with one that does address a defensible range of goals. Although conservative forces in the universities and the teaching profession would again have to be overcome, there are reasons to believe that conditions for change are more favourable now than they have been for some time. Science deans are concerned about falling enrolments, especially in physics and chemistry; vice-chancellors and school principals appreciate that they have a responsibility to ease the transition students face in passing from secondary to tertiary education; and lecturers and teachers are more aware of the shortcomings in learning that persist in the narrow curriculum. Even so, introduction of a radically new curriculum would be difficult. It is important to establish the conditions that would have to be met.

Conditions for success in implementing an innovative curriculum

A fundamental condition is that dissatisfaction with the existing curriculum has to be widespread. In order to bring university scientists to this view, educational researchers might invite them to be partners in replications of earlier studies of alternative conceptions that undergraduates and graduates hold. A previous generation of lecturers was able to dismiss the strong evidence that Gunstone and I provided of poor understanding of basic dynamics (Gunstone and

White, 1981) by asserting that the questions that we used were not fair, even though they were sensible probes of understanding of dynamics, because they differed from the lecturers' script for tests. We had a different reaction later when we had a lecturer as a co-author in a study of learning in undergraduate physics (White *et al.*, 1995) which revealed the need for the physics department to attend to problems of alienation. The presence of the lecturer meant that his department took the results seriously and acted upon them.

In addition to studies of alternative conceptions and of students' perceptions of their learning environment, educationists and scientists should join forces to study patterns of enrolments. In 1960, physics had the greatest number of students of all subjects at Year 12 in Victoria, except for the compulsory subject English expression. By 2000 it had fallen far down the list. Its fall in relative popularity was inevitable, given the rapid increase in the proportion of students at Year 12 who are female, who for various reasons have been less attracted to physics than to biology or to non-science subjects. There has, however, been not just a relative fall but an absolute one, despite the surge in enrolments in Year 12 as a whole. Whether this is due to the availability of what some see as 'soft' subjects is irrelevant; science departments have to operate in the world as it is, not as how they would like it to be. So they have to recognise the seriousness of the problem and consider means of addressing it. Their involvement in demographic research would spur progress. Educationists might have to take the initiative in inviting scientists to join them as partners in that research.

Educationists and scientists could also work together to investigate failures to complete a year of study or students' abandonment of planned major sequences in science. These investigations should uncover students' perceptions about the curriculum. Involvement in such research could have a salutary effect on decisions about the department's programmes. Non-involvement allows rejection of the implications. When Gunstone and I, in 1981, pointed out to the head of a science department that fewer than one in six of the students in his first year went on to second year, his response was that they were the few he was interested in. In the serious plight that many science departments are in, twenty years later, such a reaction is improbable; nevertheless, direct involvement in research into 'dropping out' should speed action to alter the curriculum for the school as well as for the university.

A second condition for innovators is that they must assuage universities' fear that a new curriculum will provide inadequate preparation for advanced study. It will not be sufficient to point out that US universities turn out capable graduates despite accepting students who have much less rigorous programmes in science than Australian and British universities do. The Australian universities could argue that conditions differ between countries, and what works in one need not succeed in another. What would be more convincing are local models of success. At least three lines of research could investigate the existence of such models. One is to track the paths of individuals through university.

Do some who did not study a particular science at Years 11 and 12 succeed at it in tertiary study? What reasons do they give for their success? How did they overcome their apparent lack of preparation? A second is to compare the mandated school curricula of the various states in Australia, or of the different authorities in other countries, and to see how students perform who then move to another state for university study. This sort of study would have to be fine grained, in which individuals' performances on topics that were not part of their school experience are compared with their performances on those that were part. A third line would be the evaluation of bridging courses, which some universities provide within the first year of tertiary study for science students who did not take relevant subjects at Year 12. If such courses are effective, then universities can be confident that a new school curriculum would not be disastrous for them. Universities would incur costs in putting on a bridging course, but the costs would be recouped from the income from greater enrolments that would follow from a more attractive Year 12 course. Experience at Monash University indicates that bridging courses can be effective. Students in the Faculty of Engineering who took bridging courses in physics and chemistry obtained a higher mean mark in both subjects in the examinations at the end of first year than those who entered with passes at Year 12 in those subjects.

A third condition for the introduction of a radical new curriculum is that such a curriculum has to exist and be attractive. Devising one is not a trivial enterprise, especially if the goals extend beyond basic knowledge of science to knowledge of the history of ideas and methods, ethics, social relevance, and the relation between science and technology, plus development of enthusiasm for science and a wish and the skills to learn more. It may seem impossible to package all this into a finite amount of school time. Indeed it may be, and so an approach is necessary that differs from the traditional listing of topics that teachers are to present sequentially in formal lessons. Without meaning to prescribe the form of such an approach, I have two suggestions. One is that the science curriculum for Years 11 and 12 could be based on a small number of important problems, chosen so that to make progress in solving them students would have to acquire not only a broad knowledge of science and its methods but also an appreciation of the relevance of science to society. Watts and West (1992) provide a number of examples for senior school chemistry: making soap, testing the difference between biological and non-biological washing powders, investigating the causes of fading in blue jeans, synthesising pheromones, extracting antibiotics from lichen. Other suggestions are: reducing pollution in an ecosystem, such as a pond or stream or the air; comparing energy sources for their efficiency and their effect on the environment; how to minimise the effect of a pestilence such as HIV/AIDS, malaria, or foot and mouth disease; devising biodegradable alternatives in packaging. This is not a prescription for discovery learning. Students need guidance in what to learn, and where to look. Teachers would need extensive in-service training and support to be able to manage such an approach. Though difficult to implement, a problem-centred approach would assist students to integrate knowledge of physics, chemistry, biology, and geology, and would meet the requirement for social relevance.

The second suggestion is that it is time to break from the ingrained model in which schooling takes place in a formal setting and where learning is as much the responsibility of the teacher as it is of the student. In their best practice, universities do not follow this model. They have been able to put responsibility on students, where schools have not, not just because of a different tradition but because they have greater library resources as well as more mature students who can be expected to have learned how to learn. Both advantages are less marked than they were a few years ago.

Although library support is much greater in universities than in schools, the Internet now makes available to school students vast amounts of information. Of course, access to information is not the same thing as being able to make use of it. Just as having a book is useless unless coupled with the ability to read, so is the Internet useless unless you know how to use it and to learn from it. Linn (2000), Bell and Linn (2000), and other researchers are developing tools that students can use for this.

To a large extent, students have been left to themselves to learn how to learn. Research into meta-learning (e.g. Macdonald, 1994) shows that with appropriate training students can become much more efficient and purposeful learners. The Project for Enhancing Effective Learning (Baird and Northfield, 1992) has taken this research from an experimental level to widespread practice in primary and secondary schools in Australia, Sweden, and Denmark.

The Internet and programmes that show students how to learn open the possibility of curricula that are freed from the traditional limits of time and space and local resources. Making use of that freedom will not be simple, or automatic, but will follow if school authorities and teachers see that rewards follow.

It would be naive to think that schools will discard the ingrained belief that examination scores are the major measure of success. Therefore, the rewards for good performance on a new curriculum must be largely in the form of examination marks. A radical curriculum must then be matched with a radical examination that taps the full range of goals.

Assessment and examinations

Advocates of change must recognise that examinations and the marks that result from them buttress the current script for schooling. To change that script, one has to change the system of assessment. The place to do that is in the final years of secondary school, for although teachers are relatively free in what they do in lower forms, influence in schools flows from the senior years to the junior. What happens in Grade 12 determines what happens in Grade 11, and so on down the chain. Although this downwards flow of influence is not the only way in which a school system might be organised, it is the way in which most systems operate. In Australia, the UK, and many other countries a formal assessment of students' achievements is a feature of the final years of secondary school. Teachers are constrained by this. School authorities, parents, and students acting in concert will soon remove a teacher who rebels against it. Since individual teachers are powerless, revolutionaries must then capture the whole means of formal assessment at the end of secondary school and introduce an assessment that is consistent with the goals that they intend for the curriculum. How this is to be done will vary with the system. In systems such as that in Victoria, university professors of science exercise strong influence through the committees that appoint examiners. In such systems, innovators must convince the influential professors of the worth of their proposals. Whatever the system, innovators first have to identify the key posts, and either fill them themselves or convert those that do fill them to their view.

Where goals are limited to acquisition of subject matter, without necessarily deep understanding, assessment can be restricted to items that require simple recall or selection from alternatives in multiple choice, or completion of well-drilled algorithms. Broad goals, however, require broad methods of assessment. White and Gunstone (1992) describe several innovative methods, of which Prediction–Observation–Explanation, Relational Diagrams, Question Production, and Drawings are readily applicable in science, and could be used in centralised mass testing as well as in school-based assessment.

Training

A new curriculum means change for experienced teachers, and new forms of training for those who are yet to enter the profession. For experienced teachers, a radical shift in goals requires them to learn skills that differ from those they have developed to fit the existing curriculum. This change is all the more revolutionary when the current script has been unquestioned and in place for so long. Although it is asking much for old teachers to learn new tricks, any change has to start with them. Beginners cannot carry a revolution. They have too many scripts to acquire, too much to learn in a short time about students, parents, authority structures, their subject matter, and themselves. If they try alone to act contrary to the established script of their school, they may well find themselves victims of sanctions. Brickhouse and Bodner (1992, p. 474) report a sad case of a young science teacher who had ideals of informal learning for his students, through observation and discovery in an out-of-school setting:

> I need to have my own classroom out in the woods . . . just a black spot in the woods with this old wooden house and just a place to get out of the rain if it starts raining too hard. . . . And what we couldn't learn outside we just wouldn't learn.

He was soon brought into line, and became disillusioned and unhappy. Novices tend to discard beliefs acquired in their training as their new and authoritative colleagues induct them into the existing culture of the school. Therefore, changes in pre-service training will be ineffectual unless preceded by changes in current practice.

In-service

In-service training is essential for a new curriculum to succeed. The aim of in-service training must be commitment by teachers to the new goals and scripts. Research on alternative conceptions has shown how difficult it is to shift beliefs developed through experience. This applies to beliefs about teaching and learning at least as strongly as it does to beliefs about the physical world. Change to teaching may be even more difficult since it involves change in behaviour and acquisition of new skills as well as a change in beliefs.

A key to change is ownership. Teachers will persevere with an innovation if they believe that it is their innovation, not one that an outsider has imposed on them. A change in script will come only if teachers own the curriculum. The large curricula of the 1960s were presented to teachers as final forms, to which teachers had had no input. Although the curricula did cause some change in the teaching of science, teachers adapting them to their existing methods reduced their effect. The teachers' scripts did not change much at all.

Ownership has consequences for the nature of the in-service training. The exact form of the training needs further thought, but for teachers to feel that they have control a possible arrangement is small independent groups, of around a dozen teachers from three or four schools. A curriculum officer ought to attend each group, but in a support rather than a leadership role. This arrangement favours perceptions by teachers of ownership and leadership more than a mass programme would. It also allows for trial and error, as problems and materials are tried out in classrooms. As the groups progress and their members' sense of achievement grows, their independence can reduce and communication between groups increase. The theme is that a radical change in script has to grow by experiment and support within, rather than be imposed from without.

Pre-service

For many years authorities in Australia, the UK, and the USA have considered that four years of tertiary study provide sufficient initial training for teachers. There are two common forms of the training. One form begins with three years of study of science, usually with some specialisation in one or other of biology, chemistry, or physics, then a year of study of education. In the other form the science and education studies are concurrent, but again the proportion is three-quarters science and one-quarter education. Perhaps the graduates of such programmes have a sufficiently broad knowledge of science, but it is questionable whether students can acquire in one year a substantial knowledge of the history and philosophy of education and of the psychology of learning and of child development, let alone skills of classroom management. Recent appreciation of the importance of pedagogical content knowledge (Shulman, 1986; 1987) has added to the knowledge and skills that teachers are known to need.

The reality is that after one year of study of teaching most graduates retain a script for teaching that they derived from observations of their own schooling, or soon revert to it through the advice and example of the teachers whom they join as colleagues. Probably this is inevitable with one year of training, whatever its quality and intensity. Longer training would be better, but mere length is not enough. The nature of the experience is crucial.

To advocate longer training for teachers is, in the current political climate, to tilt at windmills indeed. Western governments have reduced funding per student in universities, and are unlikely to support an extra year or more for teachers. Nor is teaching so attractive and well paid that sufficient people would be willing to pay full fees for added years. Adding a year would mean a year when there are no graduates, at a time when there is a universal shortage of science teachers. So although an increase in length of initial training before beginning to teach is desirable, economic factors will prevent it.

A more practical solution might be internships. After completion of four years' initial training, graduates could be given a provisional licence to teach for a certain number of years, say three. During the provisional period they would be required to do further study of education. This study could take various forms, with some people specialising in philosophy of education, others in teaching of children with special needs, and so on. It should, though, include two mandatory topics. One is pedagogical content knowledge, the other reflection on their classroom practice.

Without professional support, internships can regress into lower paid serfdom. They would have to involve tutors who are effective agents for change. Programmes such as PEEL (Baird and Northfield, 1992) and CASE (Adey and Shayer, 1994) show that such agents exist in experienced teachers who are not absolutely locked into the general script. The relation between tutor and intern is crucial. It should be a partnership in which both learn, and not one in which a superior directs or criticises an inferior. It is through individual relations of mutual help and respect that change can come. Without them, attempts to change the script for schooling and to implement a broad curriculum in science, or any other subject, will fail.

Suitable relations between intern and tutor are but one condition for change. Others described earlier are dissatisfaction of university scientists with the present curriculum, presence of an attractive alternative curriculum, demonstration that the new curriculum provides adequate preparation for further study, ability to show students how to learn from classroom teaching and from the Internet and other resources, introduction of a sympathetic assessment system, and availability of an appropriate course in pre-service training of teachers. The more of these conditions that are met, the greater the chance that changes can be made to the scripts for both teaching and the science curriculum. Bringing about these conditions presents a formidable but not impossible challenge, which has to be met in order to implement the programmes for science education that Fensham and others have advocated.

References

Adey, P. and Shayer, M. (1994) *Really Raising Standards: cognitive intervention and academic achievement*, London: Routledge.

Aikenhead, G. (1994) 'The social contract of science: implications for teaching science', in J. Solomon and G. Aikenhead (eds) *STS Education: international perspectives on reform*, New York: Teachers College Press.

Baird, J.R. and Northfield, J.R. (eds) (1992) *Learning From the PEEL Experience*, Melbourne: Monash University Faculty of Education.

Baird, J.R., Gunstone, R.F., Penna, C., Fensham, P.J., and White, R.T. (1990) 'Researching balance between cognition and affect in science teaching and learning', *Research in Science Education* 20: 11–20.

Baird, J.R., Fensham, P.J., Gunstone, R.F., and White, R.T. (1991) 'The importance of reflection in improving science teaching and learning', *Journal of Research in Science Teaching* 28: 163–82.

Bell, P. and Linn, M.C. (2000) 'Scientific arguments as learning artefacts: designing for learning from the web with KIE', *International Journal of Science Education* 22: 797–817.

Breakwell, G.M. and Robertson, T. (2001) 'The gender gap in science attitudes, parental and peer influences: changes between 1987–88 and 1997–98', *Public Understanding of Science* 10: 71–82.

Brickhouse, N. and Bodner, G.M. (1992) 'The beginning science teacher: classroom narratives of convictions and restraints', *Journal of Research in Science Teaching* 29: 471–85.

Champagne, A.B., Klopfer, L.E., and Anderson, J.H. (1980) 'Factors influencing the learning of classical mechanics', *American Journal of Physics* 48: 1074–9.

Durant, J.R., Evans, G.A., and Thomas, G.P. (1989) 'The public understanding of science', *Nature* 340: 11–14.

Fensham, P.J. (1985) 'Science for all: a reflective essay', *Journal of Curriculum Studies* 17: 415–35.

Fensham, P.J. (1988) 'Familiar but different: some dilemmas and new directions in science education', in P.J. Fensham (ed.) *Development and Dilemmas in Science Education*, London: Falmer Press.

Gagne, R.M. and White, R.T. (1978) 'Memory structures and learning outcomes', *Review of Educational Research* 48: 187–222.

Gunstone, R.F. and White, R.T. (1981) 'Understanding of gravity', *Science Education* 65: 291–9.

Gunstone, R.F. and White, R.T. (1986) 'Assessing understanding by means of Venn diagrams', *Science Education* 70: 151–8.

Havard, N. (1996) 'Student attitudes to studying A-level sciences', *Public Understanding of Science* 5: 321–30.

Linn, M.C. (2000) 'Designing the knowledge integration environment', *International Journal of Science Education* 22: 781–96.

Lucas, A.M. (1987) 'Public knowledge of biology', *Journal of Biological Education* 21: 41–5.

Macdonald, I.D.H. (1994) 'Enhancing learning by informed student decision making on learning strategy use', Unpublished PhD thesis, Monash University.

Mackenzie, A.A. and White, R. T. (1982) 'Fieldwork in geography and long term memory structures', *American Educational Research Journal* 19: 623–32.

Novick, S. and Nussbaum, J. (1978) 'Junior high school pupils' understanding of the particulate knowledge of matter: an interview study', *Science Education* 62: 273–81.

Office of Science and Technology and the Wellcome Trust (2001) 'Science and the public: a review of science communication and public attitudes toward science in Britain', *Public Understanding of Science* 10: 315–30.

Osborne, J., Black, P., Boaler, J., Brown, M., Driver, R., Murray, R., and Simon, S. (1997) *Attitudes to Science, Mathematics and Technology: a review of research*, London: King's College, School of Education.

Ryle, G. (1949) *The Concept of Mind*, London: Hutchinson.

Shulman, L.S. (1986) 'Those who understand: knowledge growth in teaching', *Educational Researcher* 15: 4–14.

Shulman, L.S. (1987) 'Knowledge and teaching: foundations of the new reform', *Harvard Educational Review* 57: 1–22.

Simpson, R.D. and Oliver, J.S. (1985) 'Attitude toward science and achievement motivation profiles of male and female science students in grades six through ten', *Science Education* 69: 511–26.

Solomon, J. (1993) *Teaching Science, Technology and Society*, Buckingham: Open University Press.

Watts, M., and West, A. (1992) 'Progress through problems, not recipes for disaster', *School Science Review* 73(265): 57–64.

White, R.T. (1994) 'Dimensions of content', in P.J. Fensham, R.F. Gunstone, and R.T. White (eds) *The Content of Science*, London: Falmer Press.

White, R.T. and Gunstone, R.F. (1992) *Probing Understanding*, London: Falmer Press.

White, R.T., Gunstone, R., Elterman, E., Macdonald, I., McKittrick, B., Mills, D., and Mulhall, P. (1995) 'Students' perceptions of teaching and learning in first-year university physics', *Research in Science Education* 25: 465–78.

Yager, R.E. and Penick, J.E. (1986) 'Perceptions of four age groups toward science classes, teachers, and the value of science', *Science Education* 70: 355–63.

Za'rour, G.I. (1976) 'Interpretation of natural phenomena by Lebanese school children', *Science Education* 60: 277–87.

Ziman, J. (1980) *Teaching and Learning about Science and Society*, Cambridge: Cambridge University Press.

Part VIII

Peter Fensham's impact on science education in Australia and science education research around the world

14 Impact of science education now and in the future

Cristina Padolina

The last two decades of the twentieth century saw two movements that aimed to ensure that the adventure of science learning was experienced by all. Studies which date back to the 1970s claimed that girls are disadvantaged in science classrooms and showed lower achievement in the physical sciences. There was a more general concern that the design of science curricula and instruction was focused on the elite group of students who would be most likely to go on to pursue degrees in science and technology. Thus arose the movements for achieving gender equity in science classrooms and for 'Science for All'.

In this chapter I wish to examine the relevance, particularly in relation to an Asian country like the Philippines, of these two movements today in the face of the current calls for knowledge societies and knowledge-based economies.

Knowledge-based economies

Human capital has traditionally been considered central to economic development, but its importance has been brought to the fore very acutely in recent years. President Charles M. Vest of the Massachusetts Institute of Technology recognised this when he said 'we are entering an era in which knowledge and the people skilled in its use are the coins of the realm'. This claim is supported by the increasing share of high-technology industries in total manufacturing in many countries. Non-production workers, also called knowledge workers, are in ever-greater demand and are more richly rewarded. To be competitive organisations are being transformed into cyber-corporations – able to respond to rapid change (Martin, 1996). Such an organisation requires workers who are fast learners and are capable of retooling and retraining. Abramowitz's (1989) study on long-term economic growth showed that the factor of production that has grown most rapidly is human capital.

Corporations have learned that the return on investment in knowledge and employee capabilities is very high. Motorola estimates that for every dollar it spends on employee training it gains thirty dollars in profit. Corporations know that the key to their survival is in developing people's capabilities. They compete to be the best in their industry and they know that it is their employees' expertise that keeps them competitive. Many corporations have, in fact, built their own training centres – corporate universities – each spending an estimated US$12.4 million annually in operating expenses (Crainer, 2001). In 1988 there were 400 such 'universities' with the number quadrupling within a decade (Greenberg, 1998).

Rapid technological change is considered to be the primary reason for the need for corporations to invest in the continued upgrading of their human capital. In its turn, improved ability to acquire, apply, and generate knowledge provides new impetus for technological development.

Knowledge-based economies demand multiple skills and capabilities among individuals in the workforce: for example, good communication skills, ability to work in a team, adaptability to rapidly changing circumstances, social skills, problem-solving skills, ability and self-motivation for learning throughout life, and knowledge navigation skills (Bates, 2000).

In the face of these new challenges to education, demanding what some even refer to as a paradigm shift in education, the unmet calls for 'Science for All' and gender equity seem to have been muted. The battle cry in education seems now rather to be 'Lifelong Learning'. The main support being advocated for this is the use of information and communication technologies (ICTs). For example, open and distance learning, especially in developed countries, is being equated to on-line or web-based learning.

Science education and ICT in the Philippines

In the Philippines interest in good science and mathematics education remains high, but it is in danger of being subsumed, and in some cases only justified, under the umbrella of the need to educate students in the use of ICTs.

Singapore and Malaysia in the South East Asian region are already committed to use more ICTs in education. Singapore launched its master plan for IT in education in 1997 and committed $2 billion dollars to implement a programme that calls for integrating IT into education. With IT-based teaching and learning Singapore envisages that 30 per cent of a students' study time would be with the use of IT. For countries like Singapore that make this commitment, it is very important that studies are made on attitudes and preferences in the use of computers for learning among boys and girls. Teaching approaches have been found to be one of the factors that contribute towards gender bias in science education. Teaching approaches in the use of IT should, therefore, be carefully assessed so as not to disadvantage one of the sexes. It is the responsibility of schools to minimise biases against any gender, especially with respect to teaching strategies. Awareness of social and cultural biases that may flow from the home or society into schools on the use of IT is also important for teachers to be able to provide a counterbalance in their classrooms.

The government of the Philippines is also concerned to put more computers in schools and to connect them to the Internet. The political will and the availability of resources to support such endeavours is, however, likely to be less than in Singapore and Malaysia. Nevertheless, computer laboratories are becoming status symbols among schools and universities. Not to be connected to the Internet is to be 'out of step with the times', although the vendors of computer hardware and software undoubtedly contribute to the creation of this heightened interest in ICT among educators.

'Science for All '

In 1983 Peter Fensham was part of the UNESCO ASIA regional group which produced the first major report advocating 'Science for All', and in a more detailed and argued paper he proposed a potentially exciting and powerful model for teaching and learning science in a 'Science for All' context (Fensham, 1985). It involves a holistic approach that addresses science-based issues and applications from different perspectives. It allows for the injection of social and cultural perspectives particular to the students' milieu. There are, however, constraints on the use of this model. The most significant is the teacher, who, as Fensham recognised, must be given skills and encouragement if he/she is to use such an approach.

In the Philippines little headway has been made in the intervening years in implementing such a 'Science for All' strategy and it could be thought that it is no longer relevant. Later in the chapter, I wish to argue that the model of 'Science for All' does remain highly relevant for the Philippines, and may now actually be more relevant than it was originally. First, though, it is necessary to set out some important features of school science in the Philippines.

In the Philippines science is taught as a mandatory and separate subject from Years 1 to 10. In the four years of secondary schooling (Years 7–10) the first year covers general science, the second biology, the third chemistry, and the fourth physics – a horizontal pattern somewhat like the one that is most common in the USA. Accordingly, teachers of science in the final three years are usually specialists in only one science discipline and all their teaching is in classes at the one appropriate level. The factor of teacher constraint is thus particularly acute because the 'Science for All' model requires teachers to have a good background in several sciences since socio-scientific issues usually involve more than one area of science. The structural feature that provides one year of general science in secondary education's total curriculum is also a serious constraint, compared with many other countries in Asia and elsewhere that have three or four years of general science in secondary schooling that have much more specialised resources for science teaching than do the years of elementary schooling.

Gender issues

It is now widely agreed that girls should not be excluded from enjoying the learning of science or from preparing for a career in science if they have the aptitude for it. In some countries in Asia, girls are excluded not just from science but from education generally. This is especially true of those living in rural areas or among the urban poor.

The work of Klainin and Fensham (1987) on gender learning in the physical sciences in Thailand showed that the difference in performance that was commonly observed between boys and girls in these sciences in the 1970s and 1980s is not caused by biological factors, eliminating an easy excuse for individuals, institutions, and nations not to exert any effort to scrutinise their educational policies, social and cultural practices that may be discriminating against girls and women.

When I asked science educators in the Philippines if there had been any serious study of gender and science they replied that they were not concerned because they felt that girls were not disadvantaged. It is true that participation of females in degree programmes in mathematics, biology, and chemistry is very high (30 per cent higher than males), and although lower in physics, is not more than 10 per cent different. The data gathered by the Commission on Higher Education on enrolment at the tertiary level shows that in only three discipline groups – law, engineering, and architecture and town planning – is the participation of females more than 10 per cent lower than that of males, and even in agriculture, forestry, fisheries, and veterinary medicine, which are perceived by some as traditional male areas.

The organisation of the curriculum does not apply as a constraint in the Philippines since secondary schooling has a fixed curriculum, although in some schools students may take additional mathematics and science study. The mandatory nature of school science, as Fensham (1986) has noted for Thailand, avoids the gender bias about the sciences that social and cultural factors can engender. At the tertiary level the problem in the Philippines is male participation, and this may well be a reflection of the relatively low financial rewards in science-based occupations.

With the increasing use of ICTs in education it is again important to be alert for gender biases this may introduce into education. In one study, Leong and Hawamdeh (1999) looked at attitudes among boys and girls to the use of computers and ICT learning styles in a co-educational school. Working in pairs girls were observed to be more cooperative with their partner. Boys preferred to work alone and competed with their partner as to who was to control the keyboard and mouse. Girls were more thorough in reading web pages, found it easier to navigate the web, and expressed a liking for learning with computers.

The relevance of 'Science for All'

Given the interest in ICT and knowing how government support can be influenced, it is important to see if 'Science for All' still has relevance and if that relevance converges with, or competes with, the notions of knowledge-based economies, and their emphasis on ICT in education. If there is convergence it can be exploited to push for 'Science for All' while still satisfying the needs of some politicians to show that they are not depriving their constituents of what is new and exciting, and what is being advocated as potentially powerful tools for learning.

Some may decry that this involves bringing politics into the reform of the school curriculum, but this is a mechanism, and probably an inevitable one, to effect real change. Curriculum reformers must be able to convince political decision makers and their constituencies that proposed reform will have enduring and far-reaching outcomes that will contribute to the socio-economic development of the country.

In my opinion, the rationale for 'Science for All' does remain relevant and is not outdated. It can be said that science education that gives attention to those who will not specialise in the sciences is especially relevant to developing countries like the Philippines, because of the low investment by government in scientific research. The multinational corporations only set up factories in these countries for the assembly of goods or for the formulation of products. The research behind these processes is conducted at their headquarters, usually located in the developed world. Most of the research that is done locally is concerned with studies of the market, for example determining whether toothpaste should be sweeter to cater for local preferences. Thus for countries like the Philippines it is just as important, if not more so, to educate individuals, as Fensham wrote almost twenty years ago, so that they can appreciate and participate in 'the responsible use of science and technology for development' (APEID, 1983).

In the Philippines those in government who do have an understanding of science (and not just those with scientific expertise) are the ones who listen to and take advice from technical experts. They tend also to advocate and provide support for government spending in both science and science education. For example, one person who did learn science in a context akin to 'Science for All' spelt out the potential for school science as follows: (1) awareness of the importance of science in the development of a nation; (2) awareness that the application of science can be for the benefit or detriment of society; (3) informed decision making on the appropriate technology for a particular situation; (4) a desire to see that students of science continue to experience the same excitement this person experienced and therefore provide support for a 'Science for All' curriculum and instruction; (5) work for increased government spending in science research and development.

On the other hand, the governed citizens also have an important responsibility in the way they spend their money and cast their votes. They can exercise the power of their purse in the selection and purchase of consumer items and in their demand for certain product features that are important from their point of view. Training in these processes of personal and social decision making would be by-products of a 'Science for All' approach. In the same way, critical and analytical thinking would be cultivated in such a course, along with intellectual skills such as making inferences and predictions, comparing, differentiating, and classifying.

Issue-based 'Science for All' is readily suited to teaching students to use ICTs to access information, including from the Internet. Given the large amount of science-related information that is available, say on the Internet, it is an opportunity for students to learn what is necessary for their needs and, more importantly, which pieces are valid and reliable and not just propaganda or advertising.

The question 'Would a "Science for All" approach cultivate skills and attitudes for the self-driven, lifelong learning that is the mantra of the new economy and knowledge-based society?' is an important one. Apart from communication skills, those needed for lifelong learning include the intellectual skills (1)–(5) above. Such a person would be equipped for and be motivated to continue learning not only for intellectual satisfaction but also for personal achievement in the world of work.

The goals of 'Science for All', I maintain, are more encompassing than those of education for the new economy. These have been brought to the fore largely to cope with the burgeoning amount of information, and the rapid pace of technological development. 'Science for All' does not specify the means for getting and processing information, and transforming it into knowledge. Therefore, the incorporation of the use of ICTs in the classroom is open. One only has to take care that the glitter and novelty of the technologies do not blind students and teachers and affect their use for good science teaching practice.

Implementing 'Science for All'

I have already alluded to the considerable problems of implementing 'Science for All' in the Philippines. However, if it has the potential I have just argued to meet the contemporary needs of school students as future citizens, it is important that a way forward be found.

The first year of secondary schooling where students are now taught general science is the place to start. This approach has the advantage that there is a general science major in the pre-service Bachelor of Secondary Education degree programme. This is offered in all 953 teacher education institutions in the country. This then offers the venue for the long-term preparation of teachers for a 'Science for All' approach. The courses of this pre-service degree would of course need to be taught in a 'Science for All' manner. Student teachers need clear role-models since so many of them in due course teach as they were taught.

Skills that would be cultivated in the issue-based model of 'Science for All' can be identified with the skills future students will need for survival in the world of work in the new economies. Their problem-solving skills could be honed in an issue-based science course, given that the students would be trained to look at a problem from various perspectives, and to learn that it is important to make judgements about the different factors that impinge on an issue. They could also learn how the various perspectives of the issue interact with one another. They would also learn to evaluate proposed solutions to a problem – again from different points of view.

As far as the large body of existing teachers of general science is concerned, two factors may contribute to the provision of the in-service education they will need for the introduction of 'Science for All'. These are the relative slowness with which the massive resources for ICT will be made available in the Philippines, and the devastating results of Filipino students in the Third International Mathematics and Science Study (TIMSS) and in TIMSS-Repeat, conducted throughout the 1990s. Among thirty-six countries the Philippines was third lowest. As an immediate response a fast-track programme of in-service for teachers has been implemented. (*Editor's note*: It is significant that the TIMSS study has had a political impact, see also the situation in Germany, Chapter 12 of this book.)

Before teachers become distracted by the use of IT or lulled by the notion that just using these modern technologies in teaching means that meaningful learning is occurring, I believe a longer term strategy for their in-service education is needed. In the early 1990s, a model for the in-service education of physics teachers was developed as part of the Philippines–Australia Science and Mathematics Project by staff at Monash University (Peter Fensham had a central role) in conjunction with their Filipino colleagues (Fensham and Gunstone, 1995). The model was a teacher-led in-service programme over two and a half years that involved 'a long soak followed by periods of intensive swimming'. There were very positive outcomes.

The package of in-service training designed by Peter Fensham and his co-workers for PASMEP could serve as a model for in-service teacher training anywhere. It is what I call an informed action in-service programme – since the design is supported by what research has shown would work. I would like to see the training programme written in more detail and in a form that would be easier to follow by anyone who would want to undertake it. The Philippines, since the devastating results of TIMMS-Repeat (TIMSS-R), conducted in 1995, has tried to fast track a training programme for science and mathematics teachers. I believe a 'long soak' rather than a 'short dip' would have better results in producing a long-lasting and sustained improvement in science education in the country. When 'Science for All' has been established in the first year of secondary schooling it will be clearer what needs to be done to extend it to the later years.

Postlude

Peter Fensham's long involvement with 'Science for All' is consistent with what I perceive as his deep-seated concern for people. As a scientist–educator this translates into his wish that the excitement of learning the discoveries, processes, and applications of science be experienced by all. He has applied scientific thinking and methodology in his teaching, in his research in science education, in curriculum development, and in the design of teacher education programmes. For Peter Fensham, with his concern for people and his abiding faith in the realisation of their potential, education is both a science and a humanity. His research on gender and science and his interest in science and culture are further testimony to these concerns. He has what Jacob Bronowski (1977) considered as the two characteristics that make a moral person: 'a clear judgment of what is at stake and the sense that other people matter'. He can 'combine human love with an unflickering scientific judgment'.

To educate, if one goes back to the derivation of the word, means to bring out. Peter Fensham's personal quest is to bring out the best in each and every individual, by providing the opportunity and the best environment for it to happen.

References

Abramowitz, M. (1989) *Thinking about Growth*, Cambridge, MA: Cambridge University Press.

APEID (1983) Regional meeting on Science for All, *'Science for All'*, Bangkok: UNESCO.

Bates, A.W. (2000) *Managing Technological Change*, San Francisco: Jossey-Bass.

Bronowski, J. (1977) *A Sense of the Future*, Cambridge, MA: MIT Press.

Crainer, S. (2001) 'Corporate views of university', http://www.managementskills.co.uk/articles/univer.htm (accessed 2001).

Fensham, P.J. (1985) 'Science for All: a reflective essay', *Journal of Curriculum Studies* 17: 415–35.

Fensham, P.J. (1986) 'Lessons from science education in Thailand: a case study of gender and learning in the physical sciences', *Research in Science Education* 16: 92–100.

Fensham, P.J. and Gunstone, R.F. (1995) 'A long soak followed by reports of intensive swimming: a tale of inservice cooperation between the Philippines and Australia', *Science Education International* 6: 27–32.

Greenberg, R. (1998) 'Corporate u. takes the job training field', *Techniques* 73: 36–9.

Klainin S. and Fensham, P.J. (1987) 'Learning achievement in upper secondary school chemistry in Thailand: some remarkable sex reversals', *International Journal of Science Education* 9: 217–27.

Leong, S.C. and Hawamdeh, S. (1999) 'Gender and learning attitudes in using web-based science lessons', *Information Research* 5, http://www.InformationR.net/ir/5–1/paper66.html (accessed 2001).

Martin, J. (1996) *Cybercorp: the new business revolution*, New York: AMACOM.

15 The importance of being able to see 'the big picture'

A personal appraisal of Fensham's influence on science education research and development

David Treagust

In 1973, as a Western Australian secondary school science teacher who was a delegate attending the annual conference of the Australian Science Teachers Association (CONASTA) in Melbourne, I was invited to represent the Science Teachers Association of Western Australia (STAWA) at the annual general meeting. This is when and where I first met Peter Fensham in his then new role as the first national president of the Australian Science Teachers Association (ASTA). I had little idea about the workings of ASTA at the time and this coincidental opportunity arose before STAWA developed into the educational force that it soon became and is today.

Fensham's appointment was clearly a timely decision. It moved ASTA towards a management structure that provided a national identity headed by a well-known person who was 'highly respected as a science educator and researcher internationally and was highly regarded as a research scientist' (Lucas, 2001, p. 17). I do not recall a great deal about this one-off experience, but it was a valuable introduction to organisational administration in science education and to gaining a broader knowledge of science education. Upon reflection, it is quite remarkable that a professor of science education would take on this role, but it is illustrative of Peter's ability to take on new responsibilities, to hold 'big picture' ideas for the future of science education, and his sense of how events, people, and their understanding can be brought together in a synergistic manner.

Lucas (2001) reports that 'as ASTA President, [Fensham] procured active partnerships with organisations such as the Commonwealth Scientific and Industrial Research Organisation (CSIRO) . . . and the International Council of Associations for Science Education (ICASE)'. This involvement in ICASE ensured that ASTA's presence through international science education organisations in addition to UNESCO was enhanced. As is evident elsewhere in this book, such endeavours are consistent with Fensham's commitment, interest, and ability to work internationally, to learn from others, and to influence others in return. In his long career as a science educator, he has combined his many scientific, educational, social, and research interests within a broad international arena of science education. As a consequence, his work has been informed by and has influenced colleagues and curricula in a wide range of nations.

In this chapter, I will return to these aspects of Peter Fensham's work in relation to science education as I discuss two aspects of his work: the goal of achieving scientific literacy for all students and bringing diverse ideas together at a relatively early stage of their development.

The goal of achieving scientific literacy for all students

My impression is that Fensham has been more active in a much wider international arena and in many non-English-speaking countries than any other science educator and has led the way for others. These contacts with science educators worldwide and working within broad educational contexts are much more understandable when one appreciates Fensham's overriding commitment to social justice and the place of science education for all school-aged students (see Roger Cross's Chapter 1, this volume).

The notion of who a particular science education should be for is an important issue that Fensham and others (see, for example, Millar and Osborne, 1998) have raised. That the science education received by the majority of the school population should be different to that received by the minority who go on to study science at university has been of concern for many years. Fensham's way of conceptualising the problems and possible solutions to this situation in science education comes to the fore, and his 'Science for all: a reflective essay' (Fensham, 1985) provided a unique synopsis of current developments and dilemmas up to the mid-1980s. According to Fensham, the goal of 'Science for All' has been a recurring theme in science education since the 1930s and a new vision appropriate to the 1980s was needed to provide improved science education opportunities for all students, regardless of their intended work or study once schooling had concluded. This notion of 'Science for All', although not specifically expressed that way in the early 1980s, was for improved scientific literacy of all school-aged students – an issue that Fensham has returned to on numerous occasions in his writings.

Sources of the problem

Several reasons have been put forward for the lack of success of the 1960s' curriculum developments in meeting the needs of a broad spectrum of students (Fensham, 1988; Millar, 1996). These developments were dominated by upper school curricula, which had a strong conceptual orientation, and lower secondary and primary school curricula, which had a strong process skills orientation. According to Fensham (1985), even though the upper school curriculum projects provided a better science education for the 20 per cent of students who may have a science career, the remaining 80 per cent were less well served. Fensham argued that these two demands on science education are conflicting rather than complementary. In addition, one source of the problems created by the process-oriented curricula for the early years of science education was that the teachers may not have been associating these processes with meaningful and acknowledged content and therefore the processes were not assimilated in the minds of the students.

Proposed solutions

A proposed solution to the concern about less than desirable science education in schools, based on an international workshop held in Cyprus in 1982, was to emphasise the application of worthwhile science knowledge in the world outside school based on two criteria – either the content should have social meaning and usefulness for the majority of learners or it should assist learners to share in the wonder and excitement that has made the development of science such a great human and cultural achievement (Fensham, 1985, p. 429). The first criterion was strongly pragmatic such that learners, parents, and community authorities recognised its usefulness. The second criterion required a careful choice of natural phenomena made easily available to learners and their teachers that can give rise to wonder and excitement. Based on these criteria, twelve broad fields of study were listed within which the examples of mini-curricula based on particular social settings could be developed. These twelve topics were: the senses and measurement as an extension of the senses; the Universe; the human body; health, nutrition, and sanitation; food; ecology; resources (natural and manufactured); population; pollution; use of energy; technology; and quality of life. These topics, as the organisational frameworks of science textbooks, especially at the junior high school level, are quite familiar to us now, but a cursory look at secondary science texts in the 1970s compared with the late 1980s or 1990s does show a change in style of presentation from the rather dry factual science to the inclusion of aspects of application in everyday and industrial life.

Some curriculum successes

In his keynote address at an international conference in Chile, at which I was also present, Fensham (1994) cited the Canadian *SciencePlus* series of junior high school science textbooks (edited by McFadden and Yager, 1993) as meeting many of the needs of 'Science for All'. This series incorporates a number of new pedagogies such as asking questions that are not answered in the book, setting novel exercises that are outside the students' world of school, and seeking opinions and reasoning of student readers. In addition, experimental work is integrated within the text and students take letters home to parents or guardians to inform them about the science they are doing at school.

Having worked with teachers in a Michigan school system that adopted this series (see Treagust *et al.*, 2001) at the same time as using formative or embedded assessment as an integral part of their teaching, I can say that this series is indeed designed to engender an interest in science. I do not know how many studies have been conducted that investigated the impact of this series on students' learning. However, in this study of students' learning about sound and its properties, the level of interest shown by the students in the way the course was conducted, and their interest in the topic, would suggest that as far as meeting the goals of scientific literacy was concerned this was achieved, even amongst the least academically inclined students.

Successful developments also have occurred in Australia. For example, at the upper school level, in 1989, the physics curriculum in Victoria was redesigned with the subject matter overtly oriented towards contexts that were intended to be typical and significant aspects of students' physical and social worlds. How the development of the Victorian physics course was based on a change of theoretical perspectives and how the initial science–technology–society approach was not supported by bureaucrats and many in the academic community are told persuasively by Hart (2001; in press). Fensham's work gave support to these kinds of changes through his writings and international contacts. Although I suspect he was not involved in the day-to-day decisions in the design of the new physics curriculum, it is not merely a coincidence that his connection with Dutch colleagues, notably Piet Lijnse (see Lijnse *et al.*, 1990), was a valuable element in the change process. Linjse was invited to Victoria to consult on the revamped Victorian physics course because of his work on and knowledge of the Dutch Physics Curriculum Development Project (PLON), in The Netherlands, which incorporated a science–technology–society approach and was truly context based.

Future challenges

Research has indicated that secondary teachers are, by and large, conservative in deciding whether or not to support curriculum change and this is also the case for university-based scientists (see, for example, Hart, 2001; in press) as well as science educators who do research and teach pre-service and in-service courses. The current curricula and their assessment suit their needs well and the inclusion of social and environmental issues often is perceived to dilute the rigour of the discipline. As a result, the teachers' interests remain within the existing curriculum and the type of schooling that they experienced, so to invoke meaningful change is a major decision for them. Indeed, this is how teachers are able to maintain control over the subjects that they teach, thereby limiting curricula change based on the whims of education department bureaucrats. It is one way to retain some power and control over their teaching.

Recently, Fensham (in press) has stated his disappointment that the goal of different science education for various academic groups in schools has not been achieved in the majority of nations. In illustrating what has not eventuated in the 'Science for All' movement, Fensham examined changes in science education from a wide range of international perspectives, including American,

Asian, British, and European endeavours, explaining that the failure of 'Science for All' has arisen primarily because the curriculum has remained within the existing school setting, organisation, and policies. Fensham recommends that this impasse can be addressed by using information gathered from societal experts and from the media in order to develop socially derived content for inclusion in new, more relevant, science curricula that are important to citizens' personal lives.

In their review of the status and quality of teaching and learning of science in Australian schools, Goodrum *et al.* (2001) refer to Fensham's (1987) overview of the changing nature and goals of science education during the past fifty years to explain why it has failed to promote scientific literacy. Importantly in the context of this chapter is their claim that Fensham 'has been prepared to expose power plays which have continued to resist attempts in the 1990s for nationally developed curricula to take a less content-oriented approach' (Goodrum *et al.*, 2001, p. 9). An example of Fensham's involvement at the socio-political level is described in his detailed report of how the physical science course in Victoria, designed to include aspects of the interfaces between science and technology and science and society, was deemed not acceptable for entry to certain faculties in one university, notably in medicine and science, resulting in the demise of this subject innovation in science (Fensham, 1987). So despite the success of the curriculum in being designed to meet the needs of a broader section of the school population, the conservative requirements for university entrance did not enable this approach for increased scientific literacy to be achieved.

Perhaps all science educators need to become more involved in the socio-political aspects of curriculum. As I argue elsewhere (Treagust, in press), not only are teachers and university scientists conservative and accepting of the existing curriculum, but also so are science educators, even when thinking themselves not to be so! As a case in point, I see myself as contributing to the problem that Fensham describes in the lack of success of the 'Science for All' movement. This is largely because I am not active in the educational–political interface and, to a considerable extent, I am tacitly accepting of the existing science curricula. It is these curricula that provide me with my primary research agenda encompassing how students learn the existing curricula, what difficulties they encounter, and how teachers can change their pedagogy and the curricula to address or challenge these difficulties. My research usually recommends curriculum changes, and in several cases has developed new curricula, and illustrates how learning can be enhanced by pedagogical improvements such as an informed use of analogies (Treagust *et al.*, 1998). Even so, the research and its outcomes are located within the existing curriculum. I am now beginning to realise that I have been accepting of the curriculum that the teachers are required to teach (and the students to learn) by the educational system in which they work. Because some of the science is conceptually complex, I would like to think that my research contributions help improve practice in those areas, but I do acknowledge that I am not challenging the structure of the existing science curricula.

Bringing diverse ideas together at a relatively early stage of their development

My acquaintance with Fensham's work has enabled me to appreciate how he has linked ideas together, providing a relevance to science education from other fields, and vice versa. One of the foremost contributions to science education by Fensham is the manner in which he has been able to identify these connections at an early stage of their development. In essence, he is able to step back from his own position and see the relationship of others' work to science education.

What diversity of research?

In the 1970s and 1980s there was a dearth of books about the findings of science education research that brought together readings or articles concerning current developments in the expanding research literature in science education. Fensham's (1988) book *Development and Dilemmas in Science Education* brought a welcome end to this situation and contains chapters written by seventeen authors from four continents, illustrative of Fensham's broad range of international interests. I suspect that one reason that these ideas were brought together in this book is due to his identifying what he believed to be the dominant research fields then influencing the practice of science education. Indeed, the chapters describe key issues in science education at the time and in several cases these topics have served as important bases upon which others have researched and which are described in other chapters of this book.

In the first chapter of *Dilemmas*, Fensham returns to his message that the extensive curriculum developments of the 1960s and 1970s did not have the desired effect of improving science education for a large percentage of the school-aged population. A major purported explanation was that these curricula, deemed to take place in a social and political vacuum, did not meet many of society's needs as mentioned in an earlier section of this chapter. In more recent times, in many nations, the multicultural nature of the school-aged population is acknowledged and this has brought new challenges to science education.

Fensham raised specific dilemmas for the future of science education with regard to limited access to experience, issues related to language and culture, and the role of the affective domain in science education. Proposed new directions for science education in the 1990s and today address many of the issues commented upon by authors of this volume, but at the time, in 1988, to have different issues such as relating theory to practice, the role of language, practical work, and gender in science education, for example, in one volume had a very positive impact on science education research. I believe that this combination of scholarly writing has helped other researchers develop a broader conceptualisation of those issues that were, or can be, influential in the field of science education, and particularly for classroom practice.

The central place of science content

Similarly, Fensham's co-edited text *The Content of Science: a constructivist approach to its teaching and learning* (Fensham *et al.*, 1994) brought together a substantial amount of science education research written by scholars from several different nations, though on this occasion all were from Western nations. Of note in this volume is the inclusion of classroom teachers as joint authors of research conducted in their classrooms. The connecting theme for the authors who contributed to *Content of Science* was that each was involved in, and/or directed, curriculum projects that had, as the central notion, the content being learned and how it can be better taught for more effective learning. In more recent times, Fensham (2001, p. 28) commented that:

> With the hindsight of the intervening years, it is now clear, that despite the book's main title, we failed to produce a book about the problematic character of the content of school science. . . . Rather . . . we simply summarised . . . what a decade of cognitive pedagogical research had provided about the teaching/learning of the particular science topic each of [the authors] had chosen to write about.

with the exception of the chapter by White on a theory of content. Fensham's comments, made in a keynote address at the biennial meeting of the European Science Education Research Association in Kiel in 1999 (and later published in 2001), offered a challenge for researchers who are willing to consider science content as being problematic rather than simply an issue in school science. This challenge referred to several themes in European research that ask different kinds of questions and recommend the development of new directions.

In *Dilemmas*, Fensham (1988, p. 23) cited the work of Shulman (1986) with its emphasis on the content of the subject matter of the curriculum as one example of the new way of conceptualising teaching science. The focus of the *Content of Science* was of particular interest to me because my research is concerned with the difficulties that students and their teachers experience in dealing with the designated curricula and this book became compulsory reading for my research students.

The role of science content in scientific explanations

The two chapters by White and by Carr and his colleagues in *Content of Science* certainly influenced my research into explanations in science teaching. White's (1994) research on the need for a theory of content and his analysis of ten properties of school science content that can influence the types of explanations used by teachers is rarely addressed in the literature, despite content being a central issue in whatever is taught in science classes. Carr *et al.*'s chapter deals, among other issues, with that of explanations in science teaching and learning. Subsequently, Allan Harrison and I (Treagust and Harrison, 1999; 2000) reported how teachers' explanations that impart knowledge and promote student understanding are dependent, to a large extent, upon the theoretical analysis of the content of the science. Researching the relationship between the content being taught by teachers and the manner in which they go about explaining this content has important outcomes for improving classroom practice and students' learning. Expert teachers have a very special form of knowledge that transcends content per se because it is highly adaptive and is elegant, parsimonious, highly connected, and fruitful. This kind of knowledge, referred to as pedagogical content knowledge (Shulman, 1986), appears to fulfil all the criteria of expert knowledge because it transcends both subject content and pedagogical knowledge and it is consistently and innovatively used to solve classroom learning problems. Beginning teachers often despair of achieving this expert teacher knowledge.

Carr *et al.* (1994) asked if there was a single explanation for a phenomenon that teachers should aim for and proposed that the level of explanation depends on the purpose of the explanation and the background of the students for whom the explanation is provided. They also emphasised that it is 'inappropriate for classroom interactions to convey the impression that there is a single correct explanation of any phenomena or a single definition of any concept' (p. 156). Likewise, in commenting on how scientists decide to accept a better explanation, these authors pointed to the need to let students know the rules of the game for the development of ideas in science. Teachers should encourage students to evaluate whether or not a proposed explanation is better than available alternatives. These ideas led to the design of a series of questionnaires to evaluate students' understanding of how scientific models are used by both scientists and students to engender explanations (Treagust *et al.*, in press).

Analysing the lectures of Richard Feynman, an expert scientist–teacher, in terms of the nature of the content and the explanations he used, we noted how Feynman made science concepts accessible to his students and others (Treagust and Harrison, 2000). The data for this analysis is his physics lectures at Caltech in 1961–3 taken from *Six Easy Pieces* (Feynman, 1994) and the analysis was restricted to Lecture 1 entitled 'Atoms in Motion', which exemplifies Feynman's teaching; his explanatory style and simplicity may actually be the hallmark of accessibility and relevance. Feynman believed that explaining complex and abstract concepts in everyday terms was his test of understanding. The lecture is a macro-explanation composed of many micro-explanations that use physics axioms to develop a holistic explanation of atoms, molecules, and ions. The individual micro-explanations come in many forms: as scientific explanations, they are deductive, inductive, law and statistically driven, and as effective pedagogical explanations, they include many examples, metaphors, analogies, and models and use, where appropriate, anthropomorphic and teleological explanations to make the concepts seem commonplace. Still, the explanatory devices are never arbitrary, capricious, or idiosyncratic. We asserted that the macro-explanation is an excellent example of pedagogical content knowledge because it sensitively accommodates the students' characteristics and needs, is consistently true to the science, Feynman's personality and knowledge are evident, and the explanation satisfies the requirements of the freshman physics course for which it was designed.

This research showed that effective explanations need to obey certain rules, frequently related to the nature of the content, thereby transforming scientific knowledge into student-friendly terms. This apparently simple process is surprisingly complex because each effective explanation needs to be customised not only for its audience but also for the content and the context in which it is taught. While the scientist needs to be knowledgeable about the scientific content explanations, the science teacher or science educator needs to be knowledgeable about science content explanations as well as effective pedagogical content explanations to enable the content knowledge to be accessible to students. To attend to these two categories of explanations effectively, teachers need to be able to take into account factors relevant to the students, to their own knowledge and perceptions, to the context in which the explanations are made, as well as to the nature of the content. This is not an easy task and we did not claim that the incorporation of these pedagogical skills into a teaching repertoire will be a foolproof activity; indeed, the dangers of using analogies or metaphors inappropriately have been described in the literature (see, for example, Glynn et al., 1995). Rather, our argument was that without a repertoire of pedagogical content knowledge to recognise how the content can be explained appropriately to less informed people, teachers will be less equipped to do their work effectively.

Concluding comments

In this chapter, I have written about my perceptions of Peter Fensham's influence on science education in relation to achieving scientific literacy and to bringing diverse ideas together at an early stage in their development. I conclude by commenting upon some other research activities that illustrate connections to his ideas and influences, particularly in chemistry education.

Currently, I am investigating the problems experienced by learners in first-year university chemistry courses, especially bridging courses of one type or another, for which they have little background knowledge. This research is designed to overtly explain chemical phenomena and their reactions at the macroscopic, microscopic, and symbolic levels in an attempt to help students develop a better understanding of these chemical phenomena as opposed to their usual approach of memorisation. Fensham's remarks at the international conference in Kiel, when he encouraged researchers to consider science content as being problematic, have been incorporated into my current work on examining the relationship between the characteristics of science content and the nature of explanations used by students, textbook authors, and teachers. So far, we have examined the explanations used by a sample of Australian and South African teachers and textbook authors in relation to the content of upper high school chemistry and students' perceptions of these explanations (Mamiala and Treagust, 2001).

References

Carr, M., Barker, M., Bell, B., Biddulph, F., Jones, A., Kirkwood, V., Pearson, J., and Symington, D. (1994) 'The constructivist paradigm and some implications for science content and pedagogy', in P. J. Fensham, R. Gunstone, and R. White (eds) *The Content of Science: a constructivist approach to its teaching and learning*, London: Falmer Press, pp. 147–60.

Fensham, P.J. (1985) 'Science for all: a reflective essay', *Journal of Curriculum Studies* 17: 414–35.

Fensham, P.J. (1987) 'Physics science, society and technology: a case study in the sociology of knowledge', in K. Riquarts (ed.). *Science and Technology Education and the Quality of Life*, Kiel: Institute for Science Education, pp. 714–723.

Fensham, P.J. (1988) *Developments and Dilemmas in Science Education*, London: Falmer Press.

Fensham, P.J. (1994) 'Science for all; theory into practice', in *Proceedings Science and Mathematics Education for the 21st Century: Towards innovatory approaches*, Concepcion, Chile, 26 September–1 October 1994.

Fensham, P.J. (2001) 'Science content as problematic: issues for research', in H. Behrendt, H. Dahncke, R. Duit, W.M. Komorek, A. Kross, and P. Reiska (eds) *Research in Science Education – past, present and future*, Dordrecht: Kluwer Academic Press, pp. 27–41.

Fensham, P.J. (in press) 'Time to change drivers', *Canadian Journal of Science, Mathematics and Technology Education* 1.

Fensham, P.J., Gunstone, R., and White, R. (1994) *The Content of Science: a constructivist approach to its teaching and learning*, London: Falmer Press.

Feynman, R.P. (1994) *Six Easy Pieces*, Reading, MA: Helix Books.

Glynn, S., Duit, R., and Thiele, R.B. (1995) 'Teaching science with analogies: a strategy for constructing knowledge', in S. Glynn and R. Duit (eds) *Learning Science in the Schools: research reforming practice*, Mahwah, NJ: Erlbaum, pp. 247–73.

Goodrum, D., Hackling, M., and Rennie, L. (2001) *The Status and Quality of Teaching and Learning of Science in Australian Schools*, Canberra: Commonwealth of Australia.

Hart, C. (2001) 'Examining relations of power in a process of curriculum change: the case of VCE physics', *Research in Science Education* 31: 525–51.

Hart, C. (in press) 'Framing curriculum discursively: theoretical perspectives on the experience of VCE physics', *International Journal of Science Education*.

Lijnse, P., Kortland, K., Eijelhof, H., van Genderen, D., and Hooymayers, H. (1990) 'A thematic physics curriculum: a balance between contradictory curriculum forces', *Science Education* 74: 95–103.

Lucas, K.B. (2001) 'The Australian Science Teachers Association: the first fifty years', *Australian Science Teachers Journal*, 47: 8–26.

Mamiala, T.L. and Treagust, D.F. (2001) 'An interpretive examination of teachers' explanations in senior high school chemistry', in I. V. Mutimucuio (ed.) *Promoting*

Regional Collaboration in Research in Mathematics, Science and Technology Education in Southern Africa, Maputo: Educardo Mondlane University Press, pp. 202–9.

McFadden, C. and Yager, R.E. (Directors) (1993) *Science Plus: technology and society* (Blue Version), Austin, TX: Holt, Rinehart and Winston.

Millar, R. (1996) 'Towards a science curriculum for public understanding', *School Science Review* 77(280): 7–18.

Millar, R. and Osborne, J. (1998) *Beyond 2000: science education for the future*, London: King's College, School of Education.

Shulman, L. (1986) 'Those who understand: knowledge growth in teaching', *Harvard Educational Review* 57: 1–22.

Treagust, D.F. (in press) 'Supporting change, but also contributing to the problem', *Canadian Journal of Science, Mathematics and Technology Education*, 1.

Treagust, D.F. and Harrison, A.G. (1999) 'The genesis of effective scientific explanations for the classroom', in J. Loughran (ed.) *Researching Teaching: methodologies and practices for understanding pedagogy*, London: Falmer Press, pp. 28–43.

Treagust, D.F. and Harrison, A.G. (2000) 'In search of explanatory frameworks: an analysis of Richard Feynman's lecture "Atoms in motion"', *International Journal of Science Education* 22: 1157–70.

Treagust, D.F., Harrison, A.G., and Venville, G.J. (1998) 'Teaching science effectively with analogies: an approach for pre-service and in-service teacher education', *Journal of Science Teacher Education* 9: 85–101.

Treagust, D.F., Jacobowitz, R., Gallagher, J.J., and Parker, J. (2001) 'Using assessment as a guide in teaching for understanding: a case study of a middle school science class learning about sound', *Science Education* 85: 137–57.

Treagust, D.F., Chittleborough, G., and Mamiala, T.L. (in press) 'Students' understanding of the role of scientific models in learning science', *International Journal of Science Education*.

White, R.T. (1994) 'Dimensions of content', in P.J. Fensham, R. Gunstone, and R. White (eds) *The Content of Science: a constructivist approach to its teaching and learning*, London: Falmer Press, pp. 255–62.

Afterword

A new centre for research on science curriculum

Richard Gunstone

The genesis – thirty years ago

In 1970–1 Peter Fensham spent his first sabbatical year as a science education academic at the Centre for Science and Mathematics Education at the then Chelsea College, University of London, where there was the largest concentration of academic science educators in the UK. (Chelsea College later amalgamated with King's College, University of London.)

As all who know him would expect, Peter came back from that year of thinking, researching, discussing, and observing with many, many ideas. Some of these ideas became ongoing influences on science teacher education at Monash, and as such have been a very positive part of my daily work for all of my time at Monash University. Examples are (1) convincing the Education Faculty at Monash of the need for science labs in the Faculty (and today our very new labs – named the Peter Fensham Science Education Laboratories – are a continuing and wonderful legacy), and (2) encouraging methods staff to use residential camps in our science teacher education programme. As I write, our science student teachers are just back from another annual camp that has, again, been extraordinarily successful in provoking their thinking about, and actions in, science teaching.

One aspect of Peter's ideas from that year remained no more than an abstract thought until very recently. Some time after he returned from Chelsea College Peter wrote a brief report about this idea. In this report he describes how, while at Chelsea, he was struck by the number of other international visitors, and by the extraordinary range of perspectives and experiences they had. He became acutely aware of both the value in sharing these experiences and perspectives, and the extent to which standard academic approaches to such sharing (journals etc.) were not always available. To quote from his report:

> A number of that year's [1970–1] . . . visitors were from developing countries where there is not the same chance or need to write the science education story, and hence about which we know very little. Yet each of these countries has a story of policy, curriculum, resources, teachers and learners, examinations, and practical work that is quite rich, perhaps

more so than the relatively straight forward science education scenes in countries like Britain, Australia, USA and Canada, the written accounts of which dominate the literature.

One of my visions is that one day a Centre will be realised to tell these stories that would go far beyond the league tables that bodies like the I.E.A. produce through their comparative studies of science assessment.

One obvious feature of this extract is the consistency it has with an issue Peter has been centrally concerned with for the whole of his science education career, namely the significance of ideas and practices from outside the English-speaking industrial world. The emergence of a Centre that might somehow embrace the ideas expressed above has, however, taken another thirty years.

The re-emergence of the idea

As part of the ways in which Monash University has decided to see itself in the twenty-first century it has, in common with many universities around the globe, sought to become international. Monash's 'strategic alliance' in the UK is with King's College, University of London; King's College, having incorporated the former Chelsea College, has the similar distinction of having a large group of science education researchers.

In 2000, after the establishment of this close relationship between Monash and King's College, Peter regenerated this earlier ideas, this time in the contexts of the turn of the century and of a partnership between the science educators of these two institutions. In March 2000 he proposed a joint science education centre with the following possible purposes:

1   To understand and disseminate the formal operating structures for science education in different countries. For example, the forms of senior secondary examinations in the sciences and the formal and informal assessments at lower levels of schooling in the many countries we never hear about or are obscured by the endless reports from the few countries that are reported.
2   To foster visitors to Monash and to King's College, with the visitors being encouraged to focus, during their visit, on the specific interests of the Centre (e.g. themes such as are suggested in 5 below).
3   To work closely with the current networks of expertise in considerations of culture and science education in ways that would contribute to a Centre that had concerns with understanding this aspect of curriculum issues across countries.
4   To extract and make accessible comparative data on science education that exists in UNESCO, TIMSS, OECD, etc.
5   To establish annually a clearly defined theme relevant to considerations of the science curriculum, which scholars and systems would be asked to address and provide data about. If successful, this could lead to a series of 'Yearbooks on Science Education' in electronic or other forms.

6   To hold occasional *electronic* conferences – electronic to ensure appropriate participation around topics where the theme data reveals interesting aspects that need to be more widely shared.

The idea has taken hold. The professors of science education at both King's College and Monash have embraced the possibilities of a Centre with enthusiasm, as have the Vice-Chancellor of Monash and the Principal of King's College. An expanded version now includes mathematics education as well as science education. The Centre has begun its life in 2002, based at Monash, with the present author as its director.

The final section of this short piece gives some extracts from the successful application to Monash University for funding, in order to show what the new Centre will do, and how much it derives from Peter's original idea of thirty years ago.

The Monash–King's College International Centre for the Study of Science and Mathematics Curriculum

The Centre brings together two groups of science and mathematics educators, at Monash and King's College, to collaborate in research and development activity that will address issues of fundamental significance to the nature of school science and mathematics curriculum.

Governments the world over see science and technology as central to economic development. Central to actions to foster this science-based economic development, in both developed and developing economies, are interventions in the school science curriculum (e.g. Levin, 2000) (where 'science' in these contexts is inevitably a term used to embrace both the science and the mathematics school curriculum). The modern knowledge economy demands greater scientific and mathematical literacy and expertise from school leavers than ever before. At the heart of such demands is the need for greater engagement by students with school science and mathematics.

Science and mathematics curricula are central to this engagement – in the intended curriculum, the implemented curriculum, and the learned curriculum. Science curricula around the world exhibit great diversity. In part this diversity results from diversity in cultural contexts (Bishop, 1991; Gunstone, 2001). But little is known in terms of 'what this diversity is all about and why it is there' (Roberts and Östman, 1998, p. 5). In contrast mathematics curricula around the world exhibit both strong similarities and some differences (e.g. probability and statistics are not taught everywhere, unlike algebra and geometry; see Bishop *et al.*, 1996), but again the reasons for the similarities and differences are not understood.

This Centre will consider these fundamental issues of development and diversity in the intended, implemented, and learned curriculum through the study of (1) the nature and origins of intended systemic curricula, (2) systemic similarities and differences, (3) the consequences of adopting curriculum from one system/cultural context to another, (4) more sophisticated understandings of learning outcomes and systemic differences in these learning outcomes, and (5) greater understanding of the ways in which science and mathematics curricula can contribute to the development of emerging economies.

Two specific initiatives of the Centre that will enhance its research and development profile are (1) an annual visiting scholar who, while at Monash, will be required to produce a paper on a mutually agreed topic that is central to the work of the Centre, and (2) a biennial 'yearbook' comprising a series of invited papers around some relevant broad theme. Both of these products (the visiting scholar paper and the yearbook) will be published electronically, and will be available on the website of the Centre.

References

Bishop, A.J. (1991) *Mathematical Enculturation*, Dordrecht: Kluwer Academic Publishers.

Bishop, A.J., Clements, K., Keitel, C., Kilpatrick, J., and Laborde, C. (eds) (1996) *International Handbook of Mathematics Education*, Dordrecht: Kluwer Academic Publishers.

Gunstone, R. (2001) 'Physics education past, present and future – an interpretation through cultural contexts', Keynote address to 2001 International Conference on Physics Education, Cheongju, Korea, August 2001.

Levin, K. (2000) *Mapping Science Education Policy in Developing Countries*, Washington, DC: World Bank.

Roberts, D. and Östman, L. (eds) (1998) *Problems of Meaning in the Science Curriculum*, New York: TC Press.

Appendix
Peter Fensham

Selected publications

The following publications are a small fraction of Peter Fensham's scholarly output in chemistry, environmental education, sociology of education, and science education. The selection contains publications from each area but the majority are from the field of science education.

Boas, W. and Fensham, P.J. (1949) 'Rate of self diffusion in tin crystals', *Nature* 164: 1127.

Fensham, P.J. (1950) 'Self diffusion in tin crystals', *Australian Journal of Science Research* A3: 91.

Fensham, P.J. (1957) 'Semiconductivity and catalysis', *Quarterly Reviews of the Chemical Society* XI: No. 3.

Fensham, P.J. (1962) 'Educational objectives in teaching science at universities', *Nature* 1941: 142–4.

Fensham, P.J. and Cotton, J.D. (1964) 'Magnetic susceptibility changes during the adsorption of oxygen and carbon monoxide on cuprous oxide', *Journal of Physical Chemistry* 68: 1052.

Fensham, P.J. and Hooper, D.F. (1964) *The Dynamics of a Changing Technology*, London: Tavistock Publications.

Fensham, P.J. (ed.) (1970) *Rights and Inequalities in Education*, Melbourne: Cheshire.

Larkins, F.P., Fensham, P.J., and Sanders, J. (1970) 'Adsorption of oxygen on high area nickel oxide, part I, structure and properties of oxide', *Transactions of the Faraday Society* 66: 1748–54.

Fensham, P.J. and Taft, R. (1973) 'Victorian male entrants into tertiary education, 1968–1973, part I, transition and participation', Faculty of Education, Monash University.

Fensham, P.J. (1974) 'School and family factors among commonwealth secondary scholarship winners in Victoria, 1964–71', in D.E. Edgar (ed.) *Sociology of Australian Education*, Sydney: Angus and Robertson.

West, L.H.T. and Fensham, P.J. (1974) 'Prior knowledge and the learning of science', *Studies in Science Education* 1: 61–83.

Fensham, P.J. (1975) 'New approaches to the preparation and inservice training of teachers of integrated science', in *New Trends in Integrated Science Teaching, Vol. III*, Paris: UNESCO.

Fensham, P.J. (1976) *A Report on the Belgrade Conference on Environmental Education*, Canberra: Curriculum Development Centre.

Fensham, P.J. (1976) 'Preparation for research in science education', *Studies in Science Education* 3: 106–14.

Fensham, P.J. (1976) 'Social content in chemistry courses', *Chemistry in Britain* 12: 148–50.

Symington, D.J. and Fensham, P.J. (1976) 'Elementary school teachers' closed-mindedness, attitudes toward science, and congruence with a new curriculum', *Journal of Research in Science Teaching* 13: 441–8.

Fensham, P.J. (1978) 'Implications of environment and environmental education for schools', in R. Linke (ed.) *Education and the Human Environment*, Canberra: Curriculum Development Centre.

Fensham, P.J. (1978) 'Stockholm to Tbilisi – the evolution of environmental education', *Prospects, Unesco*, Vol. VIII, No. 4.

Fensham, P.J. (1980) 'Constraint and autonomy in Australian secondary education', *Journal of Curriculum Studies* 12(3): 189–206.

Fensham, P.J. (1981) 'Heads, hearts and hands future alternatives for science education', *Australian Science Teachers Journal* 27: 53–60.

Gilbert, J.K., Osborne, R.J., and Fensham, P.J. (1982) 'Children's science and its consequences for teaching', *Science Education* 66: 623–33.

Fensham, P.J. (1983) 'A research base for new objectives of science teaching', *Science Education* 67: 3–12.

Fensham, P.J. and Hunwick, J. (1983) *Environmental Education: module for pre-service training of science teachers and supervisors for secondary schools*, International Environmental Education Programme, Environmental Educational Series 7, Paris: UNESCO–UNEP.

Fensham, P.J. (1984) 'Conceptions, misconceptions and alternative frameworks in chemical education', *Chemical Society Reviews* 13(2): 199–221.

Fensham, P. (1985) 'Science for all: a reflective essay,' *Journal of Curriculum Studies* 17: 415–35.

Fensham, P.J. (1986) 'Lessons from science education in Thailand: a case study of gender and learning in the physical sciences', *Research in Science Education* 16: 92–100.

Fensham, P.J., Kemmis, S., Power, C., and Tripp, D. (1986) *Alienation from Schooling*, London: Routledge & Kegan Paul.

Fensham, P.J. (1987) 'Higher education and equity: the need for a dynamic perspective', in R. Toomey (ed.) *Passages from Secondary School to Higher Education*, *Australian Education Review No. 25*, Melbourne: ACER.

Klainin, S. and Fensham, P.J. (1987) 'Learning achievement in upper secondary school chemistry in Thailand: some remarkable sex reversals', *International Journal of Science Education* 2: 217–27.

Fensham, P.J. (1988) 'Approaches to the teaching of STS in science education', *International Journal of Science Education* 10: 346–56.

Fensham, P.J. (ed.) (1988) *Developments and Dilemmas in Science Education*, London: Falmer Press.

Gunstone, R.F., White, R.T., and Fensham, P.J. (1988) 'Developments in style and purpose of research on the learning of science', *Journal of Research in Science Teaching* 25(7): 5–13.

Fensham, P.J. (ed.) (1989) *Discipline Review of Teacher Education in Mathematics and Science*, Vol. 3. Appendices, Canberra: Australian Government Printing Service.

Klainin, S. and Fensham, P.J. (1989) 'Successful achievements by girls in physics learning', *International Journal of Science Education* 11: 101–12.

Speedy, G.W., Fensham, P.J., Annice, C., and West, L.H.T. (1989) *Discipline Review of Teacher Education in Mathematics and Science, Vol. 1, Report and Recommendations*, Canberra: Australian Government Printing Service.

Fensham, P.J. (1990) 'Developments and challenges in Australian environmental education', *Australian Journal of Environmental Education* 6: 15–28.

Fensham, P.J. (1992) 'Science and technology', in P.W. Jackson (ed.) *Handbook of Research on Curriculum*, New York: Macmillan, pp. 789–829.

Fensham, P.J. (1992) 'What has happened to intuition in science education?', *Research in Science Education* 22: 114–22.

Fensham, P.J. (1993) 'Academic influence on school science curricula', *Journal of Curriculum Studies* 25: 53–64.

Fensham, P.J. (1993) Common sense knowledge: a challenge to educational research', *Australian Educational Researcher* 20: 1–15.

Fensham, P.J. (1993) 'Reflections on science for all', in E. Thomas and S. Tresman (eds) *Challenges and Opportunities for Science Education*, London: The Open University Publishing and Chapman, pp. 107–25.

Fensham, P.J. and Corrigan, D. (1994) 'The implementation of an STS chemistry course in Australia: a research perspective', in J. Solomon and G. Aikenhead (eds) *STS Education: International Perspectives on Reform*, New York: Teachers College Press, pp. 194–204.

Fensham, P.J., Gunstone, R.F., and White, R.T. (eds) (1994) *The Content of Science Education: a constructivist approach to its teaching and learning*, London: Falmer Press.

Fensham, P.J., Marton, F., and Chaiklin, S. (1994) 'A Nobel's eye view of scientific intuition: discussions with the Nobel prize winners in physics, chemistry and medicine (1970–86)', *International Journal of Science Education* 16: 457–73.

Fensham, P.J. (1995) (guest ed.) 'Policy and science education', *International Journal of Science Education* 17(4).

Fensham, P.J. (ed.) (1995) *Science and Technology in the Post-Compulsory Years*, Camberwell, Victoria: Australian Council for Educational Research.

Fensham, P.J. (1995) 'STS and comparative assessment of scientific achievement', *Research in Science Education* 25(1): 33–8.

Fensham, P.J. (1997) 'School science and its problems with scientific literacy', in R. Levinson and J. Thomas (eds) *Science Today: problem or crisis*, London: Routledge, pp. 119–36.

Fensham, P.J. (1998) *Primary Science and Technology in Australia: a discussion paper and comparative perspective, key centre monograph no. 7*, Perth: National Key Centre for Mathematics and Science, Curtin University of Technology.

Fensham, P.J. (1998) 'The politics of legitimating and marginalising companion meanings', in D. Roberts and L. Ostman (eds) *The Many Meanings of Science Curriculum*, New York: Teachers College Press, pp. 178–92.

Fensham, P.J. and Harlen, W. (1999) 'School science and public understanding of science', *International Journal of Science Education* 21: 755–63.

Fensham, P.J. (2000) 'Providing suitable content in the science for all curriculum', in R. Millar, J. Leach, and J. Osborne (eds) *Improving Science Education: the contribution of research*, Buckingham: Open University Press, pp. 147–64.

Cross, R. and Fensham, P.J. (eds) (2000) *Science and the Citizen: for educators and the public*, Fitzroy, Victoria: Melbourne Studies in Education.

Fensham, P.J. (2001) 'Science content as problematic – issues for research', in H. Behrendt *et al.* (eds) *Research in Science Education – past, present and future*, Dordrecht: Kluwer Academic Publishers, pp. 27–42.

Fensham, P. (2002) 'Surviving science lessons is not scientific literacy', in J. Wallace and W. Louden (eds), *Dilemmas of Science Teaching – perspectives on problems of practice*, London and New York: RoutledgeFalmer, pp. 209–12.

Fensham, P.J. (in press) *Evolution of Science Education as a Field of Research*, Dordrecht, the Netherlands: Kluwer.

Index